Praise for *Everything Counts!*

"A book becomes a 'classic' when it is the definitive reference source on a subject matter. *Everything Counts!* is destined to become a classic while serving as the guiding philosophy for anyone committed to excellence."
—Brian Tracy,
Best Selling Author
How the Best Leaders Lead

"Blair convincingly validates our experience at Falcon Jet—that paying attention to the hundreds of small details has a bottom-line impact on results. When we make everything count by sweating the small stuff, profits go up while costs come down. This principle applies not only in our professional relationships with customers, business partners, and team members, but also in our personal relationships."

—Bob Fantozzi,
Senior Manager, Dassault Falcon

"Blair's insights around excellence and execution are right on the money. Paying attention to even the smallest of details is not just common sense, it's good business, as excellence builds a powerful brand, loyal customers, repeat business, and enhanced profitability. Buy *Everything Counts!*, it will inspire you to greatness!"

—Jeramy Freeman,
CEO, Well Rounded Fitness

"Read this book and find that the overarching philosophy of *Everything Counts!*, when applied in business and in life, yields immediate results in performance and satisfaction. Gary Ryan Blair has refined this concept and provides the reader with the shortest distance between understanding and actually taking on personal responsibility. Read it with a pen at hand—it's excellent!"

—David Corbin,
Author, *Illuminate: Breakthrough Results Using The Positive Power of Negative Thinking*

"I admit that I was a little dubious when Gary first asked me to write an endorsement for *Everything Counts!* After all, I am a big picture kind of guy who sees everything in my business and that of my clients from a 50,000 foot point of view. Then I started reading the book and everything in it, down to the tiniest detail, makes sense. Everything really does count. Every detail, every customer, every action we take counts. A fabulous read!"

—Tom Wheelwright,
CEO of ProVision Wealth

"Never before have I seen a philosophy resonate so deeply with how we run our restaurants than *Everything Counts!* This simple, yet profound message provides a roadmap for excellence and quality results. It will challenge you to pay attention to the details of your work while enjoying each step of the process. My advice to anyone who is determined to build a legacy of excellence is to read this book. You'll be glad you did!"

—Jason Thomas,
President, Papa Gallo's Restaurants

"*Everything Counts!* strikes at the heart of the Martial Arts as it's a commitment to excellence and focus on detail which help to create a Black Belt Champion. As a Master in the Martial Arts and entrepreneur, I'm a strong believer in repetition of solid fundamentals. Gary is an expert at getting you excited about those simple yet necessary skills for success and achievement."

—Kyoshi Steve LaVallee,
8th Degree Black Chief Master Instructor CEO,
USA Black Belt Champions

"In life, everything you do creates who and what you are. Gary Ryan Blair's book *Everything Counts!* is a must read for anyone who truly wants to raise their game. He has crystallized the true meaning of excellence and quality by stressing that very small differences, consistently practiced, produce superior results. Read it; use it; and don't loan it out (because you won't get it back) . . . most importantly, make everything you do count!"

—Dr. Len Schwartz,
CEO, Chiropractic Marketing Solutions

"Adopting the *Everything Counts!* approach has greatly impacted the daily work I perform as a parent and educator. Espousing these essential core values has lead my students and family to greater focus, better use of time, and inspiration to try new things. Teaching kids the important link between all actions and consequences cannot only produce immediate, positive changes; it is also great practice for life. Easy to read, practical, and inspiring, this book belongs on every living room, boardroom, and classroom shelf!"

—Katie Post,
Executive Director, Your Partners in Education, Inc.

"What do Olympic Gold Medalists, Academy Award winners, and Nobel Laureates have in common? Answer: They all have a passionate obsession with excellence, and they all make everything count. Buy this book . . . it will show you how to become one of the great ones!"

—Dr. Lyle Koca,
Koca Chiropractic Clinic

"In writing *Everything Counts!* Gary Ryan Blair has given us a much needed blueprint for defining excellence while reminding us that small is indeed beautiful. This book brilliantly demonstrates how very small differences, when consistently practiced, produce quality results."

—Bobbi DePorter,
President, Quantum Learning Network

"*Everything Counts!* is a manifesto for unleashing exponential performance improvement in organizations worldwide. This powerful philosophy has transformed the success of my law practice and lent itself to the redefining of the way I look at the practice of law."

—Tom Anelli,
Managing Partner, Anelli Law

"*Everything Counts!* is a profoundly important message for succeeding in school and in life. Blair brilliantly points out that excellence is achieved via qualitative—not quantitative—shifts in developing skills. This is an important book that matters."

—Randy Tarkington,
Senior Director of Residential Education,
Vanderbilt University

"Blair brilliantly focuses on excellence as a sustainable, competitive weapon. Like the air we breathe, we too often take this critical intangible for granted. As Blair makes perfectly clear, we do so at our ultimate competitive peril."

—Steven P. Sitkowski,
President, Dynetech

"In life and business, a commitment to excellence is one of the wisest decisions you'll ever make. In *Everything Counts!*, Gary Ryan Blair convincingly demonstrates how excellence is the fundamental building block for running a great business and enjoying a wonderful quality of life."

—Donna Curry,
Development Director, Subway

Everything Counts

Counts

52 Remarkable Ways to Inspire Excellence and Drive Results

Gary Ryan Blair

WILEY

John Wiley & Sons, Inc.

Published by John Wiley & Sons, Inc., Hoboken, New Jersey.

Published simultaneously in Canada.

For general information on our other products and services or for technical support, please contact our Customer Care Department within the United States at (800) 762-2974, outside the United States at (317) 572-3993 or fax (317) 572-4002.

Wiley also publishes its books in a variety of electronic formats. Some content that appears in print may not be available in electronic books. For more information about Wiley products, visit our web site at www.wiley.com.

ISBN: 978-0470-50456-7

Printed in the United States of America

10 9 8 7 6 5 4 3 2 1

For Erika, Ryan, Libby, and Oscar.
You make everything in my life count!

THE GOLDEN RULE OF EXCELLENCE

EVERYTHING COUNTS!

Everything you say; every thought you entertain; and everything you do has a direction, which serves as an advance or a retreat in respect to your pursuit of excellence. Everything, regardless of size or intent, has bottom-line consequences; therefore, everything counts!

CONTENTS

Contents

Universal Concepts   189

FOREWORD

What do Olympic Gold Medalists, Academy Award winners, and Nobel Laureates have in common? Answer: They all have a passionate obsession with excellence. They realize that the true genius and magic behind every great performance is always found in the smallest of details and as a result, they make everything they do count.

In writing *Everything Counts*! Gary Ryan Blair has given us a much needed blueprint for defining excellence while reminding us that small is indeed beautiful. This book brilliantly demonstrates how very small differences, when consistently practiced, can produce quality results.

What distinguishes Gary is this: passion, focus, and energy. He inspires others by setting high standards for himself. He despises mediocrity and continually seizes the opportunity to acknowledge, exemplify, and celebrate excellence. Gary is a beacon; he shows you that striving for excellence in all of your endeavors is a noble ideal.

Gary is more than a motivator; I consider him a friend. I had the pleasure of meeting him when he was the keynote speaker at a chiropractic seminar I attended in January 2004. Before I met Gary, I had set goals throughout my life, from achieving certain standards in high school and college sports to maintaining a level of academic proficiency through my years of education. However, I had never consciously considered just how important every little qualitative detail was when it came to performance excellence.

During that first lecture and in the years since, Gary has impressed upon me that the sum of our actions COUNT. He has elevated the conscious belief that anything you truly desire, as long as it is fair with the universe and tangible, can be achieved. He has the ability to simplify what we want, why we want it, the time frame in which we hope to get it, and how to do it all, not just with good intentions, but with great, honorable, and noble intentions!

Over the years, Gary and I have maintained contact and often bantered back and forth via phone and email. Throughout our continued correspondence, he never ceases to question and challenge me on the importance of why I do things a certain way and to remind me that all of the little things are important, perhaps even more important than the anticipated big things.

Since I met Gary Ryan Blair, I have changed the way I think and the way we do business in my chiropractic practice. My colleagues and I have inspected our language, both written and verbal, and we make sure that everything we do counts—no matter how small. From the moment any one of us walks up to our door, we take care of business. It's the little things that make difference—no gum on the sidewalk, no visible trash, a clean door handle, and when clients walk in, they are greeted with a cheerful smile from my chiropractic Super Team—and addressed by name—because that counts! Furthermore, everyone puts in the effort to keep a clean, organized office, with pens that actually work! You won't find crumpled papers or instructions that have been photocopied so many times that they're now illegible. Scuffs on the floor get cleaned; markings on the wall get repaired. In short, we have embraced the philosophy of making everything count.

The greatest pleasure to my team is when a client walks in our door and before they can even be seen by an associate doctor or myself, they feel a little bit better "just by being here." To us, everyone is famous and everyone counts!

I have often heard Gary say that "excellence is a guilty pleasure" and I have come to embrace the fact that this is indeed true. A life of excellence and quality is only achieved through qualitative, not quantitative shifts in skill development. This is a much needed lesson not just for the students in the classroom, but also for the CEO in the boardroom, the coach in the locker room, and the parent in the living room.

While we the readers can appreciate the originality of Gary's work with *Everything Counts!*, it should inspire us to do more. Gary has written an important guide to raising the bar and performing to the best of your ability, but what you choose to do with it is what really counts. His exhortations are nothing if you don't apply them.

Knowing Gary, I suspect he places far more value in how we read, interpret, and apply his book than on his accolades for writing it. It is easy to follow so just go with the flow and enjoy the merits of each lesson. Although it might be tempting to read quickly, remember to pause and reflect. I suggest a second and third read with a highlighter; take lots of notes, and actively engage in the Call to Action exercises. *Everything Counts!* drives home the point that you make hundreds of decisions every day, and some matter more than others. But each one counts—each one comes with a consequence—and each one moves you one step closer to your goals and rendezvous with excellence.

—Dr. Lyle Koca, DC
Koca Chiropractic

ACKNOWLEDGMENTS

*E*verything *Counts!* would not have become reality if not for the help of some very special people, each of whom demonstrates a commitment to excellence. This book symbolizes a collaboration of like-minded people committed to a common goal—to inspire, promote, and celebrate excellence.

In that spirit, I am honored to know these people and express my deepest gratitude and thanks:

I could not have found a better advisor, ally, and editor than Lauren Lynch of John Wiley & Sons. You saw the value of this work and championed the entire process. Since the first day, you have made this a truly joyful experience.

To Christine Moore, without your edits and brilliant suggestions, this book would never have turned out this well. Your attention to detail, gift with words, and capacity to work quickly has been most appreciated.

To Dave Pemberton, who gave me a number of helpful tips and excellent overall guidance on how to improve the message.

To all of my friends and colleagues who I regret I cannot list individually. My deepest thanks for supporting the message, reading the drafts, and for challenging me to raise the bar by creating an unforgettable message.

To all of my clients who through your active participation in workshops have helped validate and fine-tune this life-changing message. Your feedback and recognition of the significance of this message is helping to impact the culture and work ethic of people and companies throughout the world.

Finally my deepest thanks to my extraordinary wife Erika, and my three wonderful children, Ryan, Libby, and Oscar, who gave me the freedom and encouragement to make this book a reality. I love you more than words can express.

INTRODUCTION

I interrupt your life to bring you this important message—if anything counts at all, everything counts, no matter how big, no matter how small and this book will show you exactly why and how to address it. *Everything Counts!* is an execution strategy for inspiring excellence and driving exceptional results. It offers a profoundly important message for running a great business and for enjoying a great quality of life. Its meaning is simple, yet powerful: *Everything you say; every thought you entertain; and everything you do has a direction, which serves as an advance or a retreat in respect to your pursuit of excellence. Everything—regardless of size or intent—has bottom-line consequences; therefore, everything counts. This is the golden rule of excellence.*

Self-knowledge grows as you subject your life to examination. Listening to your own speech, reflecting on your own thoughts, looking at your own actions—these are the processes by which you master your growth and capabilities. You shape your philosophies and abilities by observing, and striving to understand the events of each moment. A focus on virtues to attain and vices to forego is crucial.

Everything Counts! serves as a call to greater personal awareness, accountability, and self-discipline; not to neurosis. It offers a fresh, honest perspective on living; an ongoing investigation of truth. And in this investigation, *everything* counts.

One thing is undeniable: making everything count requires a conscientious and sustained effort on the part of each of us. The examined life is the life worth living. By adopting the golden rule of excellence, you'll begin to examine even the smallest details; those which in the past may have compromised performance and even contaminated your character and reputation.

You already possess everything you require for this investigation. All you need to do now is to make this potential actual, one day at a time. You do this by following your goals and embracing excellence as your ideal. Pursuit of your goals and a genuine commitment to excellence is compelling; each step offers an opportunity for growth, learning, maturity, and self-improvement.

No matter how you define excellence, it will always include exceptional quality, meticulous attention to details, uncompromising standards, and superior craftsmanship fueled by love and passion. Excellence is respected and admired, and serves as the triumphant accomplishment of those unwilling to accept anything less than their absolute best. World-class results are the product of world-class habits and activities. From start to finish, the distinguishing characteristics of success are found in the details.

One of the most impressive characteristics of all high achievers is their relentless commitment to excellence and the meticulous attention to details associated with that journey. High achievers turn over all stones, understanding and exploiting to their benefit the fact that the critical distinction between merely acceptable versus excellent results lies in the smallest of details. They acknowledge and accept that the difference between gold and silver at the Olympics can be traced to the tiniest of differences in training or execution; as a result, they make everything count.

Unfortunately, far too many people and organizations function in a suspended state of mediocrity. Reputations are damaged, brands diluted, and loyalty is lost by blatant disregard for the small stuff which negatively impacts the customer experience. The popular philosophy that instructs us not to "sweat the small stuff" is flawed, because it breeds poor customer service, underperformance, wasted opportunity, mistakes, inconsistencies, rework, and oversights.

From typos to tardiness, many people and organizations act as if details just don't matter much. The result of this mind-set is that they treat customers poorly, deliver sloppy results, and show up both unprepared and late. While mission statements and service creeds extol excellence, quality, and consistency, clients and customers tend to receive mediocrity, apathy, and—far too often—incompetence.

Quite frankly, this has to stop. If a business truly wants to create cult status with their customers, then it must embrace *Everything Counts*! as its operational philosophy! This adoption will become the driver for organizing all sales, service, and performance-improvement initiatives. It will also become a sustainable competitive weapon.

In business, the smallest of details count when it comes to creating perfect brand perception. Every element and detail in each company's communications portfolio is waiting to receive a touch of consistent branding: the language and tone used in letters, the standby music on the phone system, fax cover sheets, download time from Internet sites, the presentation of invoices . . . . The list goes on and on.

Likewise, in your personal life, no detail is too small to count—ask anyone on a diet. Success is in the details. Sometimes we get so caught up in the big race toward our ideal weight that we forget that we get to the finish line one step at a time. Each calorie-cutting gesture counts and pays off in weight loss and a better awareness of healthy eating habits.

People have within themselves the power to raise the bar of their own performance any time they wish by dumping "don't sweat" complacency and embracing an *"Everything Counts!"* attitude. An *"Everything Counts!"* mindset is today's total quality initiative for a productive and satisfying personal life, family life, and business life.

The *"Everything Counts!"* life is one lived in discipline, during which the individual takes charge of his or her own behaviors and exercises the control necessary to do what needs to be done right . . . the first time!

For those who believe in the importance of quality and meticulous attention to details, no explanation is necessary; for those who don't, no answer is satisfactory. Consider this book an invitation to support the crusade; everything you do produces a quality outcome, so make excellence the quality outcome of choice.

Life is, in some respects, like a game of chess. The opening gambit may have been made long ago and responses long set in motion. Indeed, some pieces may have been lost, but the board is still filled with opportunity. Every move has importance. Every decision has consequence. Every wasted opportunity is a tactical error. Every move counts!

Different and sometimes conflicting interests drive the competition on the other side of the chessboard of life. You are often your own greatest adversary; prone to self-destruction, sabotage, and other means of moving away from victory and into checkmate. Just as chess has its rules, so does the game of life, and while knowing a game's rules does not guarantee that you'll win every match, disregarding the rules makes playing the game difficult—and winning virtually impossible.

Make no mistake, the adoption of an *Everything Counts!* philosophy takes conscious effort, immense discipline, and a deep reservoir of commitment. If it were easy, you wouldn't need those attributes to be successful.

I encourage you to read this book as you would read a love letter, because in a love letter, everything counts. You read every single word carefully—between, above, below the lines, and in the margins as well. You notice the cute dot over the "i," and you examine the stamp for meaning. You turn over pages, hoping to find something on the other side. You smell the envelope for any hint of fragrance. You study the salutation and feel warmed by the close. Like falling in love, the pursuit of excellence may defy explanation; but you know in your gut when it's happening.

Everything Counts! is much more than a smorgasbord of psychological comfort food. It is a book about thinking and acting better—a celebration of excellence that is meant to raise your awareness, focus your attention on details—and a call to action to raise one's standards.

But the most important part of this book is what you decide to do with it. I encourage you to include your actions, contributions, decisions, and the results of those decisions. To that end—and to focus your efforts on making everything count—you are asked to act on each lesson and apply it in your life and your career.

It's my pleasure to present to you these 52 remarkable ways to inspire excellence and drive results. Embrace, inhabit, and make them your own. Most importantly, make progress every step of the way.

Everything Counts!
—Gary Ryan Blair

P.S. Before you read the rest of this book, call this number for a special message and learn how to best implement the Everything Counts message into your life and business—800.870.0248.

PROFESSIONAL STRATEGIES

Every Detail Counts

"The magic behind every outstanding performance is always found in the smallest of details."

If you long to accomplish great and noble tasks, you first must learn to approach *every* task as though it were great and noble. Even the grandest project depends on the success of the smallest components.

Many people downplay small details, dismissing them as minutia—the "small stuff" that we're encouraged to ignore. But in fact, our entire environment is simply an accumulation of tiny details. Although we measure our lives in years, we live them in days, hours, minutes, and seconds. Every action—every detail of our lives—has bottom-line repercussions, and it's dangerous and derogatory to think of any of those details as trivial, unimportant, or inconsequential.

3

Successful people, in many walks of life, understand the importance of detail:

- Crime scene investigators know that it's often the smallest, most obscure detail that results in the arrest and prosecution of criminals.
- Athletes and coaches are all too aware that one minor misjudgment can swing momentum to their competitor and result in a loss rather than a win.
- Doctors and nurses understand that the slightest mistake or loss of focus can result in a tragic situation that carries massive liability.
- Business people carefully oversee the details of their products and services, knowing that one simple slip-up can cause a series of events that negatively impacts the bottom line, brand integrity, and public perception.
- Engineers and architects know that the stability of the most gigantic structure depends on the integrity of its smallest element; a failed bolt or a misplaced pin can have huge consequences.
- Firefighters, first aid responders, and other emergency personnel are trained to focus on details even as a tragedy unfolds; every second can make the difference between life and death in an emergency situation.
- Amusement parks know that the safety and physical well-being of their guests—and the financial viability of the company—require consistent and meticulous attention to the minute mechanical details of rides and attractions.
- Computer programmers spend their careers tightly focused on detail, as one incorrect digit in a code of millions can create an operational nightmare for the end user.
- Automotive detailers make their living by restoring a car to showroom condition. This requires the removal of every last piece of lint, dirt, and grime; and the major tool of their trade is a simple Q-tip.

Ultimately, the key to quality in every aspect of our lives is doing little things correctly—all the time, every time—so that each action produces a quality result. When every detail is lovingly attended to, and each step in the process is given complete and careful attention, the result inevitably will be of the highest quality.

Passion for your work, a pervasive commitment to quality, and relentless attention to details are essential markers of excellence. Quality work and an appreciation for the importance of details benefit not just the clients a business serves; these attitudes and habits also bring joy and peace of mind to the person who delivers the work. To know how to do something exceptionally well is to enjoy it.

The magic behind every outstanding performance, exceptional meal, and fine piece of furniture, jewelry, or clothing is always found in the smallest of details. Those who enjoy the greatest success understand that it takes hundreds of small, seemingly insignificant details repeated perfectly day in and day out to create an unforgettably excellent experience.

The people who deliver superior results are not simply doing more of the same things everyone else does; they are doing *better* things. Very small differences, consistently practiced, produce superior results.

In business, it is the attention to these little things—the details—that create and build long-term customer loyalty. From the training of employees and the quality of products and services, to the type of stationery used in correspondence and the music customers hear when placed on hold, a successful company knows that every detail counts. The thread count of a sheet, the font style for a product's label, the lighting of a room, the welcoming smile, the floral display in the lobby, or the polish and shine of a doorknob— all of these are "small" details that leave big impressions. In the successful organization, no element is too minor to escape close attention. If you believe that you are too busy to focus on details, or that attending to the minutia of your business or life would make you less effective in delivering your services, then I encourage you to reexamine your thinking.

Further, I can tell you the following with confidence: No matter what business or personal activities in which you are engaged, you will be continuously challenged by larger problems that could have been prevented if you had paid closer attention to the details at the beginning. The particulars of your work affect your company's ability to compete and prosper. A careless or cavalier approach to these details is the kiss of death to success. Those committed to excellence know that the real threat to success isn't the Armageddon of some huge and horrible slip-up; it's the much more insidious danger of being nibbled to death by the smallest of mistakes or oversights.

No lapse of judgment, taste, or quality can be shrugged off by a true professional. Successful people know that everything counts. It's not that the devil is in the details, but that every small particle contains a seed that can potentially determine the difference between success and failure. Therefore, if the benefits of hard work are to be maximized, attention *must* be paid to detail.

Excellence in any endeavor is a production in which every little detail tells a story about one's intention, commitment, and character. Pay attention to the small stuff. Consistent attention to fine points produces excellence—that's why every detail counts!

EVERY DETAIL COUNTS—CALL TO ACTION

To explore your own commitment to making the details count, ask yourself these questions:

- Do you pay adequate attention to the details of your life? If so, what are the supporting benefits and how can you apply the same lessons to more areas?
- Do you believe that taking the time to focus on the details of your work would harm your effectiveness—or others' perception of your effectiveness?
- What step will you take to bring more focus to the details of your life?

PORTRAIT OF A DETAILED BUSINESS

The Ritz-Carlton Hotels

The Ritz-Carlton Hotel is a legend in the hospitality industry, with a 100 year track record of impeccable service and meticulous attention to detail.

Modeled after the grand hotels in Europe of the previous nineteenth century, the Ritz's tradition of privacy, sophistication and elegance continues unchanged, as guests continually attribute the Ritz hotel chain's personal attention to the small things that matter as the key item that sets their service apart from all others.

One story from the chain's Boston era hotel particularly illustrates how this focus supports their reputation. During the 1920s, it was a commonly known fact that glass imported from Europe underwent a chemical reaction when hitting the Boston air, and turned blue. Blue glass windows meant the homeowners could afford imported glass. The Ritz-Carlton, being quite fashionable, ordered glasses in this color; and to this day, you will still find blue glasses in their dining rooms.

Even as other hotels change hands, become homogenized and cut service to make up for lower occupancy levels, the Ritz-Carlton Company grows and prospers while remaining the industry's shining star. These hotels are places where the genuine care and comfort of guests is the company's highest mission. Every Ritz-Carlton associate knows that their role is to pay

6

attention to the small kindnesses that create the Ritz experience for their guests.

It's no surprise that the Ritz-Carlton Hotel Company has received all of the major awards that can be bestowed by the hospitality industry. In fact they were the first and only hotel company twice honored with the prestigious Malcolm Baldrige National Quality Award. Their standards of excellence serve as benchmarks for hotels and resorts worldwide.

It is the Ritz's continued attention to the little things that made them famous that reinforces their reputation for quality with their present and future guests.

2

COMMITMENT COUNTS

*"Commitment protects and strengthens your credibility
and reputation with yourself and others."*

Commitments present themselves in delineations of black and white; after all, you either honor your commitments, or you don't. Success is the result of making and keeping commitments to yourself and others, while all failed or unfinished goals, projects, and relationships are the direct result of broken obligations. It's that simple, that profound, and that important.

A commitment made must become a commitment honored, as each one counts in more ways than you can possibly imagine. Your ability to honor your promises directly impacts your credibility, reputation, trustworthiness, earning ability, and overall peace of mind. Character defines an individual; honoring commitments helps to define character.

Every day, you make commitments to customers, family members, and associates. Some are explicit, others implied; but each one ultimately results in success or failure. Nothing builds confidence and loyalty more reliably than a history of well-kept promises; and by the same token, nothing will undermine your reputation faster than a string of broken commitments.

If you look at successful people in any field, you may not discover that they're necessarily the brightest, best looking, fastest, or strongest of the bunch. What you *will* find, however, is that they are the ones with the deepest reservoir of commitment. They fully understand that all great accomplishment is preceded by great commitment. So, how great is the power of your commitment?

"Disposable" is a word suited to describe many of today's products. From razors to diapers, from milk cartons to toner cartridges, it seems that disposability is being built into the very fabric of society. Have commitments and promises fallen into the same trap? Is it really "no big deal" to make a pledge and then discard it; to make a promise and simply walk away from it?

Commitment is a virtue—one that requires fulfillment and punishes unfaithfulness. For many, it's going to take a dramatic shift to embrace the importance of commitments and internalize the meaning of permanence.

A man without his word is fundamentally worthless. It's like having a stain on your reputation that no amount of bleach could ever remove. If your word is not supported by action—if you take a cavalier attitude toward your obligations—then the party's over. You may as well stick a fork in your reputation, because no one will be interested in working with you.

Your word is a form of capital. It's money in the bank for someone who is counting on it. That being said, you should only invest your capital where and when it counts most or it will lose its value. And because your word is like currency, you must give it only when the occasion is important enough to call for it. The person to whom you are promising something must be able to recognize that your word has real value, and that it's not counterfeit. You certainly don't give money out to every Tonya, Dick, and Harry; you should treat your promises with the same level of respect. Remember, what you don't protect, you don't get to keep. A reputation is a terrible thing to waste.

You had best learn not to say you will deliver on something you know you can't—whether it's promising to pay someone back, keep a secret, or saying you'll do a favor on which you have no intention of following through. Consider this: What's the point of making a commitment or promise if you don't even plan to honor it? This question applies to your relationship with others just as much as it does to your relationship with yourself.

The greatest and most unfortunate betrayal is that of oneself. Being able to adhere to our commitments begins with self-respect. When we say one thing and do another—when we start projects but don't finish them; when we go on a diet but quit soon after beginning—then the only thing at which we become successful is sabotaging our reputation with ourselves. And when we dishonor our own commitments and lie to ourselves, how on earth can we be expected to honor the commitments we make to others? There is no backdoor to a self-made promise. There is no contractual loophole. Either you maintain the contract, or you are in breach.

By dishonoring your own commitments, you undermine and poison whatever faith you have in your own abilities. A strong, healthy, psychological immune system is essential for success; there's no better way to ensure that than by making each commitment count.

What kind of person do you want to be known as: someone who has character and a stellar reputation? Or as someone who's unreliable, untrustworthy ... even a quitter? Do you want to able to hold your head up high with dignity and self-respect? If so, adopt this philosophy:

If you make a commitment, honor it.

If you make a promise, keep it.

If you set a goal, achieve it.

Commitment is an act of pledging or engaging oneself to do or to perform. Once there is an authentic obligation—rather than just a passing interest—you will find a way to make great things happen. To translate your promises into action, and to experience the power of commitment, consider these questions:

- Are you interested in getting in shape, or passionately committed?
- Are you interested in simplifying your life, or passionately committed?
- Are you interested in spending more time with your kids, or passionately committed?
- Are you interested in writing a book, or passionately committed?
- Are you interested in spiritual growth, or passionately committed?
- Are you interested in improving your marriage, or passionately committed?
- Are you interested in paying off your debts, or passionately committed?
- Are you interested in starting your own business, or passionately committed?

Fantastic things can be accomplished once you move beyond merely being *interested* to a state of *passionate* commitment. Until you've committed to them, goals are irrelevant, dreams are useless, and hopes are no more than a pipe dream. Commitment inspires you to perform to the best of your abilities.

It protects and strengthens your credibility and reputation with yourself and others. It provides you with passionate energy and unstoppable momentum, and fills you with a sense of pride that's priceless. Commitment counts!

COMMITMENT COUNTS—CALL TO ACTION

To explore your own determination to making every commitment count, ask yourself these questions:

- Do you honor every commitment?
- Do you ever betray yourself by making a commitment and then not following through on it? How does that make you feel about yourself?
- What step will you take to make sure that every commitment and promise you make counts?

PORTRAIT OF A COMMITTED MAN

Jerry Lewis

Jerry Lewis is a man of many titles; some of which include Comedian, Actor, Film Producer, Writer, Director, and Singer. But perhaps his most important title and responsibility is as Host of the Muscular Dystrophy Association.

Lewis has demonstrated an unshakable commitment to this organization for over 50 years, and has provided inspiration for millions of people throughout the world.

He explains his passion for helping others with this quote: "I shall pass through this world but once. Any good that I can do . . . for any human being, let me do it now . . . for I shall not pass this way again."

His annual Jerry Lewis Labor Day Telethon is the world's most successful televised fundraiser, having contributed over $1 billion to help the more than one million people who suffer from debilitating neuromuscular diseases.

Through his efforts, the Association has established 215 clinics that also serve as sites for clinical trials of the latest experimental therapies and drugs, some 240 support groups for families, and summer camps where annually over 4,000 kids with disabilities can just visit and simply be "kids."

There is no way to count the thousands of lives Jerry Lewis has affected or the relief his work has brought to families, long time sufferers, and especially to the kids—Jerry's kids.

One simple commitment lived out through a life of service has made a huge difference in the world.

3

LEADERSHIP COUNTS

"Good leaders have good character and good
ethics; they do not lie, cheat, or steal."

A leader doesn't have to be brilliant, charismatic, nor charming; you can hire and buy those attributes. However, you can't buy courage, decency, or honor, and you certainly can't rent a strong moral compass. Strong character provides a leader with a commanding competitive advantage, whereas a weak character is a competitive liability that will ultimately undermine all efforts.

In the widening chasm between what we want and expect from our leaders and what we get, it is important to take a close look at leadership itself. Leadership is all about one enduring quality: character. Popularity is temporary, change is often unpredictable, and interest rates always fluctuate. The one true constant is a person's disposition—their character.

Leaders are stewards—caretakers who hold something in trust on behalf of others. Leaders exist to protect cherished values and core beliefs, sustain and inspire hopes, and help drive positive results for all. A steward is a caretaker, a person who holds something in trust on behalf of others. It is not a behavior that is motivated out of self-interest.

Leadership is truly about choosing service over self-interest. Properly performed, leadership is an exercise in outgoing and ongoing concern for others, including the definition and enforcement of boundaries as needed. For leaders to be effective, however, there must be uncompromising emphasis on integrity of character.

Stewardship is only virtuous if the steward consciously seeks out and achieves the good of the community above all else. A steward, then, can be defined as an individual who upholds what is best for all people, even if it may not be in his or her own interest to do so. In addition to protecting values and beliefs, good stewards live those values as a model and example for others to follow.

We will likely find ourselves thrust into various leadership roles throughout our lives. We are each called upon to be stewards of what is right and good for those in our care. The quality of our stewardship depends greatly on what we perceive a steward to be, on how we think about other people, on the seriousness of our commitment, and most importantly, on how we determine what is right and worth holding in trust.

Leadership is everybody's business; it is an issue that affects each and every one of us. Not only do we look to leaders for guidance and direction, but also we are all called upon to exercise leadership in any number of temporary situations. Whether we are called upon to be involved in leading government or business, coaching a team, educating young minds, running a family, organizing a dinner party/carpool/household, or standing for what is right—everyone participates in leadership roles at one time or another in their lives.

Are you the kind of person that others want to follow? The answer to that question depends on your character. A strong leader sets a strong example. No one, under any circumstances, should ever be appointed to or accept a leadership role unless they are willing to have his or her character serve as the model for others to emulate. A good steward knows that his or her character is contagious, and hopes that everyone will become "infected." A leader's nature casts a long shadow over his organization, and helps to determine the makeup of the organization itself. What you do, how you do it, and what you say sets the tone for everyone involved and creates the boundaries of acceptable behavior. The values you profess—the ones you hold in trust—must be aligned with the behaviors you demonstrate.

Leaders who possess good character are those who, through repeated good acts, achieve an appropriate balance of the *virtues* in his life. Therefore, like a successful athlete, the virtuous person plays a consistently good game. As Aristotle rightly noted, "we are what we repeatedly do."

The underlying spirit of a company or team is created from the top. If an enterprise conveys a great spirit, its top people display a positive attitude. If it decays, however, it does so because the top rots, just as a fish rots from the head.

Character is shaped by drive, competence, and integrity. While many leaders possess the drive and competence necessary to lead, far too many lack the moral compass. These types of leaders tend to be self-serving, and sabotage the spirit of an enterprise. As these people assume greater power and authority, an Achilles heel of pride and arrogance is created. This serves only to erode the trust of followers.

People have an indisputable, divine right to expect and demand good character and exemplary conduct from their leaders. The true test and strength of an enterprise is not to be found in a company's products or services, but in the character of its leaders. It serves as the conscience of the community.

Leadership is exercised through character; personality sets the example and is imitated by others in the organization. Character is not something about which one can fool people. A lack of character will "rat out" your true intentions, no matter how hard you attempt to cover them up. Good leaders have strong moral fiber and sound ethics; they do not lie, cheat, or steal. Ethical behavior is not easy, but it is *essential* to effective leadership. Ethical leaders are self-confident, not self-centered. There is no gray area when it comes to character and integrity—it's foundational. With it, a committed team can produce outstanding results; without it, there is no respect or moral authority to execute.

A leader cannot succeed if his people don't trust him. If he bends the rules and says what is convenient, he might succeed in the short run, but will come up short in the end. Good leaders fight to protect their character, integrity, and reputation.

Stewardship will always be tested. As a leader, you will forever be confronted with opportunities that conflict with your own self-interest. You must always remember that a steward is a caretaker—someone who holds something in trust on behalf of others.

Life is full of curious and meaningful paradoxes. Steward leadership is one such paradox that will serve you well in all of your leadership roles. It offers hope and guidance for the creation of better, more caring institutions, and it helps to explain why leadership counts.

LEADERSHIP COUNTS—CALL TO ACTION

To explore your own commitment to making leadership count, ask yourself these questions:

- Do you believe that the role of leadership is to serve as a steward, or simply as someone who exerts control over others?
- Do you demonstrate the type of values, character, and integrity that others would want to follow?
- What step will you take to becoming a more effective leader?

PORTRAIT OF LEADERSHIP

Truett Cathy, Founder Chick-fil-A

Truett Cathy believes that good leaders must be of good character and character is proven by daily actions.

Armed with a Depression-era work ethic, he was able to transform his chicken sandwich idea into Chick-fil-A, one of the country's largest, privately owned restaurant chains with nearly $3 billion in sales.

Cathy has always wanted his company to focus on people more than profits so they have a positive influence on all who come in contact with Chick-fil-A.

He believes leaders are servants. They must motivate themselves to do their very best, and by their example lead others to do their best.

Therefore, all company locations are closed on Sundays to give employees time to relax with their families, as well as to honor God.

Leaders are stewards entrusted with the responsibility to give back to their communities.

Leading by example, Cathy established the Win Shape Foundation that runs 14 foster homes caring for children who have been victims of unfortunate circumstances.

He believes that even as the world changes, we need to be reminded that the important things have not changed. Chick-fil-A is about more than just selling chicken. They are a part of their customer's lives and the communities in which they serve.

After over 40 years of consecutive growth, Cathy's actions have adequately proven he is a leader with character.

4

Focus Counts

"Focus serves as an absolute precondition for every success you will experience."

The guiding principle that should drive your every decision is the law of focus. Everything you think, say, and do is either taking you closer to or further away from it; therefore, it must be your key decision-making criteria.

Focus can be defined as your ability to keep your thoughts and actions trained on achieving a goal; a picture in your mind's eye of something you want to be, have, or do. Your focus captivates your attention and provokes an irresistible sense of optimism and faith for the future. It's the equivalent of Moby Dick in a goldfish bowl—just too powerful to ignore!

There are only 24 hours in a day; that's a given. It's how you focus these hours and minutes that really counts. Between the ringing phone, urgent e-mails, instant messages, drop-in visitors, tighter deadlines, endless opportunities, and ever greater expectations, concentrating on what's most important—the highest and best use of your time—has become more of a challenge than ever before.

With all the distractions that abound on a daily basis, it's rather easy to routinely lose focus and be pulled off course. Every new opportunity is a contestant for time and focus that, once lost, creates collateral damage to existing results and momentum.

Time is the most precious of life's commodities. The material possessions that you desire eventually become faded memories without sustained focus. You must jealously guard your focus, as any individual or organization for which focus is either absent or incidental is not a successful one.

Unless you're able to give complete attention to your goals and desires, your full potential will never see the light of day. Focus is the key ingredient that can make or break your career, and ultimately, your life. Yet when you look closely at most people and businesses—when you *really* peek under the covers—you will more often than not find them operating in an unfocused state. Few things are more admirable than a focused and committed individual.

Focus is a strategic asset and the key factor that drives all results. Any kind of positive outcome requires that you concentrate your efforts on the smallest number of activities that will produce the largest amount of productivity. Yet no other principle is violated as constantly, as recklessly, and as directly—or indirectly—as the basic principle of focus. The days of being everything to everyone are effectively over. You must have a sense of direction; you must have a focus.

Your primary objective in life is to find your true North, then to point all of your resources in that direction. Focus is the future, in the sense that it not only makes a prediction about where your future lies, but also propels you to take specific steps to make the future happen.

Focus is a language that speaks simply and eloquently to the fundamental human similarity between people. Why? Because everyone struggles with it! If focus is so important, then how come so few people seem to be driven by it? Why does it get so little attention in school? Why is it routinely violated and ignored by most people? The answer is much simpler than you may think; sometimes the hardest thing to do and see is often the most obvious.

Let's try giving a new twist to the old saying, "a fool and his money are soon parted": An unfocused person and his goal are soon parted. Loss of concentration is as common as the common cold. It's a fact of life that creates a serious competitive problem, but also dictates a serious competitive solution. Focus is much too important to be left to amateurs.

The moment of truth occurs the moment you begin to focus. Implementing and sustaining a drive toward a specific goal will put you in the best position (relative to others) for opportunity. It will also help you build support because you demonstrate real accountability, genuine results, and superior performance.

Focus can be seen as a preemptive strike against mediocrity. When you focus, you create a powerful force of directed energy; that is its purpose. When you lose focus, however, you lose your power. You dissipate your energy over a wide spectrum of activities, and accomplish very little of value. The moment you focus on a goal, your goal becomes a magnet that pulls you and your resources toward it. The more focused your energies, the more power you generate.

People are frequently driven by the urge to have, be, and do more in and with their lives. They feel that success demands increases in income, houses, clothes, and cars, even when these things are simply not necessary. Predictably, in order to meet these needs, people are spreading themselves way too thin. Simply put, the urge for "more" causes individuals to become unfocused.

While "more" might be an admirable result of other initiatives, the pursuit of growth for its own sake is a serious strategic error. It's the primary reason that people and businesses lose their focus. They have been paying heavily for this mistake, and there's no question we all have made tactical errors that have caused us to lose our direction.

While losing one's focus is never a *conscious* act of sabotage, living a focused life requires a high degree of concentration and consciousness. The tag team of focus and concentration is truly double trouble for your competitors. When a person or company begins to take the initial steps toward achieving a goal, usually they are highly focused. But at some point, they begin to lose this sense of direction. They become involved in a host of multiple agendas and, over time, become rather distracted. They slowly lose their way; they don't know where they're going or why. Their mission loses its meaning, and rather than finding true North, all they find is confusion.

You've probably had a similar experience yourself. Everything is going well at the beginning, you're gaining a sense of momentum, and productivity is taking off like a rocket. This sense of success and the opportunity to try new things, however, creates something else: the seeds of its own demise. You're filled with enthusiasm and energy, and feel like you could take on the world.

It never happens, though; after a while, things start to go south. What once seemed like a world of opportunity turns into a disaster. The damage takes a toll on all aspects of the project: objectives, profits, morale, self-esteem, and self-confidence. The bottom line is that it's the same drill with everyone, because everyone loses focus from time to time.

When you begin to focus, be prepared to fend off distractions. They're everywhere. Once you are focused, you must protect this drive by any and all means possible. While it is always possible to regain focus, it is far easier to remain than to regain or rehabilitate.

Focus definitely counts as it serves as an absolute precondition for every success you will experience. And of all the activities you must cram into your busy schedule, managing your focus is the one you can least afford to overlook.

FOCUS COUNTS—CALL TO ACTION

To explore your own commitment to making focus count, ask yourself these questions:

- Do you believe that focus is a competitive skill that must be developed or that it's better to be unfocused and just go with the flow?
- Do you think there's a connection between focus and excellence?
- What step will you take to lead a more focused and purposeful life?

PORTRAIT OF SUSTAINED FOCUS

Zappos.com

Online shoe company, Zappos.com has grown sales from "just about nothing" to over $900 million in eight years because of their unrelenting focus on customer satisfaction, says CEO, Tony Hsieh.

With 1,300 employees and over 6 million customers, maintaining employee and customer loyalty is focus number one.

On any given day, 75 percent of Zappos' customers are repeat customers.

Tony Hsieh's goal is to grow the company while maintaining their service-oriented culture and feel of a small company.

He feels that employees who know what they are doing are happier and happy employees provide better service to customers and that's how they will maintain their culture.

Every new employee is required to go through four weeks of Customer Loyalty Training at full salary, before starting the job that he/she was actually hired for.

After a week of training, the new employees are offered $2,000 to leave the company immediately, no strings attached. This is to ensure people are there for the love of the job and not the money. Over 97 percent turn down the buyout.

Mr. Hsieh wants their customers to associate the Zappos.com brand with the absolute best service so they can become their service company. A service company that happens to sell shoes, handbags, clothing, eyewear, watches, accessories, and just about anything.

For Zappos.com, customer service isn't a department—it's the company's entire focus.

5

CONSISTENCY COUNTS

"Consistency improves the experience for both yourself and the beneficiaries of your efforts."

Consistency—or the absence of contradictions—is one of the hallmarks of success. While variety may be the spice of life, consistency is crucial to the achievement of any goal. It is defined as the "agreement or harmony of parts or features to one another or a whole: correspondence; specifically: ability to be asserted together without contradiction." The agreement and harmony of your daily activities can indeed create synergy, making "the whole greater than the sum of its parts."

Consistency not only saves you time by helping to simplify and focus your efforts, but more importantly, it helps you to set and routinely meet the expectations you have of yourself. This equates to a positive impact on bottom-line results. Whether we like to admit it or not, as creatures of habit we all like, expect, and appreciate consistency. When we learn or experience something new, we expect to be able to apply that knowledge on a consistent basis.

Ask most Americans to name the three colors used on a traffic light, and, without a doubt, they will say, "red, yellow, and green." Ask them to name the color of a UPS truck. In unison, they will say, "brown." How about the color of a Tiffany's box? "Robin's egg blue!"

The next time you read a newspaper or magazine, take a good look at the fonts, color schemes, and margins. Then examine each section to identify differences and similarities. Where are the crossword puzzles? Where are the feature stories? How do you know that the weather is on the back page or that the lottery numbers are on page 2? How do you know that the letters to the editor are in the front of your favorite magazine or that editorials are in the back of your favorite newspaper?

ONE WORD—CONSISTENCY

It therefore follows that good engineers, designers, and architects recognize the importance of consistency. The streets in most American cities are good examples of both consistency and conservation of knowledge. Anywhere in America, yield and stop signs look exactly the same. Traffic lights use red, yellow, and green to mean precisely the same things regardless of the street, city, or zip code you may be in, thus making them clearly identifiable anywhere. It becomes difficult for people and society when their knowledge of things breaks down in the face of inconsistency. Visitors to a country with street signs differing from their own inevitability make mistakes until they learn the new signs, which are, in fact, consistent to the people of that country. Even subtle variances and inconsistencies, such as the difference between kilometers and miles per hour, can and will cause American drivers to make mistakes.

Here are several examples of how a consistent approach can maximize your performance and accelerate the rate at which you achieve any goal:

- Consistently deliver excellent work.
- Consistently show up on time.
- Consistently tell the truth and do the right thing.
- Consistently follow through on your commitments.
- Consistently go the extra mile for your customers.
- Consistently take action and avoid excuses and procrastination.
- Consistently work out and eat the right foods.
- Consistently meet or exceed quota.
- Consistently pursue your passion and purpose.

- Consistently invest your money wisely.
- Consistently acknowledge the good work of others.
- Consistently demonstrate love and happiness.
- Consistently make everything you say, think, and do count.

Consistency is wonderful when used appropriately because it improves the experience for both yourself and the beneficiaries of your efforts. But is consistency *all* there is to the successful achievement of any goal or project? We may be perfectly consistent with respect to our behaviors, moral principles, and values; yet our behaviors may be unhealthy, our principles may be incorrect, and our values may be misplaced. "A foolish consistency is the hobgoblin of little minds . . . ." wrote Emerson.

We may even be consistent in treating others as we treat ourselves, but this kind of consistency would hardly be the mark of a good life if we happen to treat ourselves poorly. We might say that while consistency is surely not *sufficient* for success, it is absolutely necessary for success! Success requires that there be consistency in our behaviors and in how we apply these behaviors. Success in any endeavor also requires a consistency between our standards and our actions, as well as among our inner desires. Finally, success requires that there be consistency between how we treat ourselves and how we treat others.

In some cases, consistency can become a self-perpetuating monster; therefore it has to be used for a purpose. A foolish consistency is one that serves no one well—neither the person acting consistently nor the one who might otherwise benefit from some kind of more functional consistency.

Consider the following examples of counterproductive consistency:

- Consistently being inconsistent.
- Consistently engaging in mediocre work.
- Consistently being late for meetings.
- Consistently lying and cheating.
- Consistently spending more than you earn.
- Consistently disregarding commitments.
- Consistently procrastinating on important deadlines.
- Consistently avoiding responsibility by making excuses.

Consistency is great because people like predictability—not surprises. Family, friends, coworkers, and customers feel comfortable when they can rely on you to do exactly what they think you will do and have done in the past. Consistency counts—especially when it comes to results. No one-hit-wonders allowed, as you only get a lifetime achievement award by building a lifetime body of results.

We have a strong preference for consistency in our lives. We want things to work the same way every time they happen. When we wake up in the morning, we want to find the floor under our feet, the sun above our heads, and coffee in our cups. Just as we expect these kinds of physical consistencies, we also expect psychological consistency. If we had marriages, families, and jobs yesterday, we expect to find them today in pretty much the same condition. Thus, we have "mental worlds" of our expectancies about the world and the people in them that define our relationships. The glue that holds all of these mental relationships together is consistency. Why should we expect our spouses to love us tomorrow? Because that behavior is consistent with their behavior today.

Consistency becomes a form of human gravity. It holds everything in place and together. It helps us to understand the world and our place in it, and that's why consistency counts.

CONSISTENCY COUNTS—CALL TO ACTION

To explore your own commitment to making consistency count, ask yourself these questions:

- Do you appreciate consistently good service, food, and conversation? Why is that type of consistency important to you?
- Are you consistent in positive ways? For example, do you consistently deliver excellent service, are you consistently prepared, and do you consistently follow up on commitments?
- What step will you take to ensure a greater sense of consistency in all of your endeavors?

PORTRAIT OF CONSISTENCY

Steven Spielberg

There are few names in the movie industry that can virtually guarantee a film's financial success. The one sure-fire guarantee is Steven Spielberg.

His films have been so popular, so consistently entertaining, that people rush to see anything he does.

Spielberg's films have consistently been megahits starting with his first real Hollywood blockbuster, Jaws, and continuing for over four decades.

In Jaws, he created a convincing 25-foot man-eating shark. The shoot ran over by 100 days—Spielberg was almost replaced—but thanks to his mastery of suspense and clever action techniques, the $8.5 million Jaws took off, making $260 million and began the trend for summer blockbusters.

Beyond this, it made the world afraid to go back in the water. Some of us haven't gone back in since.

Ironically, Spielberg was twice turned down for the prestigious film course at the University of Southern California. It was a minor bump in the road since, by the age of 22, Spielberg was signed by Universal, and the rest is history.

Moviegoers all over the world owe a debt to Spielberg for his commitment to excellence and for his ability to consistently produce some of the best movies ever including, Close Encounters of the Third Kind, Raiders of the Lost Ark, E.T. the Extra-Terrestrial, Poltergeist, The Color Purple, Rain Man, Jurassic Park, Schindler's List, Saving Private Ryan, and the list goes on.

People have come to expect consistent winners from Spielberg and he consistently delivers.

6

BOLDNESS COUNTS

"Boldness means making valued decisions and moving forward assertively for what you believe in."

Have you ever noticed who gets the most respect and the most rewards? It's not the wallflowers; it's not the people that sit back and wait for others to do things for them. Rather, it's those who act boldly who are recognizing both a fundamental right as well as a pragmatic reality. Every act of boldness accelerates the pace with which you enjoy success.

Those who have accomplished much have been men and women with a spirit of boldness and adventure. They are willing to challenge and constantly question even the existence of the comfort zone; they try new ideas, and attempt the seemingly impossible. They thrive under pressure and take the risks and actions that meeker people are simply too afraid to attempt. The men and women who reach the upper echelon of success are those who act boldly.

What exactly do I mean by boldness? Boldness eloquently describes bravery, and the act of responding to a situation in a manner that may be viewed as daring to some, but that is essential to address effectively the issue at hand. Boldness is a strategic, tactical approach to a given situation. It requires an acute awareness of one's situation, strong nerves, and craftiness. Boldness means taking risks, and when you decide upon a course of action, boldness demands that you execute it aggressively.

It takes a great deal of boldness to confront and tackle the issues in today's society with a straightforward approach. Boldness isn't inherited. It's a characteristic that will blossom with the determination you have to live an uncommon life of bravery. Boldness does not mean being rude, reckless, insensitive, arrogant, or a bully. None of these attributes is acceptable to any of us ... ever!

What boldness *does* entail is that you make valued decisions and move forward for what you believe in. By challenging individual growth and creating goals, you are bringing clarity to your dreams and energy that will revitalize your mind, body, and spirit.

Both boldness and timidity are acquired habits. They are learned behaviors, and because of this, you can choose to replace apprehension with courage. The truth of the matter is that high achievers learn to be bold in their actions, just as they can learn how to be timid. The trick is to cultivate boldness from within.

When will your finest hour come, and how will it arrive? Do you really think it will materialize without an act of supreme confidence, audacity, or boldness? What bold initiatives are you planning for?

When you are facing a decision to act, consider it an opportunity to prove your worth. The first thing you must do is to decide whether you want to take action or not. This is where the spirit of boldness comes into play. The person who consistently displays bold behavior will far outperform the person who does not. Boldness helps propel a person beyond what he or she might otherwise achieve. In fact, it has such a profound impact on the effectiveness of one's performance that I find it curious that this trait is not talked about more frequently as a fundamental ingredient of success.

You don't have to be a big shot to be bold. Often the most normal people suddenly achieve great heights because they learn the power that lies in acting boldly. When David faced Goliath, he was more than just the underdog, he was potential road kill. But you know how that turned out. David acted boldly—even though everyone else thought he had a screw loose—and slew the mighty Goliath. The story is now legend; an example to the world, which shows that it's the bold who make history. The timid? Well, they can read about it in the papers and live their lives in agonizing mediocrity.

Any action you take is an opportunity to improve yourself, advance your lot in life, and achieve greater success. Because people lack confidence, they also lack the aggressive boldness that is needed in order to have an impact on the world around us. Call it what you want, but cultivating boldness, audacity, or even chutzpah is no accident; nor is it an easy task. It takes guts. In fact, training yourself to act boldly usually takes a lot of blood, sweat, and tears. But it *can* be done, and if you want to be successful—if you want to be the one enjoying the fruits of your labor—then it *must* be done. Audacity has always been a component of successful ventures. More goals and dreams have been defeated because of lack of boldness and execution than for any other reason.

The surest way to get comfortable with high performance is by telling yourself: This needs to be done, I'm the one to get it done, and I'm going to get it done at all costs. Say this to yourself every time you are faced with the possibility to act and advance yourself. Make it happen, do what you have to do, and you'll gain the reputation of being a doer.

Boldness is the ability to dare to do those difficult things. It means standing out from the crowd. A bold act may not be popular, but that does not diminish the fact it is likely the right thing to do. Again, this takes courage to proceed. Popularity may only come when the prudence of an act is recognized.

We can't find satisfaction in our own lives by relying on the bold acts of others. Only the actions we take personally will change or better ourselves. Deciding to do what we know is right and good can often be a feat of daunting proportion. But when we step up to the challenge with boldness, the proportions diminish and we can face obstacles with assurance of success.

We must always be bold and assertive in each act, and seize every initiative … to move forward and to improve because every act of boldness counts!

BOLDNESS COUNTS—CALL TO ACTION

To explore your own commitment to making boldness count, ask yourself these questions:

- Do your actions demonstrate bold convictions, or do you passively go about your life taking whatever comes your way? Why?
- What bold initiatives are you planning for?
- What step will you take to demonstrate more boldness and moxie in your life?

PORTRAIT OF BOLDNESS

Ted Turner, CNN

"Early to bed, early to rise, work like hell and advertise!"

These words of fatherly advice have shaped Ted Turner's business life though his father committed suicide because of falling revenues in his billboard advertising business.

It fell to 24-year-old Ted to take over and take over he did.

He grew this business dramatically and used its success to propel his way into the media industry where he became one of the most amazing personalities of our time.

His accomplishments are many: The largest land owner in the United States (interesting because his grandfather lost his own farm during the Depression), revolutionized the television business with the creation of TBS and CNN (the first all-news network no one thought could work), winner of the America's Cup, a World Series championship trophy as owner of the Atlanta Braves.

Always bold, always colorful. He has been known to wear a Confederate officer's uniform with the accompanying sword to corporate negotiations.

An innovative entrepreneur, outspoken nonconformist, and groundbreaking philanthropist, Ted Turner is truly a living legend.

Ted Turner has always been willing to risk whatever it takes to accomplish something that he believes in and his acts of boldness have changed the way we watch the news throughout the world.

No matter how bold his vision, it is a good bet he will succeed.

!

7

QUALITY COUNTS

"A commitment to quality means never having to say you're sorry."

Quality is about love; it's a passionate obsession with perfection. It is the result of good intentions, uncompromising standards, sincere effort, intelligent design, attention to detail, and skillful execution. Quality is the calling card of greatness, and it represents the wisest choice among many alternatives.

True quality is only achieved through continuous improvement in performance that ensures the highest standards of your products, services, processes, and technology. If you intend to be competitive, then quality—in the broadest sense of the term—must become an obsession. Dynamic, sustainable results will only be achieved through an obsession with quality.

High achievers are essentially scientists whose laboratories happen to be any of a variety of places—the kitchen, athletic field, courtroom, classroom, and boardroom. They test assumptions, experiment with new concepts and ideas, and search through the minutia looking for the needle in the haystack that can lead to a breakthrough and competitive edge. In the pursuit of quality, high achievers bring a methodical, pragmatic, and demanding approach to work. Because these individuals only want to produce the best results, their personal standards are uncompromising. In their pursuit of perfection, they pay rigorous attention to detail, expect greatness, and consistently deliver superior results. In their efforts to perform at the top of their game, they show no mercy to themselves or others. They understand that quality is a competitive weapon, and they use it with great authority. For example:

- World-class chefs must fully comprehend the blending and interaction of ingredients down to the microscopic compounds in the dishes that they create. They are passionate about food, and strive to create a visual presentation that is as satisfying as the meal.
- Award-winning actors, artists, and other performers inhabit their work; they are students of their trade and strive to create perfection in every performance and rehearsal.
- Champion athletes approach their work with the precision of a surgeon and the brilliance of a military strategist. They know that success comes down to the smallest of details, and they look for the slightest edge in order to deliver a quality performance. They expect and play to win each time they compete.
- Superior teachers and professors never forget the significance of their role. They approach teaching with a sense of love, duty, and awed responsibility. They constantly and passionately look for ways to educate and inspire their students.
- Exceptional computer programmers use a series of digits to create a work of art. They search for ways to make the complex simple, visualize the perfect outcome, and work with an obsessive sense of conviction to make that vision a reality.
- Passionate wine makers accept nothing less than perfection. They tend to their grapes like mother hens, lovingly watching over each quality detail of their craft, and always look for ways to make their best product even better. Nothing is sacrificed, all is given, and no exceptions are ever allowed.
- The finest jewelers and watchmakers live by a highly stringent set of standards. Their commitment to quality materials, craftsmanship, and design is incredibly admirable. Their values are respected at all times, and reflect their preoccupation with quality and perfection at every level.

Quality is about doing things right the first time. It's easier and far less expensive to succeed right away because failure is more expensive in terms of time when you have to do the job over. Success eliminates the embarrassment of mediocrity and defeat, and money spent to fail must be spent again to succeed. It's easier to do things correctly right off the bat because credibility, once lost, is difficult—if not impossible—to regain. A commitment to quality means never having to say you're sorry.

The goal is simple: Make your own and your organization's name synonymous with quality. Strive to render ever more perfection to the form and function of your work. Ensure that each and every aspect of your work receives a finishing touch. The final attention to detail must be given to the polish. Every single facet of quality must be polished and buffed in such a way that the result exceeds all customer expectations.

Quality comes from putting your heart and soul into your work. It means that you are lovingly doing all of the things that bring out your absolute best. The word "love" is appropriate, because it is precisely right in both the meaning and the feeling that it carries. Do all things lovingly; that is the secret to quality.

Expecting nothing but perfection is the first step toward achieving it. A loving devotion to quality allows no detail to be overlooked. It wants everything to be just so; nothing that might affect that which makes the performance spectacular can be neglected or regarded as trivial. A compulsion to be tidy, orderly, and well-organized is a natural impulse and by-product in a workplace where quality is taken to heart.

To pursue quality is to aspire to perfection. While true perfection is unattainable, the passionate pursuit of perfection is what drives quality and fosters ongoing improvement. We can set high standards and strive to meet them, yet no matter how brilliantly we perform, our execution can always be improved.

While the ideal of perfection is always humbling, it should never be defeating. There is no rest when it comes to quality; therefore quality must be an obsession.

The passionate pursuit of perfection is what gives work meaning and gratifies the human soul. When the work we do is the work we love, the results are a shining testament of quality. Quality first, quality always is the mark of greatness.

Our obsession for quality in our work should be a model for the rest of our lives as well. Drinking life from a full cup is a noble ideal. We must do all things lovingly and quality of life will follow. That is the secret to virtue, and that is why quality counts!

QUALITY COUNTS—CALL TO ACTION

To explore your own commitment to making quality count, ask yourself these questions:

- Do you believe that quality must become an obsession?
- How has your ability (or failure) to deliver quality results shaped your reputation?
- What step will you take to deliver exceptional quality in your professional and/or personal life?

PORTRAIT OF QUALITY

Starbucks

In his book, *Pour Your Heart Into It*, Starbucks CEO Howard Schultz said this about his commitment to quality:

"Holding yourself to a higher standard is expensive and time consuming. It requires you to spend enormous amounts of time and money dealing with issues that others ignore. My justification for quality has always been: 'Everything Matters.'"

In a speech announcing he was stepping away from his CEO role, Schultz attributed Starbucks' longevity to the ability to provide customers not with products but with quality coffee experiences.

He always knew that their customers weren't looking for a cheaper cup of coffee so they took pains to reward their customers with consistently better service.

When Starbucks was at its peak, it had nearly 16,000 stores in 44 countries with 50 million people entering each week. All of this added up to sales of $10 billion.

With Starbucks' chief barista facing penny-pinching customers, a plunging stock price, and enough bad news, Schultz resumed the post of CEO.

He announced that the road back is "to keep innovating but get back to providing the quality coffee experience our customers want."

Starbucks is working "with laser intensity" to get back to where it all began: the quality coffee experience.

Gone are the distractions of breakfast sandwiches, poor-tasting lattes, and CDs at the cash register.

Back is their commitment to quality by making sure that "Everything Matters!"

8

PLANNING COUNTS

"Life will not go according to plan if you do not have a plan."

A well-defined plan—one that is properly executed—is your meal ticket to success. You significantly increase the odds of success in any endeavor if you know who you are, what you want, where you are going, how you will get there, and what you will do once you arrive.

Here's an interesting question: What makes it possible for a casino to turn a profit? Do the odds favor the house or the gambler? Even avid gamblers recognize that the odds always favor the house. Most of the people pulling levers, shooting dice, and playing cards lose most of the time. It's a safe bet that, in the view of casino managers, you are going to leave some of your earnings in their hands when you leave.

It may be something of an exaggeration, but you could say that when you walk into any casino, you sport a big "L" for LOSER on your forehead. No matter how sexy it appears, a casino is a competitively hostile environment, with the odds consistently favoring the house. This ensures that *they* win the majority of the time ... and you lose.

The same can be said for your life. Try to achieve anything without a well-defined plan (even with a commitment to achieve), and you go in with a big "L" on your forehead. The competitive odds are in favor of the prepared, the focused, and the committed; they will outperform, outhustle, and outplay you.

Though it may seem like common sense, this fact is often overlooked: your life will not go according to plan if you do not have a plan. You may lose at any given time because you're not tall enough, fast enough, or young enough. But do not allow yourself to lose because you were not fully prepared. Lack of preparation and planning screams "amateur," and it results in nothing more than mediocrity.

Planning without action is unproductive; action without planning can be counterproductive. Planning without action is like having a multiple personality disorder. You want, talk, and long to have, be, or do something, yet you do nothing about it.

The opposite is also true; the habit of action without planning carries a high degree of risk and decreased probability of success. Living this way is like playing poker without looking at your hand. You may get an occasional win, but you're still a complete knucklehead.

Planning is an art that requires practice and preparation to master. Yet for many of us, the experience of planning still ranks somewhere between having a tooth pulled and changing a diaper. As tedious as it may seem, effective planning ensures a greater sense of security in yourself and the actions necessary for success.

Far too many people and organizations are unprepared, undisciplined, and unfocused. Because they disrespect planning and lack the ability to hone these skills and appreciate these attributes, they will repeat yesterday's mediocre performance today, tomorrow, and the next day. This self-imposed purgatory must be stopped, as the consequences of poor planning are utterly ruthless.

Why not *create* history rather than repeat it? Why not commit to having the best year of your life? Why not develop a plan that allows you to experience exceptional growth? Get serious about your life and career; tilt the odds in your favor for a change. All of this is feasible through the discipline of planning.

The accommodation of success is preceded by long negotiation, made possible by intensive preparation. In addition to saving you 10 to 1 in execution, planning offers a host of other tasty benefits as well. *Among the most important*:

- *Planning promotes focus.* Planning is a disciplined thought process that produces fundamental decisions and actions that shape who you are, where you are going, what you do, and how, when, and why you do it. All of this is done with focus on the future.
- *Planning coordinates efforts.* Planning allows you to engage in best practices. Being best briefed and best prepared with the best information allows you to create the best strategy.
- *Planning provides standards.* Planning helps you size up your performance and measure your progress. Evaluating what you expect is more than a progress check; it's also quality control.
- *Planning prepares the planner.* It takes a good head to determine what you're going to do and why, and it takes a strong stomach to stick with decisions when you hit the inevitable bumps in the road. Planning teaches you to cultivate these qualities, so you have a better chance of succeeding.
- *Planning reveals roadblocks.* Planning provides a reality check on the good, the bad, and the ugly of achieving a particular goal. To be forewarned is to be forearmed, as one way to ensure victory is to be prepared for challenges and obstacles, and you do that through planning.
- *Planning stimulates thinking.* Planning provides the incentive you need to avoid dead ends and blind alleys. Comprehensive due diligence serves as a catalyst for new insights and ideas.
- *Planning fuels confidence.* Planning helps you to reduce the paralyzing effect of fear. It is the safety net for your future; without it, you're essentially walking a tightrope with a blindfold on and no net below.
- *Planning offers an exit plan.* Planning gives you a sneak peek of the price you must pay for success so you can determine if it's worth the risk. It serves as an early warning system, allowing you to bow out gracefully, instead of being thrown out later on.

While the benefits of planning might almost sound too good to be true, this time, the hype is legitimate. Effective planning allows you to do things better, faster, and definitely cheaper.

Perfect the use of planning, and you will win many battles by default. Planning means doing your homework—and running twice as fast as your competition. A lawyer works out the opposition's legal arguments. An entrepreneur puts himself in the shoes of a contractual partner. The successful negotiator is the confident negotiator, bolstered by advance knowledge and planning. As you practice and master planning, this ability will become second nature.

In every aspect of your professional and personal lives, you will think critically, examine your options, and devise a plan, leaving your competitors in awe as they scramble to pick up the pieces of unanticipated twists and turns.

Of course, not everything can be planned for. Success involves establishing a delicate balance between planning and improvisation. What should never be left to chance, however, is the ability to execute any plan.

Let's face it … we come to each stage of our lives as a novice. We all start on the bunny hill when it comes to being a successful spouse, parent, boss, or individual, even in dealing with death. With that reality in mind, it is imperative that we make planning count, as it is the greatest equalizer we will ever have the good fortune to enjoy.

PLANNING COUNTS—CALL TO ACTION

To explore your own commitment to becoming a more disciplined planner, ask yourself these questions:

- Do you believe that life will not go according to plan if you do not have a plan?
- Do you invest the proper time in order to be prepared and create effective, written plans?
- What step will you take to enforce better planning skills in your life?

PORTRAIT OF A MASTER PLANNER

Accenture

Accenture Limited is a global consulting services company with 186,000 people and revenues of $23.39 billion that helps successful leaders plan and implement strategies for high performance.

Accenture, formerly Andersen Consulting grew out of a revenue sharing arrangement with its partner Arthur Andersen that ended in 2001. Andersen Consulting was one of the pioneers in automating payroll processing and manufacturing facilities at the dawn of computers in the 1950s.

The name Accenture was chosen to represent its "focus on the future" and they have built their service portfolio around the notion of helping companies plan for the future and implement those plans to ensure high performance.

Accenture continues to grow in good times and bad.

Their value proposition is that leaders facing a downturn must "exploit the ordinary" by running day-to-day operations better than ever, and "manage the extraordinary" by quickly confronting in real-time the challenges and threats in a turbulent economy.

They help organizations to act quickly and make the right decisions with conviction—a core characteristic of a high-performance business—to benefit the most in times of change and challenge.

They know that the fundamentals of planning and sound strategy are the cornerstone of success and a prerequisite for high performance.

Accenture is by all accounts a high-performing organization, as they know that helping successful leaders plan and implement strategies for high performance is good for their business.

9

VISION COUNTS

"You will never be greater than the vision that guides you."

The eye is a remarkable instrument that processes the light we see in such a way that our minds can create meaning from it, thus supplying vision as one of our five senses. Another type of vision, however, is the light in our mind's eye, which paints the picture of a desired future state. This type of vision—the vision I speak of here—holds the promise of what shall one day be.

Vision is the capacity to see the invisible that inspires us to do the impossible—a guiding image of success. If compelling, that vision can change your life, family, business, community, and even humanity. In fact, vision is the only thing that has spurred these types of major changes. Throughout history, great accomplishments have begun as a single individual's image of what might be.

Clear vision is an essential component of high performance. The more lucid the vision, the more power and confidence it generates. Artists, designers, architects, engineers, and leaders in every field understand the importance of vision. In their head, there's a dressing room where concepts and ideas become clothed in words. Their ability to form and follow a vision is what leads them to creativity, innovation, insights, and brilliant solutions to nagging problems. Adversely, the absence of vision breeds dissatisfaction and discouragement. The future belongs to those who see possibilities before they become obvious, and who have the capacity to translate vision into reality.

A successful vision is one that's molded in terms of its contribution to society. If a strategic plan is the "blueprint," then the vision is the "artist's rendering" of the achievement of that plan. It's articulated in words, metaphors, and analogies that conjure up a similar picture for each person involved in creating the vision.

In planning, you will never be greater than the vision that guides you. Not one astronaut has ever walked on the moon by mistake; a compelling vision of their performance inevitably guided all the years of hard work. This is true for every past and future achievement.

A vision is more important as a guide to implementing strategy than it is to formulating it. This is because the development of strategy is driven by what you are trying to accomplish, your mission, goals, and purpose.

A mission statement answers the questions: "Why do we exist? What business are we in? What values will guide us?" A vision, however, is more encompassing. It answers the question, "What will success look like?" It's the pursuit of this image of success that really motivates people to work together.

A compelling vision is fueled by a compelling cause. Modern society is based on ideas and innovation. In addition, as a thinking society, we not only want to know where and what, but also why. The "WHY" is the "cause" that fuels this picture of the future.

While it is important—even required—that everyone develop a vision, embracing a cause is equally if not more important. A cause is the psychological mojo that inspires your vision. What cause demands your attention? How will your vision change the world? Is the cause worth fighting for? Does it incite a revolution? A compelling vision inspires people to stretch their expectations, aspirations, and performance.

A cause is about passion; it's a potent form of love that appeals directly to the heart. It can draw on a monumental amount of strength of a person's being. You think, feel, and become the cause. It possesses you. It drives you. It seduces you. It turns you on, and fires you up. With a cause, you expect victory and will never consider the option of failure.

Some examples of cause-driven vision include:

- Empowering women—Mary Kay Ash
- Promoting freedom, democracy and opportunity for All—Martin Luther King

- Stopping drunk-driving—Mothers Against Drunk Driving (MADD) founder, Candy Lightner
- Promoting gun control—The Brady Bill proponents Jim and Sarah Brady
- Democratizing the automobile—Henry Ford
- Finding a cure for Muscular Dystrophy—Jerry Lewis
- Fighting breast cancer—Susan G. Komen Breast Cancer Foundation founder, Nancy Brinker
- Establishing environmental-driven education—Dr. Maria Montessori
- Freeing India through nonviolence—Mahatma Ghandi
- Opposing communism—Vaclav Havel
- Promoting the Solidarity Movement—Lech Walesa

By choosing a cause about which you are especially passionate, you form an emotionally fulfilling vision. In business, creating an idea like this around a cause is a way to merge your profit center with your passion center and build something special that mirrors your personal values, beliefs, and integrity. If your cause also resonates with your target market, your activities will generate tremendous goodwill.

Cause is what ignites and sustains the fire in the belly. It is what stokes the hunger for growth and achievement. It is what gives you an intense desire to achieve, to make progress, and to excel. It is what gives you the strength and energy to overcome great adversity.

A vision coupled with a cause fills people with pride, morale, and loyalty. Enlightened leaders in every profession are beginning to realize the benefits of closely aligning themselves and their brand with a particular social issue. They are developing comprehensive social commitments that have become an integral component of corporate reputation, brand personality, and organizational identity. As it becomes more difficult for companies, political leaders, and even countries to separate themselves from the competition, strategic visions fueled by emotional causes or social issues will become an increasingly valuable leadership and differentiation strategy.

A cause-infused vision means more than simply communicating *where* you are heading. You also need to convey exactly *why* that vision is important, and why you are moving in a particular direction. If that vision is not presented in a compelling, cause-related manner, then why should an employee dedicate his body, mind, and soul in helping the company realize it? Why should consumers spend their hard-earned money with your firm? Why should a politician get your vote?

While monetary benefits can buy time and skills, in order to ensure that the employees commit their heart and soul to the endeavor, a company needs a cause—a strong cause, one that strikes an emotional chord with the rank and file, and one to which every employee can relate. That is what will drive excellence and resilience in employees, and therefore, in the organization.

A clear and cause-driven vision provides a unique and lasting competitive advantage that's virtually impossible to copy—and too irresistible to ignore. This type of vision goes far beyond the short-term efforts made by marketing and manipulation, and serves to maximize a wide range of business practices including advertising, public relations, strategic philanthropy, and community and employee relations.

As our vision continues to evolve, so too will the expectations of consumers regarding company, political, or personal involvement in social issues. Now and in the future, "What does your vision stand for?" will become one of the most asked questions by potential consumers, employees, investors, and business partners before they vote, enter into a relationship, or even go out on a date.

A compelling vision is mental eye candy that not only looks good; it sounds, tastes, smells, and feels good as well. Connecting your vision with a compelling cause most assuredly counts.

VISION COUNTS—CALL TO ACTION

To explore your own commitment to making vision count, ask yourself these questions:

- Is your performance guided by a clear and cause-driven vision?
- Does your vision of the future fill you with great passion?
- What step will you take to develop a compelling vision that inspires you to break through your comfort zone and reach for new heights?

PORTRAIT OF A VISIONARY

Walt Disney, Disneyland

Walt Disney better than any other could see the possibility that dreams could come true—"if you just wish upon a star."

Though celebrated for his many accomplishments in the entertainment business—48 Academy Awards and seven Emmys—Disney foremost wanted to make children happy.

One day he had a vision for an amusement park where children and parents could have fun together.

Inspired by the possibility, he rapidly drew sketches. He assembled a team of Disney planners and engineers called his "Imagineers," and over the next five years, the concept became a reality.

The more Walt dreamed of a "magical park," the more imaginative it became.

He needed rivers, waterfalls, and mountains; flying elephants and giant teacups; a fairy-tale castle, moon rockets, and a scenic railway; all inside a magic kingdom he called "Disneyland."

The Magic Kingdom was a $17,000,000 dream, an enormous amount at the time.

Walt once said, "I could never convince the financiers that Disneyland was feasible, because dreams offer too little collateral."

He prevailed and the plaque at the main entrance of the park embodies the intended spirit of Disneyland: To leave reality and enter fantasy.

Over 50 million guests visited the park in the first 10 years—now that many come from all over the world each year to enjoy his vision come true.

10

Teamwork Counts

*"Success depends on a combination of good timing,
natural advantages, and harmonious teamwork."*

Sustainable competitive advantages, such as patents, licenses, brands, and leadership, are the unique characteristics of a company that cannot be replicated by competitors. Teamwork is the ultimate competitive advantage; it plays a determining role in the success of any enterprise, and is far more important to success than strategy, finance, and technology.

Teamwork consists of two or more people coordinating their activities to accomplish a common goal. The moment you start doing anything at all with just one other person, you've established a team. Begin a conversation—pick up the phone, brainstorm an idea—and you're engaged in teamwork.

Teamwork is a force multiplier that is central to virtually every activity of every business. It's a way of organizing people to support interdependence and cooperation. Team performance includes both the outputs produced by the group as a whole, as well as the contribution of individual team members to the success of the team.

While many companies and leaders hail teamwork as a core value, most neglect to establish true group unity. These companies fail at teamwork because they underestimate its benefits and power; because their level of commitment is not sustained or serious enough; and because they become overwhelmed by the difficulty and amount of time required to make teamwork a reality. Executives get bogged down in tactical decisions; managers retain most of the control; supervisors make most of the operational decisions; and people on the team do just enough to meet externally imposed standards of performance.

Developing winning teams begins with a decision to take teamwork seriously; a unified commitment to jump into the deep end is mandatory, not optional. Supported by conscious effort and immense persistence, the benefits of teamwork can and will help any organization to maximize potential, productivity, and profits. Great teamwork and team unity make things happen more than anything else in organizations—more than skills, processes, policies, annual appraisals, management-by-objectives, the suits from head offices—more than anything. That's why it's the ultimate competitive advantage.

Teams become great when they *decide* to become great, not because someone says they should. Something inspires the team to action; a collective mental switch is flipped, and the magic begins.

Great teams believe in their cause; they are committed to making a difference, and to moving mountains. When each team member works to the best of their ability, they look out for each other, and the team succeeds beyond expectations.

Every business requires team unity; as united teams stand, divided teams fall.

- United nations are strong, dynamic, and powerful. Divided nations are vulnerable.
- United organizations are successful, innovative, and profitable. Divided organizations are uncompetitive.
- United armies are strong, flexible, and responsive. Divided armies are weak.
- United departments are effective, efficient, and fast. Divided departments are undisciplined.
- United efforts are engaging, enthusiastic, and energetic. Divided efforts are unproductive.
- United churches are faithful, loving, and inspiring. Divided churches are soulless.

- United families are strong, dependable, and protective. Divided families are dysfunctional.
- United teams are powerful, productive, and proactive. Divided teams are unsuccessful.

Team unity is a sustainable competitive weapon because it enables any business to solve the problems it encounters in order to win big in the marketplace. Whether in sports or in business, this kind of unanimity provides rich relations with others, and a sense of bonding, joy, or even intense frustration that is unmatched by any other dynamic. All for one, one for all is the spirit of team unity.

The first and most important step in building a cohesive and functional team is the establishment of trust. Trust is defined as the assured reliance on the character, ability, strength, or truth of someone or something. It's a critical issue in teamwork because a team without trust is not really a team at all.

Trust is the necessary precursor for feeling that one is able to rely upon another person, cooperating as a group, taking thoughtful risks, experiencing believable communication, and creating breakthrough results. In other words, trust is a value proposition that forms the foundation for effective communication, associate retention, synergy, and motivation.

Success depends on a combination of good timing, natural advantages, and harmonious teamwork. Highly functional teams possess a common task or purpose, a strong sense of interdependence, and a shared accountability, which is combined in a structured and systematic manner to achieve its successful completion.

Successful teams demonstrate these qualities:

- All team members fully understand—and are committed to—the team task, and between them, they have all the skills necessary to succeed.
- There is a recognized leader at any one time who provides motivation and a sense of common direction.
- All members work for the success of the group as a whole, rather than for themselves.
- They support each other in their efforts, and are concerned for each other's welfare.
- Team members enjoy working together.

Teamwork must be driven by a strategy, have a structure, and be implemented thoughtfully and effectively. When properly managed and developed, teamwork improves processes and produces results quickly and economically through the free exchange of ideas, information, knowledge, and data.

Strong teamwork is an essential component of a total quality organization. It builds trust, improves communication, and develops a culture of interdependence, rather than one of independence. While teamwork may not be a virtue, it nonetheless possesses virtuous qualities. It is a sustainable competitive advantage that requires a sustainable commitment; it must be carefully nurtured and faithfully executed.

Great things happen when teamwork and unity occur. In families and businesses, from sports arenas to battlefields, on factory floors, and in the halls of government, teamwork is the key to optimal performance and it most certainly counts in the creation of any success.

TEAMWORK COUNTS—CALL TO ACTION

To explore your own commitment to making teamwork count, ask yourself these questions:

- Do you surround yourself with a strong team, and are you fully leveraging all resources that come from working together?
- Do you foster team unity through your own actions and commitment to team performance?
- What step will you take to build a greater sense of teamwork in your life?

PORTRAIT OF TEAMWORK

Roger Penske—Penske Racing

Roger Penske, founder of the Penske Corporation manages businesses with revenues over $20 billion, 1,700 locations, and 40,000 employees.

But Penske Racing is his passion and winning is his mission.

And win they do.

Penske Racing has the most successful teams in auto racing history. Cars prepared by his teams have 306 major race wins, including 14 Indianapolis 500 victories, 363 pole positions, and 22 national championships.

Racing fans know his drivers—they are the most famous, the best in the business—but Penske knows it takes a whole team to win a race.

Regardless of the talent of the driver, the quality of the pit crew can be the difference between winning or losing, life or death.

A fast pit stop can mean millions of dollars more in prize money at the Indy 500 where cars scream by at over 200 miles per hour—that's 2½ miles in seconds.

What may look like a bunch of people running nuts around the race car is in actuality a well-choreographed affair like a ballet.

Everyone has a role—each works in flawless fashion to pump fuel, change tires, adjust wing settings, check gauges, and keep from causing a fire or explosion when every second matters.

Penske knows that winning at this level requires teamwork, talent, and a strong work ethic.

11

ETHICS COUNTS

"A code of ethics is one way of making sure everyone bases important decisions on the same standards. "

A compass is a navigational instrument that provides a known reference point—one that is of great assistance in providing direction. In essence, a compass helps us to find True North. Similarly, a code of ethics is a moral compass that serves as a fixed reference point for behavior. The "true north" of our moral compass of ethics points us to what is right, true, just, or morally appropriate.

Ethics can be defined as the body of principles or standards of human conduct that govern the behavior or actions of individuals and groups. When our moral compass is distorted—or completely absent—then our standards and actions are based on self-interest and personal gain.

Most of us have a moral compass; however, not everyone's points to True North. If your moral compass is spinning, this means you are having trouble getting a fix on what is right or ethical. Knowing the right thing to do is ethics challenge number one; a secondary challenge is actually *doing* it.

The pressure to succeed often tempts us to behave immorally or unethically. In a world of increasing expectations, rapid communication, global economics, geopolitics, and robust technology, our successes and failures are both magnified and leveraged. We live in a world where the unethical actions of a single CEO can leave hundreds, thousands, and even millions of people in a state of complete economic devastation.

We must individually and collectively elevate ourselves above the lying, cheating, and abuse so readily accepted in our society. The notion that nice guys or gals finish last is not the lesson we want to be passing on to future generations. Ethics and values demonstrate what's right with the world. They need to be appreciated, celebrated, and emulated. Unfortunately, there are people in this world who will claim that character doesn't count; that ethics and values are naive and outdated notions. They will tell you that results and the bottom line are all that matter. These people are examples of what's wrong with the world, and they must not be applauded or emulated.

The message that we must demonstrate through our actions and pass down to future generations loud and clear: character *does* count; integrity *does* count; and honor *does* count. We can—and *must*—demonstrate that success can be achieved without lying, cheating, and stealing your way to the top!

The paradox of our time is that on many levels, society is enjoying monumental financial surpluses. Yet at the same time, we are experiencing moral deficits, ethical erosion, spiritual bankruptcy, and the decay of traditional values. Most people develop their own ideas—shaped by their environment—of what principles to live by, and what they think is right and wrong. Unfortunately, more and more people today grow up in an environment where their sense of moral obligation is either twisted or not present at all. When a moral compass is distorted or absent altogether, standards are based on self-interest and personal gain.

Most of us know what our values ought to be, and we profess allegiance to them. Most of us know right from wrong, can differentiate good from bad, and have a well-developed moral compass and an internal set of checks and balances. However, there appears to be a gap between knowing and doing—something that has caused an erosion of our conduct. Poor ethical behavior should not become routine, nor should it become the accepted norm. This frightening disconnect between our values and ethical behavior manifests itself in our schools, family, government, churches, sports, and business.

We must instead embrace an inside-out perspective. Individuals and society must be concerned that we do not destroy ourselves from within by moral and ethical decay.

The challenge of leadership in any institution is not only the necessity for the leader to act consistently based on a standard of ethics, but to promote

similar standards for everyone within the institution, regardless of title or responsibility. A code of ethics is one way of making sure everyone bases important
decisions on the same standards.

One of the greatest examples of ethical leadership can be found in the first
president of the United States, George Washington. Washington was renowned
for his habit of telling the truth, and no one described him better than his fellow
founding father, Thomas Jefferson. After Washington's death is 1799, Jefferson
proclaimed:

> "His integrity was the most pure, his justice the most inflexible I have
> ever known . . . . He was, indeed, in every sense of the words, a wise, a
> good, and a great man . . . . On the whole, his character was, in its mass,
> perfect . . . it may truly be said that never did nature and fortune com-
> bine more perfectly to make a man great . . . ."

Make sure your own sense of ethic duty is above reproach, for without a
commitment to only the highest of ethical behavior, the ultimate result is failure; loss of reputation; and if not public, most certainly personal shame.

Living by our values and high ethical standards is more than the right thing
to do; it is absolutely essential to our success as individuals and a society.

So what can we do? Specifically, how can we reverse the tide and restore
our ability to live ethical, values-based lives?

Here's a two-part solution:

1. Awareness: We must be aware of the consequences of unethical behavior, and mindful of our own behavior and any unethical compromises
   we have made.
2. Shared Concern: We must have a shared concern for our children,
   future generations, and for one another, and let our ethics guide our
   behavior to form, in turn, a model for the behavior of others.

This second step will require a level of commitment and determination
that may defy explanation. It demands a sustained and unshakable resolve,
and a collective will to effect a meaningful change in society's standards and
behavior.

The deterioration of sound ethics and values is the greatest single danger
to current and—even more so—to future generations. It must be taken seriously. When looking for solutions to the problems of our society, let's be sure
to focus on the right question. The question is not, What can we do to prevent

moral decay and its consequences? But rather, What can we do to motivate and *maintain* ethical behavior in society and ourselves?

Finding the answer to that question is your challenge, the challenge of leadership, and the challenge of every parent, educator, coach, politician, business, and clergy. Why? Because practicing good ethics counts!

ETHICS COUNT—CALL TO ACTION

To explore your own commitment to making ethics count in your life, ask yourself these questions:

- Do you follow a nonnegotiable behavioral code?
- How do you perceive people who do the right thing, who believe in an honor code, and who are guided by a strong moral compass?
- What step will you take to lead a more ethical and transparent life?

PORTRAIT OF AN ETHICAL INSTITUTION

West Point

In the military, where life is endangered by virtue of the institution's mission, trust becomes sacred and honorable action becomes a requisite quality for each professional.

Leaders must be honorable and act honorably to be trusted by troops who must carry out their commands.

In business, the cost of dishonesty is dollars; in the military the cost is measured in lives; hence, an officer who cannot be trusted cannot be tolerated.

West Point is a world-renowned military academy whose mission is to educate, inspire, and develop cadets to become outstanding leaders intellectually, militarily, and ethically.

Success is predicated on cadets accepting the functional necessity of honesty, ethical behavior, and the commitment to a lifetime of honorable living.

To enforce this belief, cadets adhere to the Cadet Honor Code, which states: "A cadet will not lie, cheat, steal, or tolerate those who do."

Honor is understood to be a fundamental attribute of character.

Honor is a virtue that implies loyalty and courage, truthfulness and self-respect, justice and generosity. Its underlying principle is truth.

A cadet's spoken or written word must always be acceptable without question!

Noteworthy is the fact that for its success, the Honor System depends more upon the Corps of Cadets than upon the supervision of the officers.

12

GOAL SETTING COUNTS

"If you want to get better outcomes, you must prioritize every action and activity you undertake."

There is no purer form of success, no more exact and demanding test of what you are capable of, than to achieve a desirable outcome. A quality life is an example of what can be accomplished when thoughtful attention, goal setting, and purposeful action come together without compromise.

Goal setting is both exciting and important because of the results it achieves. But the ultimate reason for setting goals is to entice you to become the person it takes to achieve them, for you'll soon find that what you become is so much more important than the goal itself.

Although the definition of success varies for each individual, the fundamentals for achieving a goal are always the same. It is a process that begins with decisiveness, proceeds to focus, advances to action, then carries on with persistence and follow-through before ending in victory. There is no other way.

Goal setting takes your life and gives it direction as it helps you to determine:

- *What* you specifically want to achieve
- *Why* this achievement is so important
- *Who* will help you to achieve this goal
- *Where* you stand in relation to this goal
- *How* you plan on accomplishing this goal
- *When*, on what date will you achieve your goal

These are questions that only one person can answer: you!

If time is money, then goal setting is invaluable. Goals keep you focused, on time, and on schedule. You are responsible for your own success. Either you work hard for what you want, or you don't. If you want to be successful in any endeavor, you must take complete ownership of the process, which begins with goal setting.

A life lived without direction is as foolish as going to sea without a compass. A ship with a broken rudder may maintain a full head of steam, but it will never reach a port, unless by accident. If it does somehow find a port, its cargo may not be suited to the people, climate, or culture it encounters. Your life, much like a ship, must be directed to a definite destination for which your cargo of core skills and aspirations are best suited. If you want to succeed, you must not drift aimlessly.

Though it seems to be out of vogue to speak of goal setting, there is nothing more fashionable than success, which owes its very life to goals. Success requires that you pass the test before learning the lesson. It requires patience to create anything of lasting value, and it requires hard choices, complete commitment, and total focus. Success wants you to pursue your goals with great devotion and passion and says no to you when you are unprepared to appreciate it. Success demands dedication, discipline, hard work, and courage. It requires your utmost attention and will not allow itself to be taken for granted. Success must be earned, deserved, respected, and appreciated. Success plays by specific, nonnegotiable rules; *it will always require that goals be clearly identified, plans be set in place, and action consistently enforced.*

The basics of goal setting and results orientation are simple. If you want to get better outcomes, you must prioritize every action and activity you undertake. You must compartmentalize everything you do in order to remain focused on the goal at hand. You must maximize your time and energy to capture the goal.

No one has the market cornered on success—it's unlimited as to what you can be, do, and have. But to enjoy success, you must learn the fundamentals of goal setting and be willing to invest a lifetime of discipline to continually enforce those fundamentals. Like any other good habit, you must do a few things and repeat them consistently to ensure that it will stay with you for life. Most people have no training on how to successfully set and achieve a goal. They may try various strategies, finally acquiring some knowledge through the bitter pill of experience. This is like learning to drive by having a series of accidents. Keep this in mind: if you do not profit from your mistakes, someone else will!

Your mind, while blessed with permanent memory, is cursed with lousy recall. Written goals are catalysts—transforming agents for success and achievement. You must put them down on paper (or computer), because those that are kept only in your mind have an uncanny way of remaining figments of your imagination.

From eureka to achievement, the evolution of a goal begins in the mind and immediately takes shape when pen is put to paper. It progresses from thought to sketch, from sketch to action, and finally from action to achievement, in real time. The achievement of a goal is an exemplary tale of power, purpose, and potential.

A goal is more than a thought in your head. It's a profound message about who you are and what you are capable of. To enjoy the fruits of victory, begin by visualizing your goal and continue with that image until completion. If you go there first in your thoughts, your body will soon follow. I assure you, every astronaut walks on the moon thousands of times in their mind before their feet ever touch its surface.

Embrace a small, select list of goals that gratify your passion and beg for your attention—the ones that say "come and get me." But remember that no goal is complete until it's entirely finished. Halfway doesn't count, nor do good intentions or high hopes. For a goal to be achieved, it must be saturated with personal integrity and ample doses of follow through.

Success begets success, as it begets a strong desire to continually seek new adventures. A goal achieved is a mark of personal growth and mastery. It means that you have accomplished what you set out to do, that you have grown in ability and ambition, and that you are now prepared to take on new challenges.

Will goal setting ever become nonessential? If history is any judge, the answer is a resounding no. This practice is a responsibility for those who seek success, and for everyone who wants to continue to develop personally and professionally. Goal setting is a responsibility that counts!

GOAL SETTING COUNTS—CALL TO ACTION

To explore your own commitment to setting and working toward meaningful goals, ask yourself these questions:

- Does goal setting provide direction, meaning, and purpose for your life?
- Do you actively write your goals, develop detailed plans for achieving your goals, and execute those plans to the best of your abilities?
- What step will you take to develop the good habit of goal setting and to pursue the goals you are most passionate about?

PORTRAIT OF GOAL MASTERY

The GoalsGuy

The motto says it all, "Our Goal Is Simply to Help You Achieve Yours!"

The GoalsGuy is a professional training, coaching, and management consulting organization that has a singular focus on goals and goal achievement. Their purpose is to help their clients build and sustain superior performance.

They accomplish this objective by helping their clients increase their sense of direction, confidence, and capability in all areas of their personal and professional lives.

The GoalsGuy has a keen interest not just in helping companies to perform better. They also have a passion for kids and teens and have sponsored National Kids Goal Setting Week since 1989 to teach parents, teachers, and coaches how to teach their kids and students to master the art of goal setting.

They believe learning how to set and achieve a goal is perhaps the single most important thing a child can learn to prepare for school, adulthood, and for future employment. The more adept your child is at understanding this important life skill, the more options he or she will have throughout their life!

Whether your child grows up to be a surgeon, computer technician, teacher, nurse, or engineer, the reliance on goal setting never stops.

Your child will be expected to apply high levels of skill and increased technical knowledge. Intense competition awaits your child in the workplace;

therefore it is imperative that they learn these skills in order to get the results they desire in life.

If success truly is your destination, than let The GoalsGuy help you make the journey, as they know goals! Visit The GoalsGuy at www.GoalsGuy.com.

!

13

INNOVATION COUNTS

"Through innovation, what you are in fact saying is that what you do produces differentiation and real business value."

The essence of strategy lies in creating tomorrow's competitive advantages faster than anyone can mimic today's. To do this consistently, you must embrace innovation as a core competency. Core competencies are different for every person and occupation, but the one that we *all* need to make count is innovation.

The basis of competitive advantage has shifted at least five obvious times over the last few decades: from price and volume to quality, then to speed, over to mass customization, and finally on demand. Each shift has incorporated the innovative attributes of its predecessors, and then added new and progressively more challenging requirements. Innovation *is* the creation of new value and new satisfaction for the customer. The three tests of innovation are: does it create value for the customer; does the customer want the innovation; and, will the customer pay for it?

The genesis of innovation is an idea, which is somewhat like a baby—born small, immature, and shapeless. They initially offer more promise and hope than fulfillment. The creation of ideas is often driven by needs, yet to describe the need is not to satisfy it. But describing it does give a specification for the desirable results you seek, which in turn sparks the actual idea. Whether they are likely to be obtained can be decided in due time.

Innovation is essential in finding business potential and making the future. While innovations in technology, production, marketing, and finance all remain essential, it is innovation in management and, most importantly, strategy that is most desperately needed. Therefore, innovation must be ingrained into the culture of your operations. You must create less process and less structure, promoting more independent thinking and creativity.

Successful and sustained innovation demands a shift away from the conventional thought that claims that innovation is chiefly the domain of an R&D group. But to complete this shift, traditional enterprises face another challenge: they tend to rely on existing approaches to solve new problems. This must change, as no company can outgrow its competitors unless it can out-innovate them.

Society's problems are more profound and perpetual than ever before, which has resulted in the very personality of innovation. The nature of innovation is changing at a pace unheard of in modern history. Innovation has been innovated! It is now:

- **Global**—The widespread adoption of networked technologies and open standards is removing barriers of geography and accessibility. Anyone and everyone can participate in the innovation economy.
- **Multidisciplinary**—Because the challenges before us are more complex, innovation now requires a diverse mix of talent and expertise.
- **Collaborative and Open**—More and more, innovation is coming as the result of people working together in new and integrated ways. Within this collaborative environment, notions of intellectual property are being reexamined. The entities that view intellectual assets as "capital" to be invested and leveraged—rather than "property" to be owned and protected—will reap the greatest returns.

To enjoy the benefits of this evolution, an organization must modify their processes and practices. The first step is to abandon the belief that any advantage can be sustained. In its place, you must build a capacity to innovate and adapt repeatedly. That capacity will separate the winners from the losers.

The lesson: innovate or die! You can use the technique of "systematic abandonment" to achieve devastating effectiveness. Whenever you come up with an innovation, simultaneously set a sunset date at which you will deliberately abandon that innovation. This immediately triggers work on developing a replacement offering. The goal of this approach is to create three innovations for every one you phase out. This includes an incrementally improved old innovation, a spin-off innovation idea from the original, and an entirely unique innovation altogether.

Innovation is a lot like excellence. It's difficult but manageable to do once, and infinitely harder to produce consistently. Think about all those one-hit wonders that had a single record or very possibly, a single song. They disappear without a trace. What distinguishes a true star from his or her contemporaries is an ability to pull off feats of brilliance repeatedly.

All truly great innovators share two common traits: they have an almost fanatical desire to get out front and stay there, and they possess a determination and conviction that if anyone is going to render their products or services obsolete, it will be themselves. Another one of their unique characteristics is the ability to envision, as a system, elements that to others seem unrelated and separate. What fuels them is the successful attempt to find and provide the smallest missing part that will convert already existing elements.

To find a reason where innovation would create maximum opportunities, ask: What is lacking to make effective what is already possible? What one small step would transform our economic results? What small change would alter the capacity of the whole of our resources?

Innovation in many ways is looking at a product or process and then flipping the equation. It's the application of intellectual energy in those areas exactly opposite of where it is currently focused, in order to accelerate new breakthroughs and advancements.

- It's shifting research into the decomposition (rather than the creation) of products, such as computers.
- It's developing transportation systems that focus on the divergence rather than convergence of people.
- It's thinking of environmentally sound ways to freeze and compress a corpse rather than the old technology of cremation.
- It's creating business models that allow easier dissemination of resources and talent, rather than fostering their acquisition.

Flipping the equation is not a simple reversal; it requires moving beyond "either/or" thinking, and demands the ability to manage seemingly conflicting dualities at once. Ultimately, contemporary innovation hinges on the idea that it's not enough to choose one path over another.

It's difficult and risky to convert any radically new idea into a successful reality. That's why you should subject your ideas to scrutiny, as the best ideas will only get better by being part of a larger conversation where they can be debated, vetted, expanded, and improved. In a truly innovative environment, leaders do not say, "That was a foolish idea." Instead, they ask: "What would be needed to make this infantile, half-baked, foolish idea into something that makes sense, that is feasible, that is an opportunity for us?" Perhaps most important of all, progressive leaders create a passion for linking innovation and learning through recognition and rewards.

Ready, set, innovate. By making innovation a core competency, you are in fact saying that what you do produces differentiation and real business value for your clients. It says that you're focused not only on being creative yourself, but on helping your clients be innovators as well. Now that's innovation that truly counts!

INNOVATION COUNTS—CALL TO ACTION

To explore your own commitment to making innovation count, ask yourself these questions:

- Do you understand *why* innovation must become a core competency in business?
- Do you *actively look* for ways to outthink, outsmart, and outwit your competitors? When was your last innovative breakthrough?
- What *steps* will you take to be more innovative, and where should you begin the process?

PORTRAIT OF INNOVATION

Steve Jobs—Apple Computer

BusinessWeek gave Apple Computer, under Steve Jobs' leadership, its "Innovative Company of the Year" award three years in a row beating firms like Google and Sony.

How could one man revolutionize computers with the Apple Mac, animate movies with Pixar, explode digital music with the iPod and iTunes, and then turn millions into fanatically loyal iPhone customers?

In a word—he's amazing at innovation.

Steve Jobs defies single descriptors—genius, elitist, obsessed, driven, perfectionist, legend, self-made billionaire.

He says that his instinct for the experience of using his products is what drives and informs Apple's innovation. He does not consciously think about innovation, he thinks about how he can make great products that customers will buy.

He pays as much attention to the design of the cardboard boxes his gadgets come in as the products themselves, because the act of pulling a product from its box is an important part of the user experience, and like everything, it's very carefully thought out.

Jobs often says, "The thing that drives me . . . is that you see something very compelling, and you don't quite know how to get it, but intuitively, if you pay attention to the details, it's within your grasp. And it's worth putting in years to make it come into existence. That's how we innovate."

14

REWARDS AND RECOGNITION COUNT

"Rewards continue to inspire long after specific accomplishments fade from memory."

A funny thing happens on the way to success: You build integrity, character, discipline, and a host of other intrinsic benefits that add credence to the old saying, "the journey is its own reward."

Goals are natural value generators, often because of what you learn and become en route to their achievement. But having a reward that honors and symbolizes that achievement is a powerful motivator for continued progress. Simply put, a reward is an extrinsic symbol for the enforcement and celebration of intrinsic values.

If you want to improve your performance results, increase innovation to gain and sustain competitive advantages, create an environment that fosters social responsibility and ethical behavior, and increase energy levels, then you must make rewards and recognition standard protocol. Whether it's a war hero receiving a Medal of Honor, an Olympic athlete winning a gold medal, an author being granted a Pulitzer Prize, or a young child winning a trophy for a local spelling bee—rewards and recognition promote and define excellence. They provide an effective but uncomplicated means for reinforcing quality behaviors. They not only serve to honor the accomplishments of exceptional individual or team performance, they bolster and endorse the specific actions, behaviors, and values that you are striving to put in place.

The one magnificent and common element behind rewards is that each must be earned. To pay the price, to study long and hard, to compete fairly, and focus one's effort on a goal until achieved is part of the sweetness of life. That type of behavior is deserving of reward and significant recognition. All well-earned awards remind the holders, their families, and the world at large of acts of courage, quality, originality, and excellence. Rewards continue to inspire long after specific accomplishments fade from memory.

On the other hand, few things in life are more demoralizing than having your consistently good performance go unrecognized. The successful culture is one that provides constant recognition and applause. At the same time, it breeds a restless dissatisfaction with the status quo that keeps you challenging yourself to ever-higher performance. Rewards are beneficial positive reinforcements—they make you feel good about your achievements and the price you paid for that achievement, and they reinforce the behavior and attitudes that led to those achievements. The need for recognition and approval is a fundamental human drive, and one of the motivators behind our willingness to give and serve. The goal of rewards and recognition is to feed that motivation and to promote and define excellence. Those being recognized for excellence serve as models for their colleagues, inspirations to their communities, and leaders in their area of discipline.

The best predictor of future behavior is past behavior. When you reward the right behavior and its results, you almost guarantee a repeat performance. The trick is to identify and reward the behavior you want repeated, as poor behavior also will be repeated if rewarded.

In addition to being an indispensable self-management tool, recognition should be an integral part of every organization's business and people strategy. These aspects of professional life are essential to addressing the demographic, economic, and generational challenges that business faces in retaining and motivating employees. Prompt positive reinforcement in the form of commemoration and celebration is essential to morale. Performance is the key to success for any organization, and systematic reward and recognition programs offer one sure way to enhance performance.

Everyone realizes the value of going the extra mile—quality, persistence, follow-through, and sustained focus. But few actually take the time to celebrate the successful accomplishments associated with such behaviors. And when ceremonies are observed, they are too often carried out in a dull, hollow, perfunctory fashion.

Success in any endeavor requires that you identify and credit exceptional performance from yourself and others. Become a great believer in the importance of celebration and rewards. If necessary, create occasions to celebrate. Additionally, don't let your own achievements and the feeling of victory evaporate without some kind of reward and recognition. Rewarding yourself for your accomplishments is an essential part of the combination for success. We need markers and milestones as indicators or symbols of our progress and success; without them, we become easily lost or apathetic.

We need recognition and rewards to provide encouragement and remind us that we have achieved important goals. Think of the effort a new lover makes to get your attention—flowers, chocolates, a song dedicated to you broadcast from your favorite radio station, a surprise call or personalized card that tells you how special you are. How long has it been since you've paid yourself such consideration? After all, you probably kick yourself when you screw up. Why not pat yourself on the back when you reach an important milestone, go above and beyond the call of duty, or deliver an outstanding performance? Be proud of your accomplishments and recognize your own achievement, and do so in the following ways:

- Always reward your major achievements.
- Recognize intermediate steps and victories.
- Make rewards commensurate with the accomplishment.
- Ensure that incentives are personal and sentimental.
- Reflect on your performance, and allow yourself time to celebrate.

Anything that increases the behavior you want modeled is a reward. A well-earned reward is the poster child of commitment, quality, excellence, and best practices. Good, right, and honorable behavior deserves recognition and applause. On your journey toward success, make sure you reward, recognize, and celebrate excellence, because rewards and recognition count!

REWARDS AND RECOGNITION COUNT— CALL TO ACTION

To explore your own commitment to making rewards and recognition count, ask yourself these questions:

- Do rewards help motivate you to repeat the rewarded behavior?
- Do you regularly look for ways to use rewards and recognition to showcase, promote, and celebrate excellence?
- What step will you take to incorporate the celebration of rewards and recognition in your life?

PORTRAIT OF REWARDS AND RECOGNITION

The Medal of Honor

The U.S. military has long recognized excellence and honors the sacrifices of its soldiers who so valiantly serve in the pursuit of freedom.

The Medal of Honor is the highest award for valor in action against an enemy force that can be bestowed upon an individual serving in the armed forces.

Generally presented by the President in the name of Congress, it is often called the Congressional Medal of Honor.

During the Civil War, President Lincoln authored the production and distribution of "medals of honor" to "promote the efficiency of the Navy." Later bills authorized versions of this medal for the other branches of the military.

Since World War II, the criteria for receiving this medal states that it shall be awarded for extreme bravery beyond the call of duty while engaged in action against an enemy.

Due to this change, approximately 60 percent of the medals earned during and after World War II have been awarded posthumously.

One of the most recent recipients of the medal was Private Ross McGinnis for events that occurred in Baghdad, Iraq. When an insurgent fragmentation grenade landed in his vehicle, he covered it with his body, absorbing the explosion at the cost of his own life.

Private McGinnis joins over 3,465 recipients of this award in keeping with the highest traditions of the military service.

15

Every Customer Counts

"You can only create lasting value for your business by creating value for customers."

You'd think more people and companies would have gotten the message that every customer counts. It's common sense, obvious, transparent—isn't it? You take care of the ones who pick up the tab. Unfortunately, organizations that put customers at the center of the action are rare.

The pain and suffering to which many companies subject their customers is disgraceful. Far too often, customers are forced to deal with dispassionate employees, voice mail hell, and a begrudging attitude. They feel underwhelmed, overpromised, underserved, and unappreciated, which leads to a complete absence of loyalty. Way to go!

Since the customer is the ultimate end user of a product or service, it stands to reason that the customer is King—and that a company and its employees are his servants. This understanding calls for a genuine demonstration of gratitude and humility, as the better role you perform as servant, the more loyalty you garner in return.

No company can exist without happy customers. These are the people who pay the mortgage, put food on the table, and help put your kids through college. Loyal customers keep coming back and spending more; they become powerful advocates for your cause. Enthusiastic customers make your work fun, enjoyable and purposeful. B2B should mean "Back to Basics"—a return to business fundamentals where it's all about the customer.

The purpose of a business is to create a customer, then to deliver sustained quality service that is benefit oriented. Profitability will follow, as profit is the naturally resultant financial measure of the value of your service and a key success indicator. Business must be run at a profit, or else it is sure to become extinct. However, when anyone tries to run a business solely for profit, then the business must die, for it no longer has a purpose or a reason for existence. This skewed philosophy may bring profits today, but will lead to the presence of a white elephant tomorrow.

Looking beyond profitability and shareholder return, what is the ultimate value that a business and its people bring to the world? A business is defined by the *want* the customer satisfies when they buy a product or service. The mission and purpose of every business is to satisfy the customer; to think otherwise is irrational. The only view that matters is that of the customer; therefore we all must step back and look at our work from the point of view of our customers and the market.

You can only create lasting value for your business by creating true value for customers, and you can only achieve this by understanding what it is that customers themselves actually value. Think like a customer—walk a mile in their shoes—and you'll see that friendliness, quality, convenience, timeliness, respect, and gratitude all count.

Customer-centered leadership is the cornerstone of success. Here are seven value creation strategies that will keep your customers coming back for life:

Strategy 1: Adopt the "Everything Counts" Customer Service Maxim*
"Everything Counts" is a maxim that sends a powerful message. It means that you see every customer interaction as an opportunity to retain a valued customer, increase your value proposition, build loyalty, or strengthen a brand. It means that everything in your business counts—from the friendly hello to the appreciative thank you—as well as every little paper clip and detail in between.

---

*Learn more about the Everything Counts training program at www.everythingcounts.com/training/

Strategy 2: Take Care of Your Staff ... So They Will Take Care of Your Customers.

Without the right staff and proper training to deliver great service, other plans and programs won't amount to a hill of beans. That's why effective customer-focused leaders focus on employees first. Take care of your staff, and they'll take care of your customers. Leadership must put staff first, and staff, in turn, will put the customer first.

Strategy 3: Keep Your Promises and Honor Your Commitments

If you make a promise to a customer, keep it. If you make a commitment, honor it. The absence of this discipline is a stain on your company's reputation that is virtually impossible to remove. Take your promises and customer commitments seriously, because your customers do. Nothing annoys customers and fuels their lack of loyalty more than being lied to.

Strategy 4: Deliver Quality and Excellence

A commitment to quality and excellence breeds client loyalty. These things don't happen accidentally; they are the result of careful planning and exceptional execution. Quality and excellence create confidence and enhance your customer's peace of mind; they function as an insurance policy against mediocrity and an assurance of profitability.

Strategy 5: Focus on the Customer Experience

Making people feel good about themselves and your company makes a more conducive environment for them to spend their money. Customer centered companies provide more than just a quality product, they provide a rich experience, too.

The entire customer experience—the service, the quality, the design, the brand attributes—connects on an emotional level, keeping customers satisfied and feeling well served and loyal. That loyalty can result in the capture of substantial lifetime revenue.

Strategy 6: Practice the Golden Rule

"Do unto others as you would have others do unto you." When we show kindness, respect, courtesy, and humility, another bridge is built. Follow the Golden Rule to its logical conclusion and you will have formed binding relations with your customers.

Strategy 7: Go the Extra Mile

An organization's ability to elicit staff behavior that goes above and beyond the call of duty is a key asset and competitive weapon—one that is extremely difficult for competitors to imitate and virtually impossible to ignore. This advantage is realized only when you stay ahead of your customers' expectations and needs. Talking about focusing on the customer and actually *doing* it, however, are two completely different things. The companies that put customers first win much more than loyalty; they win advocates. As passionate advocates, customers jump on the bandwagon and freely recommend your company to friends, neighbors, and colleagues. They purchase your products and services as gifts, and they provide unsolicited praise or suggestions of improvement because they believe in you.

The customer is King. Long live the customer. Make every customer count!

EVERY CUSTOMER COUNTS—CALL TO ACTION

To explore your own commitment to making every customer count, ask yourself these questions:

- Do you truly believe that the customer is King, and do you conduct your business accordingly?
- Do your actions demonstrate gratitude and appreciation for your customers or do you view them as a necessary evil? How would your customers describe their experience in doing business with you?
- What step will you take to deliver quality service that will consistently build customer satisfaction and loyalty?

PORTRAIT OF EXCEPTIONAL CUSTOMER CARE

Capt. Denny Flanagan

These days many frequent flyers have made up their minds that the friendly skies aren't. United Airlines has been losing money and cutting services for years. With union issues, disgruntled passengers, and tough working conditions, many of their employees are barely able to disguise their dissatisfaction and passengers feel it.

But not every employee!

Capt. Denny Flanagan, United pilot, goes out of his way to make flying fun for passengers and is making fliers change their minds.

Here are some things he does consistently to show that every customer counts:

- When pets travel in cargo compartments, he snaps pictures of them with his cell phone, then goes to find the owners to show them that their animals are on board.
- If flights are diverted because of storms, he finds a McDonald's where he can order 200 hamburgers to give out free.
- When underage children are on his flights, if the flight is delayed by thunderstorms, he calls the parents to explain to them what's going on and that their children are safe.

Passengers routinely comment that he delivers service that goes above and beyond the extra mile.

Capt. Flanagan is not just an employee of United Airlines; he is an Ambassador who believes that every customer counts and that he can make a difference to his passengers.

"The customer deserves a good travel experience," said the 56-year-old Navy veteran. Passengers would agree.

16

Energy Management Counts

"Peak performance, optimal health, and genuine happiness are grounded in the skillful art of energy management."

How do you get to the next level of performance and productivity? It all begins with how you manage energy!

In order to enjoy and maintain high levels of performance, you must learn how to systematically spend and renew energy. Managing energy—*not* time— is the X Factor behind peak performance, personal renewal, and overall well-being. Every action, no matter the size, either adds or robs fuel from your energy gas tank.

We are all reservoirs of energy. Everything we do—from interacting with colleagues and making important decisions to spending time with our family—requires energy. As obvious as this seems, we often fail to take into account the critical role of energy in our lives. Absent of the correct quantity, quality, focus, and forces of energy, we all become compromised in any activity we undertake.

It is disturbing to see the immense amount of human and corporate potential squandered due to the misuse of energy. Unhealthy eating habits, lack of exercise, negativity, sarcasm, unfocused goals and strategies are all contributing factors to energy loss. On the other hand, the most productive members of society have the unique ability to both engage fully and disengage periodically. They understand that continuous engagement without proper renewal leads to progressively depleted energy levels, and it is this understanding that allows them to perform at consistently high levels. The act of disengagement allows for reflection and renewal.

Most of us, however, rarely contemplate the amount of energy we are spending, because we take it for granted that our energy gas tank is limitless. Early in our life and career we all tend to have a lot of energy, and when you have an abundance of anything, it often seems less important to use it wisely. However, when you have many talents, capabilities, and opportunities, there's a high cost to investing your energy where the return is less than excellent.

Many people eventually find themselves in unfortunate situations where they are only able to express a small part of their potential, or apply a small amount of their creativity because they have involved themselves over the years in a great number of energy-draining relationships, situations, habits, and obligations. The opportunity to continually expand your opportunities is what distinguishes high, average, and low performers, and your ability to manage your energy provides the framework for a permanent foundation on which to build goals for the rest of your life. This includes helping to eliminate the things you no longer want in your life and to build the new, better, and great things that you do.

An abundance of natural energy is your contribution to—and your reward from—other people, circumstances, and projects. High performers understand that they are free to cut loose those things in their life—relationships, situations, habits, activities, and obligations—that drain their energy. As these high-maintenance, unwanted elements are eliminated, they free up their most valuable talents and find themselves surrounded by an environment that supports and boosts their energy. This reclaimed energy makes it possible for you to grow your career or business exponentially, dramatically improve the quality of your life, and create a lifestyle that supports personal and professional success and happiness.

Problems—especially those that we create ourselves—are another huge energy drain. In fact, as we get older, we actually refine the process of perpetuating problems, coming up with much more sophisticated and complex pickles to get ourselves into, including legal and relationship dilemmas. A problem, after all, is simply an obligation without a committed solution. As our opportunities grow, we encounter greater demands on our energy, concern, and attention.

As a result, we can become accustomed to being overcommitted. This creates a breeding ground for problems.

The bigger a problem becomes, the more energy it takes to fix. Even ignoring a problem is an additional mental energy drain, as it takes significantly more energy to avoid a problem than to confront and straighten it out. When you allow problems to exist, you have less to give creatively, and your potential goes into hiding while you grudgingly spend your time and energy on damage control.

On the other side of the spectrum, every time you increase the energy you devote to more rewarding uses, you also increase the value of your life to you and to many others. Therefore, committing yourself to greater energy is a commitment to a greater life.

We all have far more control over our energy than we realize or leverage. The number of hours in a day is fixed, but the quantity and quality of energy available to us is not. We can never forget that peak performance, optimal health, and genuine happiness are grounded in the skillful art of energy management.

The challenge of peak performance is to manage your energy to achieve your goals. The following are the three key principles that drive energy, thus ensuring dramatic improvement in your results and overall quality of life:

1. Peak performance requires that you draw on multiple sources of energy.

    In order to perform at high levels, we must understand that energy is a multidimensional concept. It comes in numerous forms, and we must learn to embrace and synergize each one—physical, emotional, mental, and spiritual. Each energy source is important; each one counts, and by subtracting one from the mix you significantly reduce your ability to optimize performance.

2. Peak performance requires that you have a balance between energy expenditure and energy renewal.

    Energy diminishes with both over- and underuse. Therefore, it is critical that we learn to balance the output of energy with intermittent energy renewal. The fullest, most productive lives have the ability to perform optimally in the challenge at hand, but also to disengage periodically and seek renewal.

3. Peak performance requires that you push your energy levels beyond your current limits.

    Energy grows in much the same way that a physical muscle grows; as it is stressed beyond its normal limits, a muscle builds upon itself and becomes stronger. The same is true for our energy levels. When we consciously place ourselves in a position where we must perform, we will rise to the challenge with an intense focus and robust energy level.

Peak performance is an exotic combination of energy requirements, which include the greatest quantity, highest quality, clearest focus, and maximum force of energy. Focusing on the freedom of energy allows you to leverage your creativity and talents to create the kind of life you want in less time and with greater enjoyment.

The ultimate measure of our lives is not how long we live, but rather how we are able to manage our energy in the time we are each given, and that is precisely why everything counts.

ENERGY MANAGEMENT COUNTS—CALL TO ACTION

To explore your own commitment to making energy management count, ask yourself these questions:

- Do you have a strategy in place for how you use energy—one of your most important natural resources.
- What situations, activities, habits, obligations, or relationships are *draining* your energy.
- What step will you take to more systematically spend and renew your energy.

PORTRAIT OF ENERGY MANAGEMENT

Dr. Jim Loehr

Dr. Jim Loehr is a world-renowned performance psychologist, co-founder of the Human Performance Institute, and author of *The Power of Full Engagement: Managing Energy, Not Time, is the Key to High Performance and Personal Renewal.*

His energy management work helps participants become more productive and effective under pressure by managing their energy more effectively.

Early on, his work was centered on helping athletes discover the underlying emotional and mental conditions present when they performed at their very best. The idea was that assuming raw talent, much of sport performance is more mental than physical.

Through work with over 1,500 athletes, he was able to document his theories. He could show athletes how to replicate the conditions when they were performing at their best—when they were in the "Zone." He and his partner coined the term Mentally Tough to describe this state.

Later he added conditioning and nutrition experts and attracted more celebrity athletes. His research helps not only world-class athletes, but also more ordinary weekend warriors improve their performance. He offers his workshops at his multimillion-dollar performance center in Lake Nona, Florida to world-class athletes and "corporate athletes" who wish to benefit from his discoveries.

The good news according to Dr. Loehr is that, "We may not be able to eliminate stress in our lives but we can increase our capacity to handle more stress."

!

17

Speed Counts

"Speed is an indispensable ingredient of competitiveness, which helps you to enjoy market dominance, massive credibility, and customer loyalty."

The effective use of speed is a critical and clearly competitive weapon. You must learn to move fast or become history, because everything you do increases your competitive position or moves you one step closer to being competitive toast. When you get right down to it, there are only three viable strategies for coping with the accelerated pace of change: continuous innovation, ongoing learning, and speed.

Confronted with a constantly shifting array of customers, competitors, strategic alliances, and market volatility, the only hope for increased productivity lies in developing the ability to act and adapt *at least* as rapidly as your competitive environment. In addition, since it's become exceedingly difficult to see more than a few months into the future in most industries, you have but two alternatives to bankruptcy or unemployment:

1. Achieve a commanding enough position to dictate the changing rules of the game, or
2. Develop an ability to react immediately to those who do.

Either way, you get fast—and quickly, or you get out of business—quickly!

Accept this reality: customers, supply chains, and associates within a company want things done faster, easier, and smoother. And once they have experienced the combination of quality and speed, they ask themselves: "Why should I tolerate an inferior experience from this slowpoke?" The pursuit and hunger for speed is infectious. Once people know that they can have something quickly, they expect to have *everything* quickly, no matter how big the burden. Whoever embraces speed as a competitive weapon and delivers what people want swiftly is going to win.

Speed is the indispensable ingredient of competitiveness. It helps you enjoy market dominance, massive credibility, and customer loyalty. To beat the competition, speed must be incorporated into the culture and very fabric of a company.

Let me be perfectly clear about this: the type of speed I'm talking about here is not the defensive, keep-up-with-the-Joneses type of speed. I'm talking about proactive speed, the kind that leaders use as offensive, preemptive, competitive weapons. I'm talking about creating a climate and a culture of speed—speed of decision-making, speed of execution, speed of customer service, and so forth.

The following are a number of compelling reasons as to why you should use speed to your advantage by blasting out of the gate strong, setting a blazing pace for others to follow, while completely bewildering your competition:

- **Slow Costs More.** Every second or minute that you can take out of process or activity—such as closing a sale, manufacturing a product, and responding to customer needs—saves you time, and makes you more money.
- **Speed Is Sexy.** Speed is the ultimate customer turn-on. *Everyone* is short on time. We all dislike delays, long lines, out-of-stocks, and waiting on hold. However, we love finding what we want, and getting back to work (or play) fast. And we'll always be willing to pay for speed.
- **Speed Is Impossible to Ignore.** Speed brings with it a reputation of confidence, clarity of purpose, and execution. Once you become known for speed, both people and opportunities will seek you out.
- **Speed Trumps Size.** In today's world, the old rules no longer apply. It's not the big that eats the small, it's the fast that eats the slow. It's the one competitive advantage that the big competition can't duplicate easily.

- **Speed Empowers Action and Change.** Action is defined as "the causation of change." Whatever result you want, it's a change from what you now have. By definition, then, a change has to take place for you to get from your present status to that result. The faster the action, the faster the change.

An organization that eliminates wasted time in manufacturing, services, new-product development, and sales and distribution will cut costs, serve customers better, reduce inventories, enhance innovation, and make more money. The key is to recognize the competitive power of speed and to turn the pursuit of speed into a central organizing principle in your company and career.

You need to outthink and outhustle your competitors. To be able to think fast, you need to understand the primary drivers of change, work at staying plugged in, constantly search for new combinations, and develop a sense of heightened perception. The fastest people and companies in the world operate as they do because of their ability to anticipate. Anticipation means being aware of something in advance, and to regard it as possible. The ability to do this is one of the key ingredients of efficient speed and change management.

Being able to foresee that which is likely to occur in the next few months—and years—is enough to give you an edge over the majority of the population who simply follow what real leaders are doing.

Most people find change—particularly, the rapid and unpredictable kind—frightening and upsetting. But turbulence and change are not going away; indeed, they will become more pronounced. And the reality is that we all must get used to it.

The company or individual that does not embrace the importance of speed will be hammered. In fact, as a strategic weapon, speed is the equivalent of money, productivity, quality, even innovation. The good news is that, while we can't slow down the velocity of the external business environment, there's much we can do to speed up—to try to keep pace.

The only effective response to rapidly changing conditions is to develop the capacity to move at ultrahigh speed. While no one can realistically expect to move as rapidly as the constantly changing environment around us, those who can come closest will be best positioned to survive.

Your best chance to succeed is to be the one who's driving most of the changes. Of course, not everyone gets to be the leader. So it becomes incumbent on the rest of us to do the next best thing. Develop superfast reflexes that can react quickly, turn on a dime, and make near instantaneous adjustments to the turbulence of the marketplace. To accomplish this feat you must leverage the power of the new information technologies to move it into the right hands at the right time.

As you create and maintain an attitude that recognizes the supreme importance of urgency and speed by placing them at the center—not the periphery—of the action, you are building a gateway to long term prosperity and serve as an example of making speed count.

SPEED COUNTS—CALL TO ACTION

To explore your own commitment to making speed count, ask yourself these questions:

- What evidence do you see in your business or marketplace that speed is a competitive strength or serious liability?
- What practices or processes could you eliminate or enhance to speed up your ability to deliver results?
- What step will you take to make speed a core strength and competitive asset in your working life?

PORTRAIT OF SPEED

Federal Express

The career of Fred Smith—founder of FedEx, creator of overnight delivery—is built on an obsession with time and the pursuit of speed. FedEx is a company that truly understands that every package counts and "absolutely, positively" ensures that you get your high-value shipments with speed and certainty.

Smith realized early on that for a speed-hungry world, information about package delivery was as important as the delivery itself. So, FedEx pioneered the use of bar-code technology, put computers in delivery vans, and shared its software with customers. In doing so, the company turned package tracking into a high art and gave new meaning to the term "speedy customer service" by empowering customers to serve themselves.

Today, FedEx is the largest express transportation company in the world, with over 290,000 employees. They provide fast, reliable delivery to every US address and to more than 220 countries using their air-and-ground network to speed delivery of more than 8 million packages daily.

Fred Smith started out with an idea that business was speeding up; and for companies to stay competitive, they would need faster and more reliable options than the post office. By offering something truly different and sustainable and by delivering what they promise, FedEx has become synonymous with speed.

18

LIFELONG LEARNING COUNTS

"The only true certainty is uncertainty, and the only true source of lasting competitive advantage is knowledge."

Learning ability, intellectual capital, knowledge, and technical know-how are all intangibles. But these intangibles are among your most important assets, as everything you do to reinvent and update your knowledge allows you stay in the game and competitively perform.

People today work more with knowledge than with skill. While these two have many similar characteristics, we must focus on the dissimilar characteristic. A person's skill set changes very slowly over a long period of time, but knowledge empowers its own change. Knowledge—or what some call "intellectual capital"— is unique in that it cannibalizes itself. In a very short period of time, it makes itself obsolete, a relic and example of yesterday's strength being today's liability.

Lifelong learning rests upon the twin principles of personal development and social service. The social and economic development of a country, a company, and a community is increasingly dependent upon the knowledge and skills of its citizens in the global knowledge economy. Those who have the lowest levels of skill and the weakest capacity for constant updating will find themselves uncompetitive and most likely unemployed. Therefore, it is imperative that everyone commit to becoming a student for life, as the knowledge we currently possess is not sufficient for capitalizing on future opportunities.

Learning continually throughout life is vital if we are to make informed choices about our lives and the societies in which we live. Something new is always occurring as significant shifts in industries, technologies, and policies require interrogation and deeper understanding. This is only possible through a commitment to lifelong learning.

It would be foolish to ignore the call for lifelong learning as we discover more, and not less, need of new knowledge as we make progress. Lifelong learning rightly interpreted can have no endings and is as inseparable from normal living as food and physical exercise. It must be supported and encouraged throughout the course of life as a fundamental discipline. It must not be regarded as a luxury for a few exceptional persons here and there, nor as a thing which concerns only a short span of ones early formative years. Ongoing learning is a permanent national necessity—an inseparable aspect of citizenship—and therefore should be both universal and enduring.

A commitment to lifelong learning is more than just education and training beyond formal schooling. This framework encompasses learning throughout the life cycle, from cradle to grave and in different learning environments, formal, nonformal, and informal. Both individually and organizationally, the case for constant education—with knowledge creation as its primary goal—is fundamentally important. Propelled by the competitive imperatives of speed, global responsiveness, and the need to innovate constantly or perish, learning will be the essential hedge against extinction.

Knowledge and skills are perishable—both because they're not applied all the time, and because they can become outdated. Your life demands constant reflection upon experience and a healthy appetite for new knowledge in order for it to be vivid, strong, and creative. A failure to accept this reality and attend to the rigors of ongoing learning spells disaster.

The only true certainty is uncertainty, and the only sure source of true, lasting, competitive advantage is knowledge. The ability to learn faster than your competitors may indeed be the only sustainable competitive advantage.

When markets shift, technologies proliferate, competitors multiply, and products become obsolete virtually overnight. Successful companies are those that consistently create new knowledge, disseminate it widely throughout the organization, and quickly embody it in new technologies and products.

In short, ongoing success will come from ongoing learning!

For learning to be effective, we all need to be good and serious about knowledge generation, appropriation, and exploitation. Old cultural and psychological habits and paradigms die extremely hard. Rooting out and challenging obsolete assumptions can expose critical discrepancies between external reality and internal mental models. It is these gaps that provide much of the creative tension and dynamic energy that drives every learning initiative.

THE HALLMARKS AND PREREQUISITES OF LIFELONG LEARNING

This list is ambitious, and perhaps not even fully attainable. Lifelong learning is a journey with no end in sight, but the conscious pursuit of learning, just like excellence, is what really counts.

- **Intellectual Curiosity**—A passion to understand the changing forces swirling around you, an eagerness to learn them faster, and a recognition that learning is an unending journey.
- **Humility**—A pervasive acknowledgment that no one can have all the answers. You must have a willingness to learn from others.
- **Self-Criticism**—A logical extension of humility. A constant questioning of conventional wisdom and a keen awareness that success invariably sows the seeds of failure.
- **Tolerance for Ambiguity, Complexity, and Change**—An acceptance of the fact that change is an inherent reality. Thrive on change; don't allow yourself to be intimidated by its rough and unpolished exterior.
- **Experimentation**—A willingness to try out new approaches, to monitor the results, and to incorporate the feedback into new initiatives.
- **Hunger for Feedback**—A genuine eagerness to reach out and get performance feedback from a variety of sources, and willingness to listen to it and make changes.
- **Failure**—A view of experiments as desirable, mistakes as inevitable, and failures as offering the raw material of success. Learning is actually more a product of failure than of success.
- **Creative Self-Destruction**—No advantage lasts forever. Render yourself obsolete before others do it for you. It's the price world-class innovators gladly pay for staying ahead of the pack.

Lifelong learning provides the opportunities for you to continually expand your capacity to create the new results you truly desire.

Perhaps the most important thing you can do for yourself and your future is to know your strengths and focus on them. To know your strengths and natural talents and how to improve them and to know what you cannot or should not even attempt to do—these are the keys to lifelong learning. It is the most strategically compelling task to which everyone should dedicate themselves. While it's an asset that will not be reflected in any balance sheet or profit-and-loss statement, by making it count it automatically becomes competitive collateral.

LIFELONG LEARNING COUNTS—CALL TO ACTION

To explore your own commitment to making lifelong learning count, ask yourself these questions:

- Can you clearly see how a commitment to lifelong learning can ultimately lead to a lasting competitive advantage in your business or marketplace?
- Do you actively look for ways to grow your intellectual capital? Do you have a healthy appetite for new knowledge?
- What step will you take to make lifelong learning a key discipline in your life?

PORTRAIT OF LIFELONG LEARNING

Vistage International

Vistage International is the world's foremost chief executive leadership organization serving more than 14,500 members across the United States and 16 countries.

They serve the executive development needs of small business leaders by providing peer exchanges and opportunities for lifelong learning.

They are providing business leaders with the kinds of learning opportunities that will help our country remain the world's leading economic power.

This top executive network started from very humble beginnings over five decades ago.

In 1957, a Wisconsin businessman named Robert Nourse met with four fellow chief executives in the office of the Milwaukee Valve Company to test a simple, yet revolutionary, idea—share knowledge and experiences to help each other generate better results for their businesses.

The idea of businessmen asking each other questions, making suggestions, and working together to solve issues caught on.

Today, Vistage International is running strong. Members meet in small groups every month under the original guiding principles—to help one another make better decisions, achieve better results, and enhance their lives.

Vistage helps business leaders learn what they need to know to prosper in the future. The effort seems to be paying off as studies have shown that their member companies grow at three times the percentage growth rate of their competitors after joining Vistage.

A great testament to what happens when leaders commit to lifelong learning.

19

NETWORKING COUNTS

"Those who network and build social capital perform demonstratively better than those who do not."

Your network is your net worth. Better networking and quality relationships accelerate your personal and professional effectiveness, and expand the scope of your opportunities. The relationship component of your life must become a serious discipline, as each contact counts when you're building your personal bottom line.

Establishing a dynamic system of proven and effective networking habits is often the difference between success and failure; yet it's often overlooked and undervalued by many professionals. Have you ever wondered why some people get bigger promotions, better deals, or more sales— even when they are less qualified or experienced than you? Although you might think such successes hinge on simple luck, in many cases, it's networking skills that make the difference. The most effective professionals create and tap large, diversified networks that are rich in experience and span all organizational boundaries.

Simply stated, networks are people talking to each other, sharing ideas, information, and resources. Networking is a form of communication that creates the linkages between clusters of people. It's an essential life skill, as well as the most basic business-building tool in today's competitive market. When we truly understand the importance of networking, we can start to access the hidden treasure that will help us to succeed in our business, family, and community.

Your networking universe consists of three primary types of networks: a *Life Network*, a *Social Network*, and a *Professional Network*. Your Life Network is made up of your family, extended family, school friends, lifelong friends, and so forth. Your Social Network is made up of your active friends, people from your place of worship, fellow club members, neighbors, contacts in online communities, and so on. Finally, your Professional Network includes contacts from previous jobs, colleagues from other firms, contacts in your current organization, and mentors/coaches, to name just a few.

Although quantity counts in the networking universe—the more people in your networks, the better—the *quality* of each relationship is significantly more important. It's not what you know, or even who you know; it is how well you know each person in your universe that really counts toward building a powerful personal network. We all know or have at least heard of a person who seems to know everybody and whom everybody seems to know. You'll find a disproportionate amount of supernetworkers like recruiters, lobbyists, fundraisers, politicians, journalists, and public relations specialists, because positions such as these require certain innate networking abilities. These people should be the cornerstones to your flourishing network.

The three important factors behind each contact are: the number of people in your various networks, the depth of your relationships with those people, and your frequency of interaction with them. Unrealistic expectations of your network come from trying to *use* your network for support that your contacts might not feel you deserve, or feel they have no obligation to provide. You have to earn the loyalty, trust, and engagement of your network.

So go the extra mile for your network. Follow through in ways that surprise and intrigue the other businesspeople with whom you come in contact. This includes taking actions like clipping a news article about a topic that's of significance to the contact and sending it to him or her with a personal note and another business card.

Networking builds a trilogy of trust—the trust that one person has in another, which is then passed along to a third referred party. Whether it's a job opportunity or the name of a good doctor or mechanic, people want to do business with others that they know, like, and trust. If they don't know someone in a specific area, based on the trust they have for another person, they will almost always accept their recommendation.

When we truly understand the importance of networking, we can start to access the hidden treasure that will help us to succeed in all areas of our lives: business, family, and the community. The networks and the goodwill we create become our social capital, which is the accumulation of resources developed through personal and professional contacts. These resources include ideas, knowledge, information, opportunities, contacts, and of course, referrals.

Referral-based, word-of-mouth business is the ultimate power play. There is no exception to this rule. Other marketing tools like traditional advertising, public relations, and web sites are certainly of value, particularly if they reinforce the word-of-mouth process. The experienced professional recognizes that word-of-mouth is a far superior strategy than traditional marketing methods.

Social capital is built by design, not chance. Those who network and create social capital perform demonstratively better than those who do not; they get better jobs, better pay, and faster promotions. They are more influential, effective, and happier than those who are unwilling or unable to benefit from the power of social capital.

Therefore, learn to harness the power of word-of-mouth marketing to drive sales for fast, sustainable, business growth. The idea of growing your business through word-of-mouth marketing is a concept that crosses cultural, ethnic, and political boundaries, as we all speak the language of referrals.

Successful people understand and know how to develop rich social capital and reap the benefits in their business, professional, and personal networks. Yet many people hardly know their own neighbors, let alone the local businesspeople in town. More than ever, networking is critical to success in any endeavor. So many businesspeople that are trying to build their social capital do so with an almost vulture-like intensity. There are times when it's not appropriate to hand out your business card or ask someone the ubiquitous "what do you do?" Being sensitive to the moment and respecting the surroundings is a crucial networking skill.

Networking isn't an option. It's not just something you do when you want something from someone. Developing a style of networking that's deliberate, habitual, and finely tuned is one sure way to accelerate your progress through the development of personal networks. Your wealth of knowledge won't amount to much unless you have a network of people to share it with. You must also possess enough compassion for the people in that network to understand that your success is a direct result of their success.

Mom was wrong—it does pay to talk to strangers. We live in a relationship economy, where networking to get ahead in life most definitely counts.

NETWORKING COUNTS—CALL TO ACTION

To explore your own commitment to making networking count, ask yourself these questions:

- Do you believe that who you know is more important than what you know?
- Do you actively look for ways to build your network of personal and business relationships?
- What step will you take to become better at networking and increase your circle of influence?

PORTRAIT OF A MASTER NETWORKER

Dr. Ivan Misner

Most of us would agree that who you know can be more important than what you know . . . that having a good network can be hugely valuable.

Not as many people are comfortable networking or feel like they are good networkers.

Dr. Ivan Misner is a master networker and the founder of Business Network International (BNI), an organization that helps its members build effective networks.

BNI is the world's largest business referral organization and annually generates millions of referrals, resulting in over $2.3 billion worth of business for its members.

Dr. Misner has been called the "Father of Modern Networking" and believes that the most effective networkers start with the idea that they must offer value before they can ask for value (referrals, introductions, time).

He says that "When building your network, try to bring business and contacts to your networking partners. Do what it takes to 'earn' the help you might want down the road."

To become a good networker be visible in your community, establish your credibility, and be able to explain how others can profit from knowing you.

Your network will increase in value as you increase your skill at helping others get what they want through knowing you.

That's networking at its best—a shorter road to building trust through referrals.

PERSONAL STRATEGIES

CHARACTER COUNTS

"Having character is much more important than being a character."

There is no more essential or defining aspect of a person than their character. From the moment you open your eyes each morning until they close again for sleep each night, your character is either complemented or compromised. Additionally, there is no higher praise we can give a person than to say that they have good character. But what does that *really* mean? What makes this quality so essential to achieving personal success and fulfillment? How can we place a call for greater cultivation of character in ourselves, our coworkers, our friends, and in our children, so that we live more satisfying lives?

Suppose for a moment that you were responsible for picking a principal for your child's school, an executive to run one of your companies, a pastor to lead your church, or a coach to teach your little leaguers. What one exceptional characteristic would this person absolutely have to possess? Would it be good looking, Ivy League education, athletic, good negotiator, sharp dresser, a creative mind ... or would it be extraordinary character?

My guess is that solid character would head that list. When we have to relate to, work with, and depend upon someone, nothing is more important than personal ethical virtues like honor, reliability, trustworthiness, and kindness.

Everything we do and say ultimately arises from and reveals our character. In addition to a proper concern for improving our own character, we should also care for the character of others. While charisma and skill may lubricate the wheels of progress, true success comes from developing character. A person who has good character is thought to be especially worthy, virtuous, or admirable in terms of moral qualities.

Having character is much more important than *being* a character; substance carries much more weight than style. If we know a person's character, we can better predict how he or she is likely to respond to temptation, adversity, and success. It helps us make better judgments when we know the character of the people we date and marry, do business with, and elect as our political leaders.

It would be a mistake to underestimate the profound impact on our national consciousness of the stories of unspeakable acts of violence, callousness, greed, and deceit by people and of the never-ending barrage of scandals among high-profile leaders and celebrities. More and more, we are called upon to evaluate individuals and understand events in terms of character.

Character is comprised of those principles and values that give your life direction, meaning, and depth. They constitute your inner sense of right and wrong. Wrong is simply doing wrong—not just getting caught. Character functions as a moral compass: unshakable, rock-solid principles that define beliefs; that specify the dos and don'ts of behavior; and that point the way to excellence. No matter where you go on this earth, no matter what the situation, honesty, courage, fairness, generosity, and integrity are essential attributes of good character.

Character is not concerned with political correctness; it is only concerned with doing the *right* thing. People with character understand that what works is not necessarily what is right ... *even* when they can get away with less ... *even* when the wrong thing seems like no big deal ... *even* when no one is watching.

It is through character that personal leadership and excellence are exercised; it is character that sets the example and the standards by which you behave. Character is not something one can fool people about. Either you have it or you don't. People will forgive a great deal: incompetence, ignorance, insecurity, or even bad manners. But they will not forgive a lack of character.

The practice of good character ensures that you walk your talk, even when out of the glare of the lights and public scrutiny. It's far easier to do right than it is to undo wrong, so when others choose the path of least resistance, you must choose the high road of ethical behavior. You'll sleep better at night.

Practicing good ethics is a solo act, and the proverbial buck stops with you. Knowing what is right is no guarantee that you will *do* what is right. Indeed, whether we do what is right will ultimately be determined by the strength of our character—not by IQ, academic degree, DNA, or bank account.

So sweat the small stuff—because character is revealed in the smallest actions. You commit character assassination each and every time you choose to violate what you know is right. Some indiscretions shout and others whisper, but high standards leave no room for little indiscretions. And you don't build sweat equity in your character by talking. Behaving according to the spirit and intent of your personal code of conduct—even when you are the only one who knows what's really going on—is the key to character. Good intentions are fine, but doing right is what really matters. With enough practice, doing wrong will become unthinkable.

How many times can you demonstrate poor character before becoming too weak to overcome the big challenges you are destined to confront? Violations of honesty and integrity dilute your strength, suppress your psychological immune system, and chip away at your self-esteem.

Your integrity, honor, and reputation often precede you and linger after you move on. The greatest gift you can give yourself is the practice of good character; the greatest gift you can give to others is a model character. Character inspires and is inspiring, so strive to inspire!

When it comes to practicing good character, saying no to vices simply isn't enough. A quality life is never achieved by focusing on the elimination of what is wrong. True success requires you to focus your mental, emotional, and spiritual energies on pursuing that which is right and good. The extent to which your personal character evolves depends, in large measure, on the extent to which you pursue the positive. Trying to become virtuous merely by excluding a vice is as unrealistic as trying to cultivate roses simply by eliminating weeds. Behaving according to your beliefs, values, and good intentions—walking the talk—is one of the biggest challenges you will face.

Practicing good ethics and character is the moral equivalent of war, as it's a lot easier to fight for principles than to live up to them. Heed this warning: you will pay a price for high standards and strong principles. While people may be impressed and respect you, they won't always like you. You'll wrestle with inner conflict. Buyer's remorse might try to settle in. You are likely to obtain a few battle scars as you exercise good character. Nonetheless, carry on!

We live in an age that increasingly sacrifices personal responsibilities at the altar of personal freedoms. When we fail individually and collectively to take seriously the importance of character, we begin to self-destruct. History leaves us with enough clues to believe with confidence that we can only experience true success and happiness by making character the bedrock of our lives. When it comes to good character, everything counts!

CHARACTER COUNTS—CALL TO ACTION

To explore your own commitment to making character count, ask yourself these questions:

- Do you believe that good character is one of your greatest strengths? Why do you feel this way?
- Do you demonstrate the type of character that inspires others to become better people?
- What step can you take to demonstrate strong, consistent, and inspiring character?

PORTRAIT OF IMPECCABLE CHARACTER

Paul Newman

Paul Newman was a good man with great character. He really tried to do the right thing—and he succeeded. He lived a useful life that exemplified what good, caring, human values look like in a truly decent human being.

For all of the timeless roles he has played on the silver screen, it is as the benevolent Salad King that Paul Newman ought to be known and remembered.

He donated all his profits and royalties after taxes from his Newman's Own brand to educational and charitable purposes. With more than $200 million in charitable gifts donated since 1983, Paul Newman cooked up the concept of selling his vinaigrette and popcorn and turning all profits over to causes that mattered to him, including The Hole in the Wall Gang Camp that he founded for children with disabilities.

"All good things flow out of a salad dressing bottle," he says. The legacy of his capitalism with not only a cause but a heart bears second fruit in the work of his daughters Nell and Clea, who both volunteered as camp counselors at Hole in the Wall in rustic eastern Connecticut and now run their own organizations in what can be called a family empire of good works, great character, and extraordinary commitment to doing the right thing.

21

COMMON SENSE COUNTS

"Be committed to living by the rules of common sense, common honesty, and common decency."

Common sense is a collection of the pearls of conventional wisdom. It's the basic governing principles of life that most of us know intuitively, even though we waste valuable time trying to deny them. Common sense is the clear line that separates right and wrong, helpful and harmful; it is the simplicity that can be found just on the other side of complexity.

Common sense can be elusive, at times; after all, the obscure takes a while to see, the obvious even longer. Nevertheless, common sense is a valuable resource that deserves our attention and admiration. It tells us when to come in out of the rain; it teaches us that the early bird gets the worm, and that we must take the bitter with the sweet. Common sense also tells us not to spend more than we earn. It offers reliable parenting strategies that ensure the adult is in charge, not the child, and advises us to follow prudent dietary plans, such as rounding out the eggs and bacon breakfast with a little fiber and orange juice. Most of all, common sense encourages us to do the right thing, at the right time, for the right reason.

Life is a series of ordinary events that follow the laws of logic and probability. These events are indifferent to our fantasies and require the careful, accurate navigation of common sense. Using common sense means applying our knowledge to solve everyday problems in ways that might not come naturally to us. In trying to create a law for every situation, however, we have lost the perspective of the principles common to our society. We have allowed bureaucratic rigidity, costly and ineffective regulations, and overly complex procedural rules to supersede good judgment and common sense.

Society's overreliance on statutes and regulations as a means to creating a better society, instead has created a system of regulation that precludes good judgment and sound common sense. Instead of fostering common sense, our legal culture often undermines it. We have allowed common sense to be lost in our culture's accumulated knowledge.

Individuals can also become so tightly focused that we lose our ability to apply what we learn generally to our own lives specifically. As a result, we lack both discretion and common sense. To connect with reality and to develop the wisdom of common sense, we need to learn to be aware of our own actions and to pay attention to the world around us.

One of the first rules of common sense is that we can learn from other people's successes and mistakes. We all play the role of both teacher and student throughout our lives. Every person you meet provides a lesson in living, if you will only be aware enough to learn. Observe both good and bad actions and behaviors of others, then define where they have taken the wrong turn, or what they are doing right. Finally, determine what that lesson means for you. That's common sense in action.

Second, if you know some action or behavior that works—and yet you expect success even though you don't use that action or behavior—you have disconnected from reality. If you observe that a behavior has consistently failed, and yet you repeat that behavior with the expectation of success, you (again) have disconnected from reality.

Interestingly, humans are the only living things that can *decide* to disconnect from reality. We are inclined to do what we want to do, rather than what we know we *should* do. We can—and often do—choose to live according to unreasonable expectations, which makes no sense at all. Though it might temporarily allow us to justify repeating failed behavior, we are only kidding ourselves.

Living with reality takes an effort on our part, but it is essential that we do the things that we know must be done and stop doing those things that we know don't work. That's common sense in action. It demands an understanding of the principles of cause and effect, since all things happen for a reason. We are the sum of the decisions we have made and the actions we have taken to this point. When you catch yourself doing something that is counterproductive—something you know, from observation, doesn't work—*stop*. Make the necessary adjustment to your behavior and practice what you learn in order to create positive habits.

Take a concentrated look at the mistakes you make. Seek to understand why you've done these things, and why they don't garner the results you want. If you are doing the right thing, keep at it, whether you see immediate results or not. A successful life is made up of a series of course corrections. That's common sense in action.

Common sense also requires that you learn to step back from situations and look at each objectively. Take out all of the personalities, emotions, and egos and determine the right thing to do, then act on that determination, regardless of who is involved. Be principled and do not compromise in doing what you know to be right.

As we examine the results of our behavior and learn from the experiences of others, we begin to create a yardstick by which we can judge what we know and the knowledge with which we come into contact. We can use that yardstick to determine what ideas and behaviors are acceptable and then act accordingly. That, too, is common sense in action.

You are the only one who can apply common sense wisdom in your own life. No one can make you wise or ignorant, or guide your behavior. Any time you see, hear, or experience a lesson for better living, it's up to you to learn and follow that lesson. The job of living is, in essence, the daily task of learning and following the laws of common sense.

Be strongly committed to living by the rules of common sense, common honesty, and common decency. To get the best results—to be genuinely happy, successful, and content—you have to make common sense your common practice. Live intelligently, live with meaning, and live with an understanding that common sense counts!

COMMON SENSE COUNTS—CALL TO ACTION

To explore your own commitment to making common sense count, ask yourself these questions:

- Do you have a tendency to simplify or complicate situations in your life?

- Do you ever second-guess yourself when the solution to a vexing problem seems like such common sense? If so, why?
- What step will you take to learn and follow the rules of common sense in your life?

PORTRAIT OF COMMON SENSE

Common Sense Media.org

Today's kids spend so much time absorbing media (TV, movies, Internet) that it has become the other parent in their lives.

It used to be easy to say of bad stuff, I know it when I see it. That's just common sense. Now there are so many sources for entertainment that it is difficult for parents to know in advance what might be harmful to their children.

Everyone is busy—working long hours, rushing to soccer practices, dance classes, volunteer activities—so it's easy just to hope kids make the right choices.

Nonprofit Common Sense Media.org was founded because families need trustworthy information to help manage their kids' media lives and have a voice about the media they consume.

They provide parents with solid information via movie reviews, articles, forums, and news to help parents keep up.

Founder Jim Steyer, former elementary school teacher, public interest lawyer, father of four, and a Stanford University professor, is well versed in media choices and their impact on children.

We have to remember that the price for free and open media is a bit of extra homework for families.

Common Sense Media is a great free resource for busy parents who believe that through informed decision-making, we can improve the media landscape one decision at a time.

22

EXCELLENCE COUNTS

"Excellence is a guilty pleasure, as it creates confidence and enhances peace of mind."

The pursuit of excellence is not only politically correct, it's also highly profitable. Excellence is a form of currency. A commitment to excellence can help you capture true wealth and realize the inherent value of your potential, while a lack of commitment devalues potential, credibility, and reputation.

Each of us must determine the specific achievements we must accomplish in order to deem our own life "excellent." Your responsibilities in doing this include choosing a career path, deciding what to and what not to believe in, what to learn and apply in life, and what actions to take. You can help yourself with these responsibilities by consistently asking one simple question: How are your thoughts and actions reflective of a life committed to excellence?

What exactly *is* excellence? Well, think of it as the process of continually growing and improving yourself and your life. Excellence includes achievement of goals that can be measured by constantly asking the question, "Is what I'm doing truly reflective of a life committed to excellence?"

Your greatest responsibility in seeking excellence is to define what this means precisely in *your* life, then to choose the best course of action to make it happen. Excellence is not a relative term; it is the standard by which you must judge what you do. You will quickly discover that committing yourself to a life of excellence cannot be accomplished haphazardly.

Excellence never occurs by accident. It always comes as the result of quality thinking and purposeful execution. To become the person you were meant to be, everything you do must be done with the single purpose of achieving excellence. You must do it with the unshakeable belief and understanding that excellence counts. You must live and die in the spirit of quality and excellence. The measurement of your "best" begins and ends with the marks of excellence—nothing less.

Another way to achieve excellence is to start breaking bad habits and form good ones. But how do you break a bad habit? And how do you adopt a good one? It's easy; make a commitment to do these two things, and you'll learn to do what needs to be done. Next, maintain a focus on the new behavior and refuse to accept anything less than what you expect. That's exactly how excellence is achieved.

Some people perpetually create their own dissatisfaction by consistently slipping into mediocrity. This can easily be fixed, too, right now by simply deciding to quit doing less than excellent work. What a profound idea! Mediocrity is a choice; it's not always made consciously, but it is still a choice. You commit career malpractice every time you do things in a mediocre manner; every time you show up late; every time you are unprepared. There is no inherent value in mediocrity, so there is no reason for people to stop and pay attention to you or your work. Choose never to compromise your talent, quality, and high standards, and you will never choose mediocrity.

Being world-class has nothing to do with size, education, or bloodline; it has everything to do with decision, commitment, action, and persistence. Excellence is a destination for anyone who appreciates, respects, and demonstrates hard work and good judgment. But excellence is not something that you attain, then put in a trophy case. It is a habit—a momentary happening—a crossroad where the body, mind, and spirit all work together. Basketball players call it being in "the zone" when their athletic prowess, experience, and talent peak. Everyone has this potential to achieve excellence.

Excellence requires that a price be paid; whatever you are willing to pay in sweat to find it and keep it in good working order. Those who have legitimately reached the summit of their careers, relationships, gamesmanship, have worked harder and longer; studied and planned more assiduously;

practiced more self-denial; and overcome more difficulties than those who have not risen as far.

You can become excellent in a second—beginning right now. Start by visualizing yourself as the best teacher, artist, manager, coach, or parent that you aspire to become—and start acting the part. Put yourself in the best possible position to succeed, and then perform your script exactly as it plays out in your mind. It takes less than a second to raise your standards higher than they are right now. You must merely decide to deliver world-class quality, but it takes a lifetime of passionate pursuit to maintain it, whether you are the concierge at a hotel, the manager of a small department, or the CEO of an international firm.

One of the wonderful things about excellence is that when it is on, you'll know it because you'll enjoy the experience through all five senses:

1. ***Look:*** Impeccable grooming, solid posture, and complete preparation for a business meeting display the look of excellence.
2. ***Feel:*** An inviting smile, the fine leather of a new car, and the smooth texture of fabric demonstrate the feel of excellence and quality.
3. ***Sound:*** A rich singing voice, an expansive vocabulary, and the friendliness of a wake up call are examples of excellence in communication.
4. ***Taste:*** The design of a home, the font of a letter, and the sweetness of a chef's dessert all celebrate excellence in taste.
5. ***Smell:*** The aroma of fresh flowers, the bouquet of a perfume, and the scent from freshly baked cookies help us to experience the smell of excellence.

Excellence wastes little time in making its presence felt. It represents an example of truly great thinking. We should all appreciate the merits of rich thoughts, high personal standards, and a commitment to squeeze every ounce of ones potential.

Excellence begins as a decision—one where you look at your life, business, and relationships and ask, "What do I see that needs improvement? What do I wish I didn't see? What would I ideally like to see? What do I hear other people say about me? What do I see that rubs me the wrong way about others?" The answer to these questions, along with others like them, will provide the points of improvement you seek.

Implementing and sustaining a drive toward excellence will put you in the best position relative to others for opportunity. It will also help you build support because you demonstrate real accountability, genuine results, and superior performance.

Excellence is a guilty pleasure, as it creates confidence and enhances peace of mind. It functions as an insurance policy against mediocrity and an assurance of continuous growth. A genuine commitment to excellence allows you to bump yourself up from coach to first class anytime you wish.

We all have a range of career choices and opportunities, but we expand this range and quality of our choices when we practice excellence. Adversely, we blackball ourselves from future opportunities when we do mediocre work. Attempt to make every opportunity one of importance, because every opportunity counts.

What is considered excellent today will become the minimum cost of admission tomorrow. You're only as good as your last performance. The bar is constantly being raised. If you don't produce excellent results consistently, someone else will. There is no grace period for mediocrity, and you must have a zero tolerance policy for it. People expect the best. If they can't get it from you, they'll find it elsewhere.

Most people are not hard acts to follow, and that's exactly why a commitment to excellence is the ultimate competitive advantage. Excellence is achieved via qualitative, not quantitative, shifts in developing skills. Be part of a qualitatively different world or environment, where excellence is expected and practice is a key to achieving excellence.

Never relax the rules of excellence. When you compromise quality, you suffer physical and emotional detachment from your goals. Have the belief that the efficiencies of your business and life are infinite, that everything can be improved upon, that every project can be completed in an excellent fashion.

Why? Because when it comes to excellence, everything counts!

EXCELLENCE COUNTS—CALL TO ACTION

To explore your own commitment to making excellence count, ask yourself these questions:

- Do you believe that a genuine commitment to excellence pays handsome dividends? If so, why?
- Do your actions raise the bar for others to reach higher and to perform supremely?
- What steps will you take to commit every aspect of your life to excellence?

Portrait of Excellence

Steve LaVallee, LaVallee's Karate Studios

Steve LaVallee's passion is the martial arts.

He believes that the study of the martial arts is about more than learning technique—beyond what takes place in the ring, it's something that can transform ordinary into excellence.

His mission is to help others achieve excellence.

He began his quest for excellence at the age of 10 and spent nearly every waking moment training, traveling, and competing. He was awarded the Triple Crown" by *Karate Illustrated*, by winning championships in fighting, forms, and weapons.

He became a Sensei, a Japanese term for master, and owner of his own dojo at 18. Dojo refers to a place for martial arts students to conduct training.

As he expanded his skills, his talents and titles grew. He realized his true passion was teaching and training. He retired from active competition and focused on building a new generation of black belt champions.

His program, Excellence in Knowledge, influences students' Attitude, Behavior, and Character.

Students train with great intensity to master the martial arts and critical life skills, such as goal setting, leadership, fitness, self-defense, self-discipline, improved focus and concentration, mutual respect, and relationship building.

His programs reach more than two thousand students per day and are recognized as the leading edge in the development of peak performance.

Steve LaVallee embodies excellence as a way of life. Even better, he is helping others achieve excellence in their lives.

23

EVERY CHOICE COUNTS

"We can turn lemons into lemonade, weeds into gardens, and pennies into fortunes, simply by making a choice to do so."

Every choice must have a purpose: to move you closer to your goals!

Some people claim that you must "play the hand that life deals." But you *build* that hand largely from a deck of your own choices, and your hand improves as your choices improve. Every moment offers you a choice: to exercise this power by setting and holding a direction or to veer off course.

Every choice counts. There are no insignificant choices, no neutral actions. Even the smallest decision has a bottom-line consequence, leading you toward or away from your goals.

Choices are the meat of your daily diet. Your quality of life is a direct reflection of the quality of the decisions you've made up to this moment. Good choices move you to desirable actions. Your life immediately points "true north" when you begin making choices that lead you toward your goals.

In fact, you can decide to change it all any day—or at any moment—that you wish. You can make the decision to improve the quality of your life. You can decide to get in the best physical shape of your life. You can decide to raise your own personal standards. You can commit to doing excellent work. You can decide to say yes to your dreams.

Conversely, you can decide to do nothing at all. You can decide to make excuses rather than accept responsibility; to avoid rather than to confront a problem; to be a follower, instead of a leader; to be timid rather than bold. You can decide to settle or go for your goals. You can decide to quit, rather than press on when confronted with adversity. Simply put—the choices are yours to make.

You cannot allow a bad choice or error in judgment to be repeated, as it will lead you down an undesirable path. You must continually make and reinforce the choices that will bring fulfillment, happiness, and joy into your daily life. If by chance you don't like certain things in your life right now, change it. You're not a leopard; you *can* change your spots!

You have the ability to totally transform every area in your life—so change it now. Going from good to bad, bad to worse, and worse to life support is only a few small decisions away. It all begins with the choices you make, therefore make every choice count.

We all experience our share of both good and bad times. Yet some people can't even make a living in good times—let alone in bad times—mainly because they have failed to exercise their freedom to choose proactively. When bad times come, they sit back and fill their minds with discouragement, doubt, fear, and excuses.

In contrast, others choose to think proactively and succeed, even in so-called bad times. Choices that deliver the desired results are the key ingredient to the recipe of success.

Its charm and strength is in its simplicity. You can decide today, tomorrow, the next day, or next month but for change to take place in your life, a choice must first be made. The difference between repeating a vice and creating a new reality is determined by the choices you make. Human beings have the unique ability to mold and shape ideas—which initially are little more than vapor—into something of beauty and significance. They can turn lemons into lemonade, weeds into gardens, and pennies into fortunes simply by making a choice to do so.

The greatest form of abuse in this world is the self-abuse that results from wrong thinking and bad choices. The culprits of your struggles are your thoughts and corresponding choices—change them, and your life will turn for the better.

Washing the outside of a car does not make it run any better. To improve its performance, you must get inside. Likewise, improving the condition of your life is an inside job. By choosing thoughts and actions that move you in the direction of your goals, you are bound to improve your station in life. Unfortunately, failing to execute properly your God-given right to choose renders you a slave to the failure you hope to avoid.

The wonderful part about making good choices is that it doesn't require any special aptitude or training to do. The sooner you recognize your inborn power to choose, the sooner you will get off the back roads of life and onto the freeway of prosperity.

Every choice carries a consequence. For better or worse, each one is the unavoidable consequence of its predecessor. There are no exceptions. If you can accept that a bad choice carries the seed of its own punishment, why not accept the fact that a good choice yields desirable fruit?

If you change your thinking, you change your choices. If you change your choices, you change your life. Understanding that *everything counts* impresses upon you the enthusiasm and urgency of constructive thought and choice. Wealth, health, peace of mind, intimacy—everything in life is the germination of a choice. The single biggest determinant of your success happens between your ears—nowhere else. If there is something in your life that you do not like, begin immediately to make choices that will deliver you what you desire. You define yourself by your decisions.

Decisiveness pulls more weight than correctness. In some situations, you won't know what to do. You will want to do the right thing and have some sort of guarantee that everything will turn out fine, but you will feel unsure whether one course of action is better than an alternative. So make a decision. Whether that decision is right or wrong, you'll soon receive feedback that will help you progress.

Decision is the most important criteria for the release of and admittance to your potential. Do not allow yourself to be victimized by your own indecision.

You go through this life just once—so choose wisely. Choose to make the most of life for yourself and everyone else around you. Why? Because, when it comes to thoughts and choices, everything counts!

EVERY CHOICE COUNTS—CALL TO ACTION

To explore your own commitment to making every choice count, ask yourself these questions:

- Do you believe that every choice you make produces a consequence that is either positive or negative? What was the best decision you made today?

- Do you take the time to seriously consider the relevance of each choice before choosing a direction? What in your view is the purpose of decision-making?
- What step will you take to make sure that every choice you make advances you one step closer to your goals or desired outcome?

PORTRAIT OF GOOD CHOICES

Jim Koch

Jim Koch founded The Boston Beer Company in 1984 because he believed that Americans ought to be able to choose the beer they drink—they deserved better beer.

Jim's father, a fifth-generation brewer, left the beer business when the market for classic, full-flavored beers had all but disappeared—Boston was once home to over 30 breweries.

Jim pursued a career in consulting until his instincts told him people were starting to crave something different in their beer.

Miller was everywhere, Coors was a regional brand, and the "better beer" category did not exist beyond imports—no "microbrews or craft beers" were available.

Once he made the decision, he got things running quickly.

During the first year, Jim went bar-to-bar with his Samuel Adams Boston Lager, named after a Boston revolutionary war hero and famously independent thinker. After selling 500 barrels, it was beginning to look like his instincts were right—if you offered people a better tasting beer they would choose it.

Other small brewers were inspired and the microbrew revolution was on.

Over the years, Jim Koch has mapped each step of the way, always choosing to offer the best choices in microbeers.

The makers of Samuel Adams are always careful to remind people to drink responsibly—maybe the most important choice of all.

24

PASSION COUNTS

*"Great works can only be accomplished by those who are
intoxicated with a passion for greatness."*

The most powerful weapon on earth is the human soul on fire. Passion is hard-core devotion to a person or cause; it infuses life with meaning, joy, and unbridled enthusiasm. It's desire in your heart, fire in your belly, an indispensable virtue that is far more valuable than money, power, or fame. Whether you are tackling the issue of growing sales, adding value, focusing on results, embracing change, attracting talent, or raising performance, your passion will keep you committed to success.

Passion reflects confidence, spreads good cheer, raises morale, inspires associates, arouses loyalty, and laughs at adversity. It's a compelling emotion that enables you to go places others are afraid to go, to try things others are afraid to try, and to be the kind of person others are afraid to be. Passion gives you the will to start, the strength to continue, and the sustaining power to overcome the greatest of obstacles and setbacks.

Your life's path will inevitably hand you your share of obstacles. Common sense slows you down to investigate them, creative thinking will suggest some ingenious way of getting around them, and perseverance deliberately goes to work to dig under them. But your passion will boldly face and leap right over difficulties. Passion is closely related to perseverance, and perseverance is the strong determination to move toward the achievement of a goal. Passion is the fuel that drives perseverance.

Far too many people go through life without making any effort to truly live it, never getting that fire in their belly for enjoying life to the fullest. The worst bankruptcy in the world is the person who has lost his passion. For the individual without passion, life is irrational, unfulfilling, and even hopeless. He is missing any kind of significance, and goes through life like a blindfolded man in a strange room playing a game without knowing the rules.

The enemy of passion is apathy. It is perhaps the worst of all evils; it is a killer of ideas, hopes, and dreams. The only quality that can overcome apathy is enthusiasm. The world has no lack of good fights to fight, and it has no lack of resources to solve our problems. What many require, however, is the burning desire and enthusiasm to fight the fights and to solve those problems.

Most children clearly demonstrate their potential for passion; bubbling enthusiasm is one of their most irresistible charms. Children fully under the spell of passion see no darkness, no stop signs, no red lights, and no speed limits. They are easily excited and have relatively few fears about expressing their enthusiasm. They are completely smitten and forget that there is such a thing as failure in the world. Children are turned on by an innate curiosity that stimulates learning. And when they learn, they can hardly contain themselves long enough to tell you about their new discoveries.

The secret of genius is to carry the spirit of the child into old age, which means never losing your passion and enthusiasm. What have you done with childlike passion this week?

One of the deepest needs of human existence is to know that our lives count for something—that our gifts and talents are being used to make a difference. Since work is so much a part of our lives, we want it to be meaningful. To know that our work counts for something important is to know that *we* count. You must love what you do. Your heart must be in it.

Without passion, you will never live up to your fullest potential. Each of us has to bring our all to the game. Actively engaged hearts and minds, unwavering commitment, laser focus, and relentless determination are all motivated by passion. Doing mundane work is like allowing a vampire to suck the life out of you and leave you feeling anonymous, alienated, and defeated. You go home at the end of the day emotionally drained, with little or nothing left to give to loved ones.

To engage in work that does not cultivate your passion is completely unnatural, and sabotages your spirit. If the project you're working on now is not fueling your enthusiasm, you should transform it, reframe it, and redefine it until you fall in love with it.

Many factors contribute to building passion into your work. These include identifying what it means to be successful, transforming projects into exciting work, and defining that work in terms of a heroic or noble cause. Few things are professionally more fulfilling than doing work at which you excel and that excites you. Deep down, we all want to be involved in work that matters and—if we're really lucky—that changes the world. Compelling work stimulates passion.

So ask yourself: What is most beautiful and sacred to you? What would you feel incomplete without? When you have identified that which brings you complete joy, your unquenchable desire to achieve that goal will become your passion—the inner drive that turns your dreams into a shining reality.

Far too many people act as though comfort and luxury are the chief requirements for a successful life, when all that they really require for happiness is something to be passionate about. Those who truly live by their passions see the bigger picture and understand the ultimate value they bring to the world. These people are fully aware of the link between their individual contributions and the larger, nobler cause. I'm talking about the administrative assistant in a hospital who believes she is a part of saving lives, the photo developer who knows that she preserves peoples' most treasured memories, and the sailor who understands that the combat-readiness of his ship strengthens peace negotiations.

When people establish a connection between what they do and a larger effort to change the world for the better, their work becomes an act of passion and heroism. Everyone wants to feel heroic and noble about something; it feeds their passion and gives their life meaning and significance.

What is the ultimate value *you* bring to the world? What is the heroic cause that sparks your passions? When you define work as a cause—a movement worth fighting and feeling passionate for—you will find that there is no height to which your spirit cannot rise. You will also find that you have cultivated something that is extremely difficult to replicate, for passion is a powerful competitive weapon.

Every great accomplishment is the triumph of some great passion. Great works can only be accomplished by those who are intoxicated with a passion

119

for greatness. Vow to live completely, fearlessly, and passionately because passion counts.

PASSION COUNTS—CALL TO ACTION

To explore your own commitment to making passion count, ask yourself these questions:

- Do you feel a sense of passion and romance about your work? Do you *love* what you do?
- Do you believe you would be happier if you followed your heart and lived a life of passion?
- What steps will you take to bring more passion to your work, relationships, and hobbies?

PORTRAIT OF A PASSIONATE BUSINESS

The American Girl Company

The American Girl Company has a passion for who girls are today and who they can become tomorrow—a passion to create girls of strong character.

Their mission is to develop books and products that help girls grow up in a wholesome way, while encouraging them to enjoy girlhood through enchanting play.

The inspiration for American Girl came to founder Pleasant Rowland during a visit to historic Williamsburg where she thought about how much she loved the costumes, the everyday life—the living history.

Was there some way she could bring this history alive for young girls?

What if she could come up with doll characters dressed in historical costumes and write stories so good that the little girls would identify with and fall in love with the character?

Her musings ignited her passion for developing girls and that drove her to launch American Girl, now owned by Mattel.

This work continues with the release of "Chrissa."

The Chrissa character is a friendly, creative girl who finds the courage to stand up for herself and for others.

This is part of American Girl's effort to bring awareness to the devastating effects of bullying and give girls the skills to stand strong and speak out against it.

The passion for building character in young girls is alive and well.

25

PERSEVERANCE COUNTS

"With perseverance, we discover the depths of our commitments; without it, we merely survive."

It may lack the nobility of integrity, the charisma of enthusiasm, the grace of generosity, and the sparkle of excellence, but the beauty of perseverance is that, in time, it always makes up for all that which it lacks. There is great virtue and glory in never giving up.

Nothing concentrates the mind or tests our character like a demanding goal—the desire to be something better than we are, to be the complete person that we are meant to be. But in the course of achieving any goal, we can expect to experience both triumph and tragedy. No great achievement comes without obstacles, including physical limitations, the unpredictability of nature, Murphy's Law, or resistance from the outside world. In fact, we should be thankful for all obstacles, for they are our practice ground. Each new victory prepares us for a greater future victory. In the end, we express our greatness not by the acts we perform, but by the perseverance that made those acts possible.

Perseverance keeps hope alive. Growth of any type requires personal struggle; in the face of stern obstacles and setbacks we need to keep moving forward, however tempting it might be to give up and let go of our dreams. Perseverance is a force that stirs us and keeps us moving on toward our goals. The inner passion of perseverance, the indomitable emotional commitment to a worthy goal or an ennobling cause, is an awesome and liberating force.

With perseverance, we hurdle adversity; without it, we stumble. With perseverance, we discover the depths of our commitments; without it, we merely survive. With perseverance, we are undaunted; without it, we succumb to fear and exhaustion.

Perseverance is an unflagging commitment to pursuing a goal. It is:

- Working by day and going to school at night for a number of years to earn a degree.
- Obtaining your black belt in martial arts after six years of hard, strenuous study and practice.
- Running a marathon when you suffer from asthma or some other ailment.
- Winning a huge deal after years of setbacks, rejections, and competitive liabilities.
- A small child crawling, falling, stumbling, and finally learning to walk on her own.

We live in an age of immediate gratification. What we want, we want now, and just the way we ordered it. No delays, no substitutions, no excuses. Sadly, many view new tasks and the accomplishment of most goals that way. We want overnight growth, instant mastery, and flawless performance on the first try. But that's not the way success works; we need the core attributes of patience and perseverance to be truly successful.

Pace is irrelevant to perseverance. It does not matter how slowly you go, so long as you do not stop. Yet perseverance is more than simple constancy. Yes, we need to keep moving, but only if we are headed in the right direction. It does us no good to keep slogging into a quagmire. We must remember the difference between studied conviction and mindless stubbornness.

Steady perseverance—the achievement of a little every day—is of more value than an overly aggressive and unplanned rush forward. Patience and perseverance are two of the most difficult things to embrace for one whose commitment is being tested and tried through the fire. If you persevere in doing the right things, you will ultimately get the right results. If we fail to act with perseverance, we forfeit victory. As long as you are willing to do whatever it takes for as long as it takes, no one will be able to prevent you from reaching your goal.

Victory belongs neither to the fainthearted nor to the weak-willed—not if the enemy is great and his resolution strong. Victory necessitates that we fight on with undying, inflexible persistence. The rewards for those who persevere far exceed the pain that must precede the victory.

Quitting is the path of least persistence. There will be times when a voice within you seems to shout: "I doubt if I can continue." "Why don't you just quit and go back to safer ground." "I don't know if this will ever work." "Who am I kidding?" "Why not just throw in the towel." When you hear that voice, dismiss your doubts. Remind yourself there are always compensations for the assets you lack.

We cannot all claim genius, or beauty, or the best schooling, but anyone can have perseverance. Perseverance has no peers as a personal quality; it's more important than talent, more powerful than intelligence, and more resilient than the best strategy. Perseverance is omnipotent, and those infused with it will not be denied victory. The spirit of indomitable perseverance crowns every worthy effort.

The residual effect of perseverance sometimes doesn't happen for years. When you get into a pickle, when your back is up against the wall, when your options are paltry, and when it seems as though you could not possibly hang on a minute longer, tap your perseverance and don't give up. Everything can look like a failure in its middle stages; that perception becomes reality only when you quit before you've succeeded. Perseverance is ultimately a physical, emotional, and spiritual demonstration of how badly we want to succeed.

In your efforts to achieve your goals, you will be buffeted and pummeled, criticized and opposed, attacked and assaulted. You will struggle and fall. But you must fight one more round. Great adversity and setbacks can't defeat you if you persevere. Let them see you sweat, as perseverance is fueled by a heart-pounding, ego-bashing, soul-searching test of your limits.

Why put yourself through so much pain and uncertainty? Because if you can pass this test, you will inspire others and prove to yourself that you can accomplish anything you set your mind to.

You must rise each time you fall. You must make perseverance count!

PERSEVERANCE COUNTS—CALL TO ACTION

To explore your own commitment to making perseverance count, ask yourself these questions:

- Do you admire people who persevere in the face of obstacles and setbacks?

- Do your actions demonstrate perseverance in the pursuit of a goal or cause?
- What step will you take to ensure that perseverance is demonstrated in every aspect of your life?

PORTRAIT OF PERSEVERANCE

J.K. Rowling, Author

J.K. Rowling's Harry Potter books have sold over 400 million copies.

Her personal story proves that imagination, hard work, and perseverance triumph over adversity.

During a train journey, the idea for a story of a young boy attending a school of wizardry came fully formed into her mind. Though she could see the entire Harry Potter series, it would take her the next five years to complete the first book.

She later would describe her life in this period as a "mess."

Recently divorced, living in Edinburgh, Scotland, she was raising her young daughter in a tiny flat. She had quit her teaching job to concentrate on writing while surviving on welfare when her mother passed away leaving her clinically depressed.

Through her deep belief in her writing and by using her personal experiences to flesh out some of her characters, she was able to complete *Harry Potter and the Sorcerer's Stone*.

Of this period she would say, "I knew I wanted to get published. And since you don't really know if it's ever going to get into the bookshops once it is published, you really have to keep believing, so I persevered."

This first book was rejected by 12 different publishers. Bloomsbury, the small publisher that finally purchased her manuscript, told her to "get a day job."

In the end, she stayed true to her goals and her Potter books have inspired the imagination of millions of children and adults alike.

26

COURAGE COUNTS

"One of the most virtuous aspects of moral courage is that it can be practiced by anyone regardless of age, gender, physical ability, or surroundings."

Virtue can be defined as "habitual moral excellence." It's a highly valued character trait that is practiced at all times. Of all the known virtues, courage is the staircase on which all the other virtues step, and without courage, all other virtues become vices. The conceptual opposite of courage is cowardice. We are therefore confronted with the reality that we either habitually practice courage, or we habitually practice cowardice.

What good is a conviction about honesty or fairness if no willingness exists to habitually put hem into action when faced with adversity? Of what use is a code of ethics that hangs on the wall, unimplemented? What good is a vision, a core set of values, principles, and beliefs if you don't have the courage to enforce them habitually?

Courage is unique in that it takes on the form of every virtue at the testing point. When moral courage is tested, it manifests itself in the form of character, honesty, respect, responsible behavior, and compassion. And when moral cowardice is tested, it presents itself in opposite forms to include bad character, dishonesty, disrespect, irresponsible behavior, and lack of compassion. No gray matter exists when it comes to moral courage.

Courage is a universally admired virtue. Every culture, religion, philosophy, and school of thought is dependent upon it, and subsequently breaks downs without it. All habits and muscles are strengthened by use, and courage is no different. Through the process of practice and repetition, we can learn to become courageous. Likewise, all habits and muscles atrophy through the lack of use, and none of us can afford a courage deficit.

The subsets of courage are physical and moral. Each is unique, and each is intertwined. Physical courage is the willingness to face serious risk of life or limb instead of fleeing from it. It is the firmness of one's resolve that confronts danger or extreme difficulty without fear and with resilience. It seems that in modern society, physical courage has been replaced with ease and convenience. Rarely will we be called to exercise physical acts of courage. Where we once faced dark, mysterious, and uncharted frontiers, we now experience each new journey in clear and precise detail, which is evident in the use of the global positioning devices that provide a guaranteed safety net.

Even in time of war, when the truest form of courage is tested and found, advanced technology and weaponry used from a safe distance has significantly removed the necessity for physical courage. While technology can be used to reduce or offset acts of physical courage, it is up to us individually to perform heroic acts of moral courage.

Moral courage is best defined by firmly and confidently facing mental challenges, crises of conscience, and ethical dilemmas that could harm one's reputation, emotional well-being, self-esteem, and other intrinsic characteristics. It is doing the right thing—even if it's unpopular—without flinching or retreating. It's refusing to stand idly by while others engage in unethical behavior. Moral courage is synonymous with moral excellence. It is concerned with the defense of the intangible. It is not property but principles, not valuables but virtues that moral courage rises to defend. Acts of moral courage carry with them the risks of humiliation, ridicule, contempt, unemployment, and loss of social standing. The morally courageous person is often going against the grain, acting contrary to the accepted norm.

For many, the rule says that in order to get along, you go along. But that philosophy is unacceptable for the morally courageous person. There's risk associated with moral courage, but that's exactly the point. If you don't risk defending your principles, you are guaranteed to lose them—that's a risk not worth taking.

One of the most virtuous aspects of moral courage is that anyone—regardless of age, gender, physical ability, or surroundings—can practice it. A child can stand up to her peers in defense of a principle in the same way her parents could. A physically challenged person can fight for what's right just like anyone else.

The type of courage we must call on in business and in life is primarily moral, not physical. It is commonly displayed in a steadfast adherence to fundamental values. Moral courage is a necessary element in the ethics equation, as without courage you cannot possibly demonstrate values with complete authenticity. An absence of moral courage leads to moral decay as greed and selfishness, and stupidity takes over. There will be a growing distain and contempt for your services, which is never healthy for your future.

Moral courage can only exist on a strong moral culture. But that statement raises questions: Why create a strong moral culture? Why bother being morally courageous? Why should we care about simple moral misdemeanors?

Here are a few important points:

- All growth and maturity require that we pass tests and master each lesson. Moral courage plays itself out throughout our lives. It begins the moment we awake, and is tested by the instant, with every choice we make and every action we undertake. Each day provides you with an endless stream of opportunities to habitually demonstrate moral excellence.
- A culture built on a foundation of moral courage is a transparent culture. No one has to second-guess for ulterior motives. Decisions are easier, faster, and universal, since everyone is committed to doing the right thing.
- A morally courageous culture requires action and responsible behavior. When we commit to doing the right thing, we must physically engage in the activities that enforce the moral commitment. As a result, we strengthen our mental and physical capacities.
- Joy is the natural result of moral courage. When you demonstrate the courage of your convictions, you feel good about yourself. Your self-confidence and self-respect rise considerably.

Without moral courage, all virtue is fragile. While we may admire, profess, and look for it in others and ourselves, most hold it cheaply and surrender it with little fight. Behavior never lies, and without the courage to act, virtuous conviction is completely meaningless.

We must have the moral courage to defend our convictions. If we lack the courage to hold on to our beliefs in the moment that they're tested—not just when they harmonize with those of others, but also when they confront opposition—then they're superficial and add nothing to our self-respect or our society's respect for the virtues we profess. We can admire virtue and abhor corruption, but without courage, we are corruptible.

Now and in the future, more emphasis needs to be placed on courage—specifically moral courage. The true heroes in our families, neighborhoods, schools, boardrooms, and elected offices are those who habitually practice acts of moral courage. When we do that, when we uphold and celebrate that which is right and virtuous, we are making courage count.

COURAGE COUNTS—CALL TO ACTION

To explore your own commitment to making courage count, ask yourself these questions:

- Do you acknowledge acts of courage in those with whom you live and work?
- Do you ever second-guess your own courage when making decisions and taking action?
- What step will you take to live a life of strong, moral courage and conviction?

PORTRAIT OF COURAGE

Coleen Rowley

"I have to put my concerns in writing concerning the important topic of the FBI's response to evidence of terrorist activity in the United States prior to September 11th."

These 29 opening words in a letter to FBI Director Robert Mueller by Special Agent Coleen Rowley led directly to her becoming a former Special Agent.

Prior to the attacks of September 11, 2001, Rowley's field office received a lead from French intelligence that extremist Zacarias Moussaoui (later identified as the 20th hijacker) had paid cash to learn how to fly a Boeing 747. Rowley requested a warrant to search his laptop computer, but her superiors refused.

During Congressional hearings following September 11, Director Mueller made statements to the effect that if the FBI had only had any advance warning of the attacks, it may have been able to take some action to prevent the tragedy.

Knowing this misstated the facts, she decided to take action.

Three years later, Agent Rowley retired from the FBI after 24 years of service.

Americans have long valued honesty, character, and personal integrity. But somehow, when it comes to reporting wrongful actions, we are less appreciative.

To blow the whistle on wrongdoing takes deep moral courage, knowing that job loss and character attacks may follow. Moral courage suggests that we applaud whistle-blowers for having the internal constitution to do the right thing regardless of the consequences.

PATIENCE COUNTS

"Patience is, in a real sense, the guardian of all virtues,
in that it clears obstacles from their path."

As we've likely heard many times throughout our lives—patience is a virtue. The ability to endure waiting, delay, or provocation without excessive frustration is an admirable character trait. Patience is a reward. The willingness to overcome temptation, endure adversity, and embrace temporary suffering is rewarded with grace and maturity. Patience is a blessing. The capacity to persevere calmly when faced with difficulties is blessed by increased peace of mind, enlightenment, and love. Patience counts.

Most of us recognize that patience is a key success habit; we're just in no hurry to obtain it. The word *patience* is derived from the Latin word *pati*, which means to suffer, to endure, to bear. Already that tells us much about the nature, meaning, and necessity of the virtue of patience.

Patience is one of the moral virtues that falls under the umbrella of fortitude, which strengthens the soul and sincerity of our commitment to sustain and overcome the difficulties and dangers that beset us in our daily lives. It keeps us from giving up when the going is hard. It brings a spirit of strength that is required of every virtue.

Patience is a divine gift that we give ourselves. It helps us to encounter adversity and hardships without losing serenity, or becoming irritated or despondent. It helps us not to be upset or stressed by trivial incidents and events like waiting in line or sitting in traffic. We could never learn to be brave and patient if there were only joy in the world, and that is why adversity must be viewed as an opportunity for disciplined patience.

Patience is the ability to maintain self-control over the impulse that rises suddenly when something disagreeable happens. It is not just disregard of or indifference to life's daily irritations or upsetting incidents—it's a real control of self, of one's feelings and impulses.

Impatience, on the contrary, is the lack of self-control—something that can grow into other, greater faults, like anger, irritability, harsh words, unpleasantness toward others, and so on. Many a serious quarrel starts with impatience over little annoyances or inconveniences.

Anger, frustration, and impatience are serious problems in the home, on the job, in the community. The solution is a loving patience that each member of the family must show in dealing with others. Husbands and wives, parents and children must all be patient with each other. In the workplace as well, we need to show patience to one another throughout our daily interactions.

Patience is a humble virtue; it is, in a real sense, the root and guardian of all virtues, not causing them, but removing obstacles to their operation. If you do away with patience, the gates are open for a flood of discontent and unhappiness. Patience touches every aspect of human activity; nothing can be brought to completion in all our strivings unless patience endows us with that power.

Although patience is an important and much-needed virtue in daily life, it is not an easy one. It demands much diligence over our emotions and impulses. It is acquired by slow, continual repetition of patient control, in spite of many failures. However, it is unfortunate that many do not grasp the value of patience, for its natural fruit is emotional balance and peace of mind.

To understand patience in its purest form, observe nature. Nature makes patience an art form; it has its own rhythm, pulse, and cycle for growth, maturity, and gestation. Nature is made up of great diversity and those differences require different gestation periods and degrees of patience for events to occur. In nature, a mango cannot be forced to bear fruit until it is fully matured. The cycle for growing radishes is different to that for cultivating roses. The gestation period

132

for childbirth is much different than in the animal kingdom. What runs through all of nature is the patience of each strand of nature. Whether it be the beauty of a garden, the perfect grape for a fine Bordeaux, or the majesty of a breathtaking sunset—nature is never in a hurry to move to its next stage. It has the patience for the child to advance from crawling, to stumbling, to walking, and then finally to running.

Nature shows us that the secret of life is to know the gestation period for whatever the issue is, and then to have the patience to wait for the period to expire. Yet far too often, people believe that their objects of desire should be available to them immediately, and with little effort. This false belief is perpetuated by technology, which feeds the inner child of instant gratification. In fact, it glorifies it. The speed of the Internet, the immediacy of instant messages and e-mail, the convenience of shopping online, and the plethora of on-demand services are powerful tools; tools that come at a great cost to everyone in society. These modern conveniences allow people to pack more into their life, but they are losing patience in the process. People have managed to compress time to such an extent that they are now painfully aware of every second that they have to wait for anything.

It's not just cell phones and call waiting that drives our inability to exercise patience. It's extended to elevators where you can get the news on the fly, gyms where you can surf the Net and pedal at the same time, and even at the gas station where you can pump fuel and get sports updates in real time.

Technology has outpaced humanity, and the result is a delusional view of reality as many people attempt to run their lives and business on the same terms and conditions of technology and that violates the very laws of nature.

When there is no time to wait and be patient, there is often no time to think, to connect to other people at deep levels, or to create lasting memories. Emotional and spiritual maturity requires patience—the absence of patience is impatience, and when impatience rules, immaturity follows.

Good things come to those who exercise disciplined patience and common sense. Our patience will achieve more than our force. Every activity and relationship will bear fruit in time, so long as we are patient. From teaching a child to ride a bike to learning a new language, from giving a presentation to writing computer code, we will experience greater success when we are patient with others and ourselves.

Adopt the pace and lessons of Mother Nature, for patience is what she teaches. Patience requires that you take the time to think carefully and thoroughly as the consequences of impatience are real and over the long haul have the potential to be devastating. Making patience count in your everyday life won't be instantaneous, but isn't that the point?

133

PATIENCE COUNTS—CALL TO ACTION

To explore your own commitment to making patience count, ask yourself these questions:

- Do you admire patience in others?
- Do you maintain a sense of calm composure when confronted with challenges and adversity; or do you easily lose your cool?
- What step will you take to be more patient with yourself and others?

PORTRAIT OF PATIENCE

The Seghesio Family Vineyard

What can a winemaker teach you about patience, excellence, and quality?

Started in 1895, the Seghesio Family Vineyard has carved a rich heritage in the California wine industry. Seghesio is one of the oldest wine-growing families in Sonoma County.

Their vineyards, stretching over 600 acres, produce old Zinfandel wines consistently rated at the top of *Wine Spectator*—testimony to their passion for winemaking and caring for the land.

Peter Seghesio, fifth-generation CEO, says that having land owned for so long is a blessing. "We own land that's been farmed for many decades with very old vines that have limited vigor in their root system. The yield is half of other vineyards but greater concentration which allows us to produce more intense, more elegant wines."

Quality is first. They are not worried about making lots of wine and they want to make wines responsibly so the Seghesio family tradition will live on.

The Seghesios love the family business. It's a family and it's a business.

The family knows that their lives and work are marked by the seasons and linked to the harvest and wine production. Their tradition is to make great wines while they enjoy their family.

The secret of the Seghesio family is that they grow great wine by patiently guarding the traditions of family and winemaking.

HUMILITY COUNTS

"Acts performed with genuine humility also put so much more goodwill into circulation."

Humility is a virtue that many preach, but few know how to find. No man or woman can truly love, serve, persevere, dare mighty deeds, hope for the future, or honor the past without a humble heart. To serve well is to serve humbly.

Humility is to virtue as a foundation is to a house. For a house to withstand pressure, weight, and environmental stress, it needs to have a solid base that begins deep in the ground. The foundation of humility is modesty, selflessness, and respectfulness. Humility once established in our character makes us strong; and our strength is built in humility.

So what does it mean to be humble? Well, let's answer a question with six more just like it. See how the practice of humility can be the source of strength and effectiveness as a leader, at home, at school, and in the marketplace.

THE WHO, WHAT, WHERE, WHEN, HOW, AND WHY OF HUMILITY

1. *Who are we when we practice humility? Who are we when we are not practicing humility?*

   A humble person is generally thought to be unpretentious and modest, someone who does not think that he or she is better or more important than others. It's someone who demonstrates true humility, and does so quietly and subtly. Those who do not practice the virtue of humility tend to embrace the vices of arrogance, pride, and pretense. Arrogance is a state in which we are convinced that we have the right to think of ourselves above others. When we are impressed with our deeds and take ourselves too seriously, we are of no value to anyone else.

   The causes of arrogance and pretentiousness sometimes include education, knowledge, religious piety, fame, family nobility, beauty, physical strength, wealth, and achievement. But in reality, none of these qualities are *themselves* the causes of arrogance. After all, they are positive values. The real cause of arrogance is ignorance, and there is no medicine but humility that can cure it.

2. *What is the purpose of humility?*

   A fundamental tenet for people with a humble worldview is that we should *want* to do something that elevates others, regardless of the impact it has on our own situation. By simply making it a habit of giving with nothing to gain, acts performed with genuine humility also put so much more goodwill into circulation. This goodwill fosters social kindness—something that could certainly use a renaissance.

3. *Where will we be if we do not practice humility?*

   Quite frankly, we have gotten out of the practice of showing any deference to one another. That must change as wealth, power, or status gained at the expense of others brings only anxiety and negative self-worth; never peace, love, or respect.

   The humble qualities of courtesy, patience, and forgiveness have such a prominent place in the world. A humble demeanor is exactly what we need to live in peace and harmony with all other persons. Humility dissipates anger and heals old wounds, allows us to see the dignity and worth of all people, and distinguishes the wise leader from the arrogant power seeker.

136

4. *When should humility be employed?*

Humility isn't employed because of its competitive advantage in business or life. Becoming a humble person makes you a more effective human being. It is how we develop the people skills that are essential to success in our world.

Don't get a psychological hernia over this, but in order to succeed, you must take a greater interest in others. You must be honest, transparent, and genuinely concerned about other people, and you can't fake it. Impersonal warmth will expose the weakness of your character, while undermining your reputation.

5. *How is humility best demonstrated?*

Humility is best demonstrated by focusing on meeting other people's needs and desires. It's having the confidence and comfort to know that it is infinitely more satisfying to focus on enhancing your friends', families', and colleagues' lives than it is trying to achieve our own peace of mind. We are all guilty of allowing ourselves to be so focused on our own desires for self-made happiness, self-made wealth, and celebrating a self-oriented worldview, that we rarely consider the even greater satisfaction that comes from focusing outward.

6. *Why are we afraid to practice humility?*

Very few think of humility in strong, positive terms. This leads many to believe in the notion that authentic humility means that one must be a doormat. Terms like *subordination, obedience,* and *servanthood* are counterintuitive, as most people associate meekness with weakness, and we are generally turned off by weakness of any sort. We crave strength, because we perceive that strength facilitates success, and success is believed to be key to our pursuit of happiness.

However, nothing could be further from the truth. The perception that humility is a sign of weakness is false. In fact, it's just the opposite. Humility never connotes weakness. Reserved? Absolutely. Wimpy? Not a chance.

We must come to the understanding that our strength, position, or influence is not marginalized when we consider our own interests to be secondary to those of others. It requires tremendous strength and character to place the interests of others before our own.

How will practicing gratitude help us as well as those we meet?

Like its cousin, mercy, the quality of humility is twice blessed. It blesses he who gives and he who receives. Humility liberates both parties. If you try to calculate being more humble like you calculate buying a car, then you are about to ruin what little reputation as a decent human being that you have left.

Humility begins with a sense of subordination, so get used to it. It knows when to lead and when to follow. If humility does not precede all that we do, our efforts are fruitless. Life is a long lesson in humility and each lesson counts!

HUMILITY COUNTS—CALL TO ACTION

To explore your own commitment to making humility count, ask yourself these questions:

- Do you like your friends and family to be self-centered braggarts, or do you admire and appreciate humility?
- Do your actions demonstrate someone who is humble or as someone completely full of themselves?
- What step will you take to exercise greater humility and modesty in your life?

PORTRAIT OF HUMILITY

Tony Dungy, Retired Football Coach

Tony Dungy walked away from cheering crowds, a salary over $5 million a year, and a team ready for another Super Bowl run. He announced his departure with the same calm and quiet demeanor he brought to professional football so many years ago.

In an era of celebrity coaches and millionaire prima donna athletes, his peers describe Dungy as the picture of humility and a coaching genius, capable of changing losing organizations into winners.

Even though he has experienced bitter losses, firings, and the personal tragedy of his son's suicide, he retains his quiet, calm demeanor.

He has stood tall during the low points of his life and remained humble during the times of celebrated triumph.

Upon his retirement he said, "I've always felt that there's more that I could do besides coaching football players. I want to change lives. In life, it's the journey that matters. Learning is more important than the test. It's about the journey—mine and yours—and the lives we can touch, the legacy we can leave, and the world we can change for the better."

As the best-selling author of two books about life and character, he is incredibly busy, but he finds time to help the Abe Brown Ministry's work with young people in prison prepare themselves for life on the outside.

And he is doing it humbly.

29

SELF-DISCIPLINE COUNTS

"Self-discipline transforms you into the best you can be, which makes you feel confident, capable, and unstoppable."

Success in any endeavor consists of a few simple disciplines practiced every day, while failure is simply a few errors in judgment, repeated every day. It is the cumulative weight of our self-discipline and judgment that leads us to either excellence or mediocrity.

First, you establish your goals, and then you enforce a strict program of self-discipline in order to cross the finish line of achievement. Every act of self-discipline moves you toward your goals, and every disruption takes you off course. There are simply no exceptions to this rule.

Before you brush aside this statement as something too obvious to matter, ask yourself this important question: "Based on my goals and expectations, am I on target?" The answer to that question hinges on your willingness and ability to remain focused on the habit most necessary for success—self-discipline. The only sure way to grow and to accelerate your progress is to bring a new discipline to your current activities.

Self-discipline is based on pride, functions through a meticulous attention to details, relies on mutual respect and confidence, and represents an unswerving commitment to excellence. The habit of self-discipline must be so ingrained that its influence is stronger than the excitement of the goal or the fear of failure.

You may spend your life fighting the temptations of to do or not to do, but here's a thought you can sink your teeth into: True success comes from living a disciplined life. Self-discipline transforms you into the best you can be, which makes you feel confident, capable, and unstoppable.

To those around you, your life will serve as a prophecy of excellence—or excuses of what could have been. Your life can be seen as the sad consequence of neglect, self-pity, poor character, lack of direction, and ambition, or it can be an example of talent put to use, and of a disciplined life spent in the intense pursuit of clearly perceived objectives.

If you don't discipline yourself, you are sure to be disciplined by others. Don't believe me? Then try this: Run up your credit cards very high, be late on a few payments, and see how quick those companies are to teach you a thing or two about discipline. Be unprepared for a few meetings, and you won't have to wait too long before your manager unapologetically tells you what it means to be a professional and encourages you to get with the program.

Why wait for things to deteriorate so drastically that someone else must impose discipline in your life? Self-discipline is infinitely more valuable than discipline imposed by others. You can be proud of living a disciplined life, but how can anyone be proud of the fact that they required someone else to force them to get up early, to be on time, to be accountable for their own actions? Discipline is always better on your own terms.

The manifestation of self-discipline is self-control. Contrary to popular belief, freedom does not arise from "letting it all hang out," freedom is the result of a personal triumph over excuses and bad habits. To experience true freedom, you must prove to yourself that you are the master of your own destiny. Never are you less free than when you are held hostage by your excuses and lack of discipline. When discipline is lax, enslavement and mediocrity follow!

Bad habits hold a gravitational pull on your emotional life; overcoming them isn't easy. Surrender is always a tempting option. And surrender gets easier and tastier each time you compromise what your intellect tells you, every time you make an exception to your rules of self-discipline.

One exception leads to a second, and a third usually takes you around the bend. Neglect self-discipline, and there will be a price to pay. A lack of discipline in the small areas of life can cost you heavily in the more important arenas. If you want to have lasting success, you have no choice but to make a serious commitment to the enforcement of self-discipline.

Self-discipline is an act of cultivation. One of life's greatest challenges is appreciating both the immediate enjoyment of the benefits of today's good work and the anticipated enjoyment of fruits not yet earned. Self-discipline requires you to connect today's actions and tomorrow's results. As we've been told, there's a season for sowing and one for reaping. Self-discipline helps you know which is which, and prepares you to enjoy both.

Everything of value requires care, attention, and discipline. Learn the discipline of looking for solutions rather than focusing on problems. Learn the discipline of honoring your commitments. Learn the discipline of writing a thank you note to a customer. Learn the discipline of paying your bills on time. Learn the discipline of preparation, of consistency, of healthy living, and of self-control. Learn the discipline of proper money and time management. Learn the discipline of giving more than you receive. Learn the discipline of self-discipline.

One of the great benefits of self-discipline is that each act comes with a corresponding reward. For each book you read, you gain knowledge. With each success you achieve, your confidence grows. As you overcome each challenge, you gain new understanding. For each failure you experience, you find new lessons and wisdom. With each loss, you gain empathy. Every act of a disciplined life bears desirable fruit.

Discipline is the road less traveled, the path that leads to excellence as it empowers you to do what needs to be done when it needs to be done. Quality living requires you to make difficult choices and sacrifices; it demands that you do the hard work first. You cannot arrive at true success without an understanding and consistent application of self-discipline.

True self-discipline is a habit. Anyone can be self-disciplined on occasion, but to get constantly positive results requires consistency. It is the day-in, day-out practice of self-discipline that determines your future. After all, a lifetime is an accumulation of moments, days, weeks, months, and years. What you do during each moment counts; it influences the degree to which you judge your life to be a success.

Everyone struggles with self-discipline. The discipline you establish today determines the successes you'll enjoy tomorrow. The strenuous life tastes better. When it comes to self-discipline—a key driver of success—everything counts!

SELF-DISCIPLINE COUNTS—CALL TO ACTION

To explore your own commitment to making self-discipline count, ask yourself these questions:

- Is it easier for you to discipline yourself, or to submit to the discipline of others?
- Do you apply self-discipline on a situational basis or as a fundamental rule of excellence? Are your acts of discipline consistent?
- What steps will you take to enforce a greater sense of self-discipline to your life?

PORTRAIT OF SELF-DISCIPLINE

The Ironman Triathlon World Championships

"Swim 2.4 miles! Bike 112 miles! Run 26.2 miles! Brag for the rest of your life!"

This warning on the rules sheet might be the last thing you see before you dive into the surf to start the "Ironman" Triathlon World Championship in Kona, Hawaii.

Think about it—a 2.4 mile ocean swim through the waves, short bike ride with lovely scenery over 112 miles, and finish with a 26.2 mile jog over rugged lava rock terrain—with no break in between.

The Ironman competition was born in 1978 following a disagreement at the end of a running race as to who were more fit—cyclists, runners, or swimmers.

The first Ironman took place with 15 competitors. The winner was given the title "Ironman."

Now 1,800 participate, but to get to the starting line you have to be very lucky by winning a lottery or talented by winning a qualifying event. What makes this event so unique is that average people get to compete alongside the best in the world.

If you're thinking about it, you will need unbelievable physical and mental stamina, strength, and endurance just to compete—to finish is a victory.

143

The current Ironman course record was set in 1996 by Luc Van Lierde (Belgium), whose winning time was 8 hrs 4 mins 8 sec.

The winner may be called the Ironman but anyone who participates has demonstrated the iron will and self-discipline to be called a "Winner."

30

ETIQUETTE COUNTS

"Proper etiquette is a legacy we want to pass on to those who will be the leaders of tomorrow."

Good etiquette is one of the easiest and most influential social skills to develop, and almost nothing is more profitable. Yet the very word *etiquette* is one of the most misunderstood in the English language. Most people assume etiquette involves merely knowing which glass to pick up at a dinner party or making sure to send a thank you note after a wedding shower or Bar Mitzvah. While such discretion is a part of etiquette, there is much more to it.

Etiquette in its purest form is simply *being nice*—an attribute that seems to escape a lot of people. It is a code of behavior acquired by learning and constant practice. It can be more simply defined as everyday manners and is foundational to the making of a good, successful, and happy life.

We are living links in a chain of wisdom handed down through history. One axiom developed in that chain that best manifests good etiquette is the Golden

Rule: "Do unto others as you would have others do unto you." Practicing the Golden Rule is practicing etiquette and it proves that we appreciate and respect the rights of others.

Practicing good etiquette builds a bridge through our expressions of kindness to one another. Follow the Golden Rule to its logical conclusion, and you will have formed relations with the many people for whom you harbor good feelings. If more of us tried to build bridges through proper etiquette, there's no telling where such kindness might take us.

Etiquette is a powerful, practical, and profitable skill you can use when it counts most—to get, keep, or succeed in a job. The skills you use to communicate courteously and intelligently are thus among the most significant you can use to advance in any profession. Using the wrong word, at the wrong time, or in the wrong way has lost many a plum opportunity. No one can afford to blow their chances of success by making etiquette mistakes that could easily be avoided.

When it comes to winning and keeping business, it's the little things that matter most, like a firm handshake, good posture, a warm smile, and professional attire. The implications of business etiquette lead to enormous competitive advantages as customers flock back to businesses that go out of their way to make them feel happy, special, and comfortable—something quite naturally accomplished when employees have good manners.

Administering etiquette, like administering law, entails more than just knowing a set of rules. Even the most apparently trivial etiquette rules are dictated by principles of manners, which are related to—and sometimes overlap—moral principles. Respect and dignity, for example, are two major principles of manners from which many etiquette rules are derived.

The absence of etiquette is the cause of some of our most serious social problems. For instance, our school systems have broken down from what many call a lack of discipline. What does that mean? It means that such etiquette rules as sitting still, listening to others, taking turns, respecting your elders, and not hitting others have not been taught. Nor will the business of government be done well (if at all), by people who can't work together in civil, statesman-like ways. That is why we have all those highly artificial forms of speech for use in legislatures and courtrooms.

We have a legal system that bars us from acting on natural human impulses to pillage, assault, and so forth. Whether we appreciate it or not, we also have another form of law—a moral law called etiquette that does many of the same things. Law is supposed to address itself to the serious and dangerous impulses that endanger life, limb, and property. Etiquette addresses provocations that are minor but can grow serious if unchecked.

Etiquette has some very handy conflict resolution systems—such as the apology, admitting that you were wrong, sending flowers in the morning, saying "I don't know what I was thinking"—that help settle things before they have to go through the legal system. But when people refuse to comply with proper etiquette and civility, the law must step in. A classic example is smoking. We've had to use the law to explain such simple etiquette rules as: You don't blow smoke in other people's faces, and you don't blow insults in the faces of others pretending its health advice. Sexual harassment is another area in which the law had to step in, because those in a position of power refused to obey and enforce such basic values as "Keep your hands to yourself."

It's a dangerous practice to keep asking the law to do etiquette's job. When we have to enlarge the scope of law to enforce manners, it really does threaten freedom. Trying to live by law alone does not work, as every little nasty remark would be labeled a slander and taken to court, meanness or rudeness would get dressed up as mental cruelty, and everything else that's annoying is declared a public health hazard. That's why we need a system of moral law and it's exactly why etiquette counts.

While the world grows ever more complex and competitive, there is one constant: etiquette. Proper etiquette is a legacy we want to pass on to those who will be the leaders of tomorrow. Our individual and collective goal should be to bring good etiquette practices back in style and make our homes, classrooms, workplaces, and communities better places to be. Now, that's really making etiquette count.

ETIQUETTE COUNTS—CALL TO ACTION

To explore your own commitment to making etiquette count, ask yourself these questions:

- Do you believe that etiquette and civility are important virtues worth pursuing? If so, why?
- Do your actions show the world that you understand and practice proper etiquette, or do you simply not care about your behavior and how it intrudes upon others?
- What step will you take to lead a life of proper etiquette and civility?

PORTRAIT OF ETIQUETTE

Emily Post

Emily Post was born into privilege. As the only daughter of a famous Baltimore architect, she attended Miss Graham's finishing school in New York.

Finding herself divorced with two young sons, she needed to support her family, so she took up writing and found success.

An editor citing her background as a writer and woman of society suggested she write a book on proper social behavior.

Etiquette—The Blue Book of Social Usage, first published in 1922, quickly became a best seller, bringing her fame and fortune.

Today a book on etiquette seems like an unlikely subject.

Nowadays people who behave badly in public are unashamed—they post the evidence on YouTube.

But it wasn't always this way.

For 30 years, Emily Post handed down rules of social behavior guaranteed to keep you in polite society.

Mrs. Post often said etiquette had much more to do with "instinctive considerations for the feelings of others" than with using the right fork. She was long considered the authority on everyday manners.

In 1946, she founded The Emily Post Institute to study problems and issues of gracious living, which today serves as a civility barometer for American society, and continues her work.

When you hear the name Emily Post or the Post Institute, you are in the right place for advice on civility and politeness.

31

OPTIMISM COUNTS

"No matter how realistic and rational we are, we have no choice but to focus our attention and attitude."

Optimism is an active, empowering, constructive attitude that creates conditions for success by focusing and acting on possibilities and opportunities. Optimism is the attitude of champions, the fuel of hope, the enemy of despair, and the creator of the future. Developing and strengthening this dynamic life skill is one of the most effective ways of adding to your personal power.

Optimism is a general disposition to expect the best possible outcome or dwell on the most hopeful aspects of a situation. It is a positive and empowering rational attitude toward our individual and collective possibilities. It is the belief that our future will contain desirable outcomes.

Optimism and pessimism affect your entire worldview. Your whole approach to living is either empowered or neutered depending on which style of thinking predominates. The principles of optimism provide keys for unlocking your full potential. An optimist cannot be stopped, spooked, pushed aside, or bullied. An optimist will respond to all obstacles, all attacks and setbacks with calmness, determination, and a creative, problem-solving attitude.

Tenacity is essential when you encounter setbacks on the way to any goal. Optimists learn from the setbacks and then try a different approach. In contrast, pessimists throw in the towel, concoct an excuse, and succumb to depression and apathy. Optimists direct their thoughts and actions toward constructive problem solving and purposeful activity; they do not stagnate in the distractions of pessimism and worry.

Many people feel virtuous and justified by complaining about problems rather than focusing on solutions. Destructive criticism feels easier than constructive thinking. While we all experience negative events, the difference between optimists and pessimists is that the latter takes less action to prevent bad things from happening, and when negative events *do* occur they make them seem worse by thinking persistently negatively and helplessly about them.

We must also come to acknowledge the dangers lurking in a half-hearted approach to optimism. We do others and ourselves no favors if we replace a pessimistic mentality with a passive optimism that assures us that all will work out well without personal effort. You must integrate the motivating, uplifting effects of optimism with an active, responsible approach to living. Merely *believing* that everything will work out fine without taking action makes one a foolish rather than a dynamic optimist. For optimism to give us the power to overcome the limits in our lives, it needs to fully recognize reality, not hide from it. For optimism to maximize our abilities and happiness, we have to take responsibility for our thoughts, our attitudes, and our actions.

Optimism forms a core part of emotional life expansion. If we wish to live effectively, we will have to root out self-defeating pessimism and replace it with a rational, active form of optimism. Becoming an effective optimist requires more of us than putting on a forced smile and telling ourselves "everything will work out for the best."

Living at full capacity—a capacity beyond what most of us imagine possible—asks us to go beyond superficial formulas such as "Don't Worry, Be Happy!" and to understand an intelligent form of optimism. We will only expand the vitality and achievement in our lives if we understand what optimism is, why pessimism holds us back, and why some kinds of optimism actually restrain us rather than project us forward.

In claiming to be an optimist, you are saying more than the fact that you simply expect life to get better. Optimists go beyond holding certain beliefs about the future; they also display certain *attitudes*. A hopeful attitude allows you to remain optimistic during uncertain times and to transform the negativity of any situation into opportunities for growth, progress, and achievement.

No matter how realistic and rational we are, we have no choice but to focus our attention and attitude. Optimists choose to focus primarily on thoughts, events, and interpretations that induce joy, encouragement, pleasure, and constructive activity. They will look at the same world as pessimists but notice different things, and see the same things in different ways. One admires a well-tailored suit; the other cannot see anything but a tiny stain in the jacket. One enjoys the colors of a beautiful rainbow; the other complains about the rain. Optimists spend most of their time focused on opportunities, on being with people who they enjoy and benefit from, and on thoughts that energize them. Optimists can look at a frustrating event, fully accept its reality, and then choose to interpret the event in a way that leads to action, growth, and mastery.

A child's irresponsible behavior, for example, can give a parent an opportunity to improve his communication skills, while the pessimist often focuses— excessively and pointlessly—on the frustration itself. The optimist keeps the event in proportion, enjoys the rest of the day, and looks for solutions to the challenge.

Effective optimism requires that we understand the part we play in bringing about the results we want. An optimist realizes that goals and excellence can be reliably achieved only through personal effort. Wishful thinking cannot substitute for active pursuit of the life we want.

Taking responsibility for our actions and attitudes requires a strong sense of purpose. Without a clear vision of our destination, we will find it hard to get anywhere. Being responsible necessitates self-discipline—as we make our choices through the day, we need to keep our goals and values in mind, remain focused, and resist distractions. More than that, taking responsibility means *persisting* at working toward what matters to us. Persistence and perseverance are virtues of character found in all successful, optimistic people.

Optimism involves personal commitments to certain modes of thinking and behaving. By mastering these modes of thinking and adopting optimistic attitudes, you can profoundly influence your thinking, behavior, happiness, and achievement.

Optimists believe that a positive approach can make all the difference in the world. They brighten spirits and create hope and confidence in the future. During difficult times, taking a positive approach, maintaining an upbeat outlook, and making a commitment to creating a more optimistic future will differentiate you from the majority of people.

This world is full of possibility. We can achieve almost anything we can conceive. Yet we will move forward only by turning goals into practical, rational, responsible thinking. This kind of thinking will naturally generate productive activity.

Through positive action in their communities, business, and personal life, optimists believe they can create a better tomorrow. It is imperative that you cultivate a climate of optimism throughout your life because an optimistic attitude counts!

OPTIMISM COUNTS—CALL TO ACTION

To explore your own commitment to making optimism count, ask yourself these questions:

- Do you believe that there are significant health and performance benefits to optimistic thinking?
- Do you always look on the bright side of the world? Is your glass half full or half empty?
- What step will you take to bring an enlightened sense of optimism to your life?

PORTRAIT OF OPTIMISM

Life is Good

"Life is Good" is more than a slogan to brothers Bert and John Jacobs.

These words describe a belief, an attitude, and a brand that helped them transform an unsuccessful business hawking T-shirts in the streets of Boston into an international success story.

They began selling T-shirts out of an old van at street fairs on the East Coast. With good intentions but no business knowledge, they lived on peanut butter and jelly, slept in their van, and showered when they could.

A drawing on the wall of their apartment gave them an idea that would change their lives.

The drawing was of a smiling stick figure man with the words "Life is good" scrawled below. "Jake" and his contagious grin, simple as it was, seemed to express everything the brothers believed in.

They printed up 48 Jake shirts, set up their rickety card table, and sold out by noon.

Soon Jake and his simple message of optimism were embraced like nothing the brothers had ever seen.

Today, their Life is Good company stays close to its roots, with an emphasis on simplicity, humor, and optimism even though sales have grown well over $100 million.

They believe that if you stay focused on the good things and help others to focus on the good things you will be successful.

32

HEALTH COUNTS

"Excellent health is not merely physical—it is a condition of the mind and spirit as well."

Mother Nature does not bend her rules; Father Time does not grant pardons. There are no exceptions, no reprieves. You must take care of your body; or the day will come when your body will no longer tolerate your indifference.

Without cause, there is no effect, so there is no sickness without violation of the laws of nature. Nature has a bias toward health and vitality; however, we bring on sickness by continuous violation of the natural laws. The natural laws are relentless. There is no mercy when it comes to blatant violations of these rules for taking care of the body.

Life is precious and ever so short. Choose optimum health; make a commitment to your life. If you wear out this body before its time, where do you go from there? Life is not a defensive struggle of restricted options; it's a game of vitality, imagination, and excitement.

Optimal health—that which gives one the greatest chance for a long, active, vital life—is much more than simply the absence of disease. It means being the very best you can be. It means not being incapacitated or wasting away physically, physiologically, emotionally, or mentally.

Success is not for the weak of body or the weak of mind, as everything that enters the body and mind counts. The way you look and feel tomorrow is a direct reflection of the thoughts and actions you engage in along with the foods you consume today. Carefully and consciously, avoid consuming anything that negatively affects the body or mind.

Excellent health is perhaps your most valuable possession. Fitness and health is not just a new and passing phenomenon, and neither are the ways to achieve and maintain good health. The fundamentals of good health—known and proven for so long—are available to anyone who decides they want to enjoy fully the enormous benefits of healthy living.

Your body is meant "To Protect and To Serve" you, but the door swings both ways, and to protect your body, you must protect your mind. Strong, pure, and positive thoughts build vigor and grace. Excellent health is not merely physical—it is a condition of the mind and spirit, as well. Additionally, the benefits of health and good nutrition go well beyond just improving your appearance. You widen your moral purpose as well—vow to live better, to have more energy, self-worth, and clarity. Preserving your health is *your* duty, yet few seem conscious that there is such a thing as physical morality.

Health is joy, and it is wealth; it impacts every aspect of life. Without excellent physical health, enjoyment is never complete; one cannot fully maximize their earnings, and one compromises their physical activities. Without excellent physical health, energy levels become sabotaged; life becomes more demanding and difficult.

On the contrary, *with* excellent physical health, you have the ability to be fully engaged and can pursue your goals with the confidence that you will be able to accomplish them. Therefore, foremost attention should be given toward keeping perfect health. Live physically at the top of your powers by taking a proprietary interest in your body. The goal should be to live your life with as little down time as possible. Taking good care of your body gives you bragging rights; neglect brings another day of indignity. Our greatest challenge is often found in withstanding the effects of our own bad habits.

Physical activity builds physical vitality. With every year of your life, you have more to gain from being physically active. As your age-related risks of chronic disease increase, regular exercise generally slows or reverses that trend. In fact, you're even more likely to notice the benefits of regular exercise if you already have a chronic condition.

Focus your attention on your body. Actively avoid excess. Practice economy of regimen. Remain alert for disturbances and dysfunction and try to abstain from or cut back on alcohol and other stimulants. Consider all factors—season, climate, diet, and lifestyle—that may disturb your body's balance, and act in your own best interest. Exercise today to preserve and enhance the self you attained yesterday and to secure the self you desire to be. There can be no respite here. If you do not exercise, you will eventually lose all that you gain, and your future along with it. The athletic life protects you as long as possible. There is simply no other way. The effects of exercise are temporary; you cannot put them in the bank and save them for later. If inactive, your muscles will atrophy. Since having good health affects every aspect of your life, you must exercise daily. Otherwise, you will slowly experience reduction of your mental and emotional well-being.

Life is not a spectator sport—it's an adventure to be lived, experienced, and enjoyed. The success or failure you experience each day has far more to do with your body than many think. The body is the source of energy. You either respect it or abuse it.

Are you ever going to be fit again as long as you live? The answer is: unless you *decide* to get fit, you're never going to be—ever. The choice is yours; it begins by opting for the stairs instead of the elevator, fruit in place of chocolate, and active rather than sedentary activities.

The secrets to good health are not complicated. They are known and waiting for you to discover them and, even more importantly, to put them into practice. The blessings and joys of good health and fitness can be yours when you choose to make them priorities in your life.

You may spend your life fighting temptation. But here's a thought you can sink your teeth into: true self-indulgence is living the healthy life. Becoming the best you can be makes you feel the best you can feel. From a renewed body comes a renewed mind.

If a mind is a terrible thing to waste, let's make sure that optimal health and energy are wonderful things to attain, save, and enjoy. When it comes to your health and energy, everything you do to, and for, your body counts!

HEALTH COUNTS—CALL TO ACTION

To explore your own commitment to making physical health and vitality count, ask yourself these questions:

- Do you believe it's important to be in good physical shape? What, in your opinion, are the main benefits to physical vitality?
- Do you respect your body through proper food, exercise, and sufficient rest?
- What step will you take to living a life of greater physical vitality?

PORTRAIT OF HEALTH

Jenny Craig

When Jenny Craig had her second child, she was thrilled. That excitement, however, quickly turned to depression when the weight she had gained during the pregnancy refused to go away.

Her mother had been overweight and died of a stroke when she was only 49. Looking into a mirror, Jenny saw her own mother and decided that if she wanted to raise her two daughters, she had to lose that weight.

Exercise wasn't enough—she wasn't losing weight. Doctors just said eat less.

She joined a gym, cut back on her food portion sizes, became more selective about what she ate, and slowly got back into shape.

Not only did she lose her own excess weight, but she created a business empire in the process.

Doing her own research, she realized she was not alone and that insight led her to start her Jenny Craig Centers where women could come for education, meal design, and support.

Today, with over 650 centers around the world, Jenny Craig Inc. has become one of the largest and most recognized companies in the weight management industry.

Jenny Craig, the mom, is a hero to legions of women around the world who thank her for helping them achieve healthier eating habits and happier, fuller lives.

33

GRATITUDE COUNTS

"As you practice gratitude, you also enhance your peace of mind and quality of life."

T hink for just a moment of all the things that require practice—grammar, arithmetic, cooking, learning a particular sport, and even playing the guitar well. Practice is probably something you think you're done with when you leave school or when you've stopped taking music lessons. However, having or showing gratitude is also a fine art that comes with practice. The art of displaying gratitude is an act of simplicity that can be very powerful. There is a special kind of magic in the practice of showing gratitude. It raises our consciousness, recharges our energy, enhances our self-worth, and strengthens our spirit.

It's quite possible to attain great wealth, the best education, and an exceptional quality of life, and still be unhappy. This occurs when people live with an absence of gratitude. Success is a process that includes both peaks and valleys, but the one constant in a truly successful life is gratitude.

A successful life requires ongoing growth, and gratitude ensures this growth. Gratitude heightens awareness and expands your interaction with the world. Once gratitude becomes part of your nature, you begin to see the connections between your successes and creature comforts, and the talents and contributions of others.

- The farmer plants, waters, fertilizes, and harvests the tomatoes you enjoy.
- The truck driver delivers the food to the market that will soon feed your family.
- The baker kneads and bakes the bread for the sandwich you'll eat for lunch.
- The engineer and architect design the bridge that allows you to get to work.
- The furniture maker's handiwork creates the furniture in your living room.
- The plumber fixes your leak, clears your drain, and plunges your toilet.
- The teacher educates and inspires your children to be the best they can be.
- The customer provides the support that enables everyone to receive wages.
- The performer engages the imagination and entertains your senses.
- The seamstress sews the beautiful clothes that make you look great.
- The physician and nurse help to bring your beautiful baby into the world.

Pause for a moment, and begin to think of the connections between people. You will immediately understand the important role that gratitude plays in the creation of a happy, productive life. We live in a world where we have much to be grateful for, if we would just stop and look around.

It's quite humbling to think of all the roles that complete strangers play in our daily existence. The sheer ingenuity and effort required of others is one of the most compelling reasons why we must make gratitude a daily practice. In fact, humility is a virtue integral to gratitude; we cannot recognize the need for gratitude without it.

You may be tempted to believe that success and happiness is the result of karma, fate, design, destiny, or pure luck, but gratitude offers the best guarantee of success. As you practice the fine art of gratitude, you automatically enhance your peace of mind and overall quality of life. Finding something good in each and every day harnesses the power of gratitude. Do you light a candle or curse the darkness? Do you bless each and every thing that comes your way, trusting that its meaning will become clear—even if you can't possibly see how in the moment?

One of the best ways to cultivate gratitude is to count your blessings by thinking of all the good in your life, as well as acknowledging the contributions of others. This is important for three reasons:

1. **Positioning.** By focusing on the positive things in each and every day, you position gratitude so that it has top-of-mind awareness.
2. **Perspective.** By looking for goodness and nobility in yourself and others, you are reminded that there are many good people with good intentions in the world.
3. **Power.** By being appreciative for challenging lessons and adverse situations, you are demonstrating grace under fire. That grace results in greater personal power, self-confidence, momentum, and energy.

Practicing the fine art of gratitude is among not only our most important positive emotions, but also one that links directly to our physical and mental well-being. It's in our self-interest to feel gratitude, because it makes us better people. When we consciously practice grateful living, happiness follows along with an ability to withstand negative events. An attitude of gratitude provides immunity to anger, envy, resentment, and depression.

While forgiveness heals the heart of old hurts, gratitude opens it to new love. Gratitude bestows many benefits. It dissolves negative feelings— anger and jealousy melt in its embrace, fear and defensiveness shrink. Gratitude deflates the barriers to love. It also evokes happiness, which is itself a powerfully healing and beneficial emotion. When we are happy, we like to make others happy, and this fosters kindness and generosity.

Like other attitudes, gratitude can be cultivated. We don't have to wait for someone to shower us with gifts before feeling thankful. We can develop gratitude by reflecting on the gifts that are already ours. This reflection can be done for a minute, a day, or throughout a lifetime. Most people celebrate birthdays, anniversaries, and holidays, but those who cultivate gratitude celebrate and rejoice every day. We can be grateful because we are happy, but we can also be happy because we are grateful.

We tend to forget how very different the laws that govern the mind are from the laws that operate in the physical world. In the physical world, if we give something to another person, whether it is a toy, a book, or a diamond, we lose possession. Yet in the mind, the opposite is true. Whatever we intend for another person, we first experience ourselves; whatever we give we gain; whatever we offer, flowers in our own mind. If you feel hatred toward someone, that hate boomerangs back and scorches your own mind.

160

On the other hand, if you offer love and gratitude to someone, that love and gratitude first fills and heals your mind. The phrase "As you give, so shall you receive" is a profound statement about the way our minds work.

Enjoy every moment with gratitude and the next time you are eating fruit, remember to give thanks to the person who planted the tree. That's making gratitude count!

GRATITUDE COUNTS—CALL TO ACTION

To explore your own commitment to making gratitude count, ask yourself these questions:

- Do you believe that you have many things to be grateful for? What are they?
- Do you share your gratitude; or do you take many things and people for granted?
- What step will you take to demonstrate sincere gratitude, to whom and for what reason?

PORTRAIT OF GRATITUDE

The Gift of Life

"You have 6 to 12 months left to live. Your only option is a heart transplant."

Though these are not words you want to hear, heart transplants have been saving lives since 1968.

The United Network for Organ Sharing administers the nation's only Organ Procurement and Transportation Network and they report that approximately 2,800 people in the United States receive heart transplants each year.

Recipients uniformly say that it's amazing to be alive. They are thankful and grateful for all things in life, what they have, and what they can do!

Given another chance for life, they feel sad for the person who lost their life but this emotion gives way to their overwhelming gratitude for the donor who freely gave them the gift of life that now beats in their chest.

Donor families say the act of donation helps them in their grieving process. It does not take away their pain of loss; however, it does help them to know that someone is alive because of their loved one's donation.

Over 109,000 people are waiting for organ transplants each year and approximately 6,200 die while waiting for an organ transplant.

You have the power to give life at the time of your death by becoming an organ donor.

Remember the principle of gratitude says that "As you give so shall you receive!"

34

REPUTATION COUNTS

"A good name, like good will, is earned by many actions and lost by one."

Your reputation is your most important asset. It's an intangible advantage that is far more valuable than money. And as it is with any asset, what you don't protect, you don't keep. Your good name is a terrible thing to waste. You must protect and polish your reputation, as one slip of the tongue, one wrong move, or one moral misdemeanor can tarnish or even destroy a lifetime of hard work.

A favorable reputation has a positive impact on almost every aspect of running a business: share price, sales, customer loyalty, recruitment, and retention. It is what sets a company apart from its peers. In an age of corporate scandals, paranoid customers, sky-high expectations, and almost zero tolerance for small mistakes, there is simply no substitute for a sterling reputation. Competition for reputation has always been a significant driving force that propels every economy forward.

Your reputation is a critically influential factor in your ability to achieve success and sustain any competitive advantage. The crown jewels of your success include your character and reputation; they give people the confidence to do business with you, and help you and your company weather the tough times.

Your reputation is a deeply held, emotionally driven view of the people and customers with whom you come in contact. Simply put, reputation is what people think of you. And this depends on not only what you are, but also how much they know about you, in what context they know you, and how all of this fits into their personal set of values. Like beauty, your public perception and reputation resides in the eye of the beholder.

In any business, an individual's reputation is directly impacted by whether or not the person is considered trustworthy. A bad reputation is undoubtedly shadowed by questions about this quality. Professionals never take trust for granted; they know that the easiest way to grow a business is to have happy and trusting clients tell family and friends about their experience.

We each know that our personal reputation is important to us. It is the currency that allows us to operate freely in the world. Simply having a good reputation makes everything you do that much easier, and the same is true of organizations. A company that has a good name generally succeeds where ones with no name—or a bad name—may fail. Companies with good reputations tend to ride out storms and crises far better than those with less impressive reputations.

It's your company's reputation that gets your salespeople through the door and winning business; it's your reputation for quality service, quality products, attention to detail, and timely delivery that get you repeat business. Your reputation for going the extra mile garners recommendations from your customers. And it's a company's reputation as an employer that gets them the best—or worst—staff, which in turn affects the reputation they give you when dealing with the outside world.

Associate with men and women of good quality if you esteem your own reputation. Invest time and attention in your name, because when push comes to shove, the court of public opinion is most certainly interested in the character and reputation of the people and the companies with whom they do business.

If Intellectual Capital consists of *what* you know, and if Social Capital is based on *whom* you know, then Reputational Capital is dependent upon who trusts you. That's why trust matters, and it's exactly why serious consideration must be given to your reputation and how you intend to protect it.

And although corporate reputation matters, your personal reputation matters even more. After all, people buy from other people. In a world of change and constant innovation, is there any permanence to be found? Unifying forces such as loyalty and pride of ownership are being supplanted by trust, reputational capital, and pride of contribution.

Think of reputational capital as a kind of accumulated trust; a standard of accountability that enables diverse and often virtual networks of people to confidently strike partnerships with one another. While overlooked by many, the only real and constant permanence in a career lies in your personal reputation.

Individuals are not much different from companies. Having a trusted personal brand or reputation nets you the same advantages as a company. You're likely to foster loyalty, be trusted, be forgiven for occasional mistakes, and earn more money. We all build our personal brand each day through our character, attitudes, and actions.

You begin to build your professional reputation on the very first day that you start working. It develops with every phone call you make, every meeting for which you are on time and fully prepared, every negotiation in which you engage, and every extra mile you go for your customers. Every detail of every relationship combines to form your reputation. Whether good or bad, each exchange you have at or about work says something about you. And while the business world may be a big place, your industry—and company—are much like a fishbowl. Sooner or later, everyone finds out who can be relied on, who engages in gossip, who delivers on time, on budget, and who does not.

Your reputation is a permanent factor in your professional life. Jobs may come and go, but your reputation sticks to you everywhere. The reputation you build over time, consciously or otherwise, can be a staunch ally or a looming problem. The fact that a reputation is permanent is seen in how incredibly hard it is to change it.

A solid reputation is built on solid values. So ask yourself: What is it for which you want to be known? What are the values—personal and professional—you want to stand for? How can you develop cult status? It's worth thinking about this deliberately. When you can define what you'd like your reputation to be, you've effectively defined the values you wish your career to articulate. That will help you to make better choices. It will draw you to like-minded people. Think of it as the North on your professional and personal compass; it will point you in the direction that you need to go.

Build care for your reputation into your future by inserting one simple question into your decision making process: "How does it affect our company or my personal reputation if it goes wrong?"

Reputation, trust, and integrity have never been more important than they are today. Protecting your reputation is a lifetime exercise. A good name, like good will, is earned by many actions, and lost by one. It takes many years to establish a reputation, yet only minutes to ruin it. So look after it with great care.

Does reputation count? There's only one answer—yes, it does!

REPUTATION COUNTS—CALL TO ACTION

To explore your own commitment to making your reputation count, ask yourself these questions:

- Do you pay attention to how habits, behavior, and the quality of your work impact your reputation?
- Do you use and leverage your reputational capital to seize new and better opportunities?
- What step will you take to protect and sustain a stellar reputation?

PORTRAIT OF A STELLAR REPUTATION

Lexus

The Lexus was born out of a simple mission: to build the world's finest luxury car.

The launch of Lexus' flagship sedan in the United States shocked the industry. The idea of a Japanese luxury car that would compete fender-to-fender with Mercedes-Benz, BMW, and Cadillac seemed preposterous.

And compete it does, becoming the top-selling luxury nameplate in the United States in a few short years.

After six years in development, the work of more than 1,400 engineers, hundreds of prototypes, $1 billion invested, and the support and close collaboration with the industry's top dealers, Lexus charted new territory.

Lexus reinvented the luxury car and Lexus also reinvented the luxury car market with their reverence for luxurious materials, unrivaled attention to detail, new levels of service, customer satisfaction, and quality that other automakers scrambled to emulate.

With the mantra "the relentless pursuit of perfection," Lexus moved from an unlikely outsider to become the industry leader, as renowned for the experience of buying and owning its cars as it is for the vehicles themselves.

Lexus earned its reputation in the most discriminating segment of the market by consistently delivering what they promise.

The engineers and designers may have redefined the luxury automobile with the introduction of the Lexus, but its thousands of satisfied customers are responsible for perpetuating their reputation for excellence.

35

Personal Development Counts

"We get better when we do better. And we do better when we know better."

Every morning when you wake up, you can—and should—embrace the notion that there is something about you, your life, your business, or the way that you carry yourself that could stand to be improved. Every day requires dedication, discipline, good judgment, energy, and the feeling that there's something about yourself that you can make better. Each day offers an opportunity for improvement, and each moment serves as an opportunity to advance or to retreat in the pursuit of your goals.

Personal development is a lifelong pursuit, because life is a work-in-progress. You never totally arrive; there is always some polishing to do, some knowledge to gain, and a love to deepen. Self-development ends only when we run out of time. You are and will always be the self in evolution. Who couldn't progress a little as a parent, child, spouse, friend, citizen, or employee? No one is perfect; no one walks the straight and narrow line *all* the time.

And this absence of perfection leaves the door open for improvement. Our fight is not external; it lays internally in mastery over self. If we are to dominate events and experience greater levels of performance, we must first dominate ourselves.

Let there be no doubt: as long as you continue to blame others instead of assuming your responsibilities, you will make no meaningful and enduring change for the better. What kind of people are we if we don't have the character to own up to our own shortcomings and responsibilities? To have and enjoy certain liberties requires us to hold each other and ourselves accountable for our actions.

Here's a truth you can lean on: All personal development is dependent upon your growth as a person. It's a solo act that requires contemplative thought and behavior modification, along with a healthy dose of humility. So in order to enjoy a better life, you must first become a better person. If you want to be a more influential manager, a more caring parent, a more attentive doctor—become a better person. If you aspire to greater spheres of influence—*become a better person.*

One well-executed idea or one person who's attracted to you because of what you've become has the potential to change your life forever. Goal setting should primarily focus on oneself. Strive to become the best person you can possibly be, so that your life attracts the kind of people you'd like in it.

You must continually seek ongoing personal development and self-mastery for developing a balanced philosophy of life, and you must then live in accordance with the dictates of that philosophy. The only sure source of lasting competitive advantage is knowledge. Any ability to improve and learn faster than your competitors may indeed be your only sustainable competitive advantage. Propelled by the competitive imperatives of speed, global responsiveness, and the need to innovate constantly or perish, personal development and ongoing learning has become the essential hedge against extinction.

Perhaps the most difficult notion to face is the fact that personal development requires you to reexamine all of the assumptions that currently operate in your life and business. It's about more than simply acquiring new knowledge and insights; it's also crucial to unlearn old knowledge that has outlived its relevance. Thus, forgetting is probably at least as important as learning.

Self-improvement begins with just a few questions: How should I live my life so that I am fulfilled and content? Am I becoming the person I was meant to be? In order for me to make more money, what habits must I begin to initiate? What should I begin doing today in order to leave a lasting legacy once I'm gone? Which behavioral vices must be removed and replaced with virtues? How can I can contribute and make myself more useful as a human being? Answers to questions like these require an intense evaluation of your life.

Nothing can be more valuable than finding a weakness early in your career and dealing with it before it has a chance to spread and negatively affect future opportunities. Pay special attention to the patterns you see yourself repeating. Judicious self-development means you no longer draw the blinds on what you abhor, or settle only for a small squeak of what's possible. Concentrate your energies on what needs development and how you can perform better. Don't play games by denying the reality of a certain part of your character or personality through the creation of false perceptions because it's easy and convenient. Expect skepticism. Personal development is somewhat of a "damned if you do, damned if you don't" situation. If you don't improve, people will say that you should; but when you do change, they are disbelieving. So improve anyway!

Habits—good and bad alike—are lifelong companions that hold court and act as both judge and jury over personal development. Your challenge is to withstand the effects of your own bad habits, which are like landmines strewn through the landscape of your life. The only problem with good habits is that they're so easily given up.

Based on perspective, the passage of time does not bring age but rather maturity. We reach a stage, master it, and pass on to the next. If we fail, that failure will persist until we rectify it. No amount of years will rid us of that necessity and that is exactly why personal development is necessary. The great treasures of life are found in the smallest events in our daily living. This is the setting and stage for our own drama. We fail or succeed according to how we handle the ordinary, commonplace events. It is in apparently trivial and routine events that we most clearly show who we are and how we have matured.

So spend your life learning *how* to live. It is an ongoing journey, with lots of beginnings and continuations. We never get to a point when all knowledge is attained and understood, when our bodies function flawlessly, when we completely honor our values, and achieve every goal.

We get better when we do better. And we do better when we know better. Personal development is the way that we purposely make everything count!

PERSONAL DEVELOPMENT COUNTS—CALL TO ACTION

To explore your own commitment to making personal development count, ask yourself these questions:

- Do you believe that each day offers an opportunity for improvement and that each moment serves as an advance or retreat in the pursuit of your goals?
- Do you reflect on your past performance and constantly look for ways to improve and get better?
- What step will you take to ensure that personal development is practiced in your life?

PORTRAIT OF PERSONAL DEVELOPMENT

Napoleon Hill

American-born Napoleon Hill is considered to have influenced more people into success than any other person in history. He has been perhaps the most influential man in the area of personal success and development, primarily through his classic book *Think and Grow Rich*, which has helped millions of people and has been important in the lives of many successful people such as presidents and heads of state.

He began his writing career at age 13 as a "mountain reporter" for small town newspapers and went on to become America's most beloved motivational author. His early career as a reporter helped finance his way through law school. He was given an assignment to write a series of success stories of famous men, and his big break came when he was asked to interview steel magnate Andrew Carnegie. Mr. Carnegie commissioned Hill to interview over 500 millionaires to find a success formula that could be used by the average person.

These included Thomas Edison, Alexander Graham Bell, Henry Ford, Elmer Gates, Charles M. Schwab, Theodore Roosevelt, William Wrigley Jr.,

171

John Wanamaker, William Jennings Bryan, George Eastman, Woodrow Wilson, William H. Taft, John D. Rockefeller, F. W. Woolworth, and Jennings Randolph, among others.

Hill passed away in November 1970 after a long and successful career writing, teaching, and lecturing about the principles of success. His work stands as a monument to individual achievement and is the cornerstone of modern motivation.

You can get started by reading his book *Think and Grow Rich*. A free e-book is available for you at www.EverythingCounts.com/GrowRich.

36

SUSTAINABILITY COUNTS

"Sustainability is not just about doing well by doing good; it is about doing better by doing good."

As defined by the Brundtland Commission, an organization convened by the United Nations in 1983 to address the growing concerns of the deterioration of the human environment and natural resources, "sustainability is a shared responsibility to proceed in a way that meets the needs of the present without compromising the ability of future generations to meet their own needs." Or, in the words of countless parents and teachers, "Don't take more than your share." Sustainability seeks to provide the best outcomes for the human and natural environments so that each can exist in productive harmony. In fact, there may be as many definitions of sustainability and sustainable development as there are groups trying to define it. Regardless, all the definitions share these similar characteristics:

- An acknowledgment that all resources are finite, and that there are limits to growth.
- An understanding of the interconnections among the economy, society, and the environment.
- An ability to weigh costs and benefits of decisions—including long-term costs and benefits to future generations—fully.
- An equitable distribution of resources and opportunities.

Concerns about the environmental and social impacts of corporate activity are moving sustainability and social responsibility from important yet peripheral problems to issues debated in the boardrooms, classrooms, and around the kitchen table. Some may view sustainability as companies' misguided efforts to meet rising public expectations, or even more cynically, see it as the corporate world's renewed moral agenda to save the whales and become "tree huggers." But the fact is that a sustainable business—one that fully accounts for global environmental and social impacts—has already become a mainstream reality. When companies of all sizes are willing to tackle the worldwide challenges of climate change and the widening gap between the rich and the poor—not simply as moral obligations, but as a strategic business opportunity—everyone should sit up straight and pay close attention. Because this clearly indicates that there is a lot more going on than just regulatory compliance or slick public relations campaigns.

Sustainability is not just about doing well by doing good; it is about doing *better* by doing good. It no longer just means conducting business responsibly. Rather, it encourages professionals to embrace social and sustainability challenges as opportunities for innovation and business development.

REWARDS OF SUSTAINABILITY

Companies that adopt a pro-environment policy will see a variety of tangible and intangible positive results, including the chance to:

- Earn positive publicity with the local, regional, or even national media
- Attract consumers in the rapidly growing green marketplace
- Differentiate themselves from competitors
- Become preferred vendors in green supply chains
- Transform their companies into industry leaders
- Create significant competitive advantage
- Attract the interest of top job candidates

- Develop brand distinction and recognition
- Build credibility with stakeholders
- Enhance employee satisfaction
- Reduce operating costs
- Attract investors

Far from being a cost and an ongoing headache to society and business, sustainability is emerging as a huge opportunity for both. The key sustainability is innovation, and that, in turn, spells competitive advantage. Sustainability is undoubtedly the single greatest untapped source of competitive advantage in the twenty-first century. And the people who get the sustainability message are the ones who are going to win big.

IMPLEMENTING SUSTAINABLE PRACTICES

If sustainability means using resources at a rate that can be renewed—or, using the earth as a sink at a rate that does not exceed its capacity—then how can a business, community, or even a family start putting green initiatives to work? The key to understanding sustainability and turning it into a value proposition is by getting out of the gate and up the learning curve as quickly as possible. The following is four-step approach that anyone can implement to make any institution more efficient, more cost effective, and greener:

1. Challenge Your Paradigm to Recognize Sustainability as a Human Problem

    Once you recognize that sustainability is a human problem rather than an environmental one, you'll see that the true challenge is to change human behaviors. The environment did not put us in this situation; humans did. The good news is that we have the technology and resources we need to solve it, we just need to change our behavior. Easier said than done!

    Making an institution more sustainable requires that we encourage others to stop doing some things they currently do, and start doing things they are not doing. The fact is there is a person behind every building code, inefficient supply chain, carbon-polluting plane, cigarette butt, and any job or function that takes more than it puts back. Changes in these kinds of practices are what we want to see in the world, and the leaders of any business, institution, or family needs to be the catalyst for that change. Once we can all recognize that sustainability is a human problem, we can begin to focus on changing behavior, which takes us to the remaining three points in your sustainability plan.

2. Reduce or Eliminate Your Rubbish

Waste is a sign of inefficiency, and our ultimate goal—while very challenging—should be moving toward 0 percent waste. The use of the term 0 percent waste includes "0 percent Solid Waste," "0 percent Hazardous Waste," "0 percent Toxics," and "0 percent Emissions." 0 percent waste suggests that the entire concept of waste should be eliminated. Instead, it should be thought of as a *residual product* or simply a *potential resource* to counter our basic acceptance of waste as a normal course of events. Advantages like reduced costs, increased profits, and diminished environmental impacts are found when returning these residual products or resources as food to either natural or industrial systems.

This process may involve redesigning both products and processes in order to eliminate hazardous properties that make them unusable and unmanageable in quantities that overburden both industry and the environment. You also can reduce or eliminate your rubbish by taking simple steps, like using reusable shopping bags, lunchboxes, and reusable coffee cups instead of disposable packaging.

3. Reuse Your Rubbish

Waste prevention—also know as *source reduction*—is the practice of designing, manufacturing, purchasing, or using materials (such as products and packaging) in ways that diminish the amount or toxicity of trash created. Repurposing items is another way to stop waste at the source, because it delays or avoids that item's entry in the waste collection and disposal system.

Source reduction and reuse can help decrease waste disposal and handling costs, because they elude the costs of recycling, municipal composting, land filling, and combustion. Source reduction also conserves resources and reduces pollution, including greenhouse gases.

So focus on turning your rubbish into someone else's treasure. Give away or sell your unwanted items, and cut down on the rubbish that goes to landfills.

4. Recycle Your Rubbish

Recycling turns materials that would otherwise become waste into valuable resources. Collecting used bottles, cans, and newspapers and taking them to the curb or to a collection facility is a simple yet significant step that generates a host of financial, environmental, and social returns. Some of these benefits accrue locally as well as globally. Some of the notable benefits of recycling include:

- A decline in the need for land filling and incineration.
- Pollution prevention caused by the manufacturing of products from virgin materials.
- Energy savings due to reduced or eliminated decomposition.
- Decreased emissions of greenhouse gases.
- Conservation of natural resources such as timber, water, and minerals.
- Sustaining the environment for future generations.

If performed correctly, sustainability delivers a triple bottom line for people, planet, and profit. It captures an expanded spectrum of values and criteria for measuring organizational and societal success—economic, ecological, and social. Better living for all—now *that's* making sustainability count!

SUSTAINABILITY COUNTS—CALL TO ACTION

To explore your own commitment to making sustainability count, ask yourself these questions:

- Do you believe in the importance of sustainability and its impact on society? If so, why?
- Do your actions demonstrate the convictions of someone who truly believes in sustainability or as someone with a half-hearted commitment?
- What step will you take to help make a more sustainable lifestyle for yourself and future generations?

PORTRAIT OF SUSTAINABILITY

UPS

UPS is a $49.7 billion corporation focused on enabling commerce around the globe in a sustainable fashion.

UPS delivers over 11.5 million packages for over 1 million regular customers daily.

Pioneers in the sustainability field, they are working to reduce their environmental impact as they operate their business.

They know companies have to account for their environmental and social impacts and that sustainability allows them to do better by doing the right thing.

UPS protects the environment and boosts profitability while saving millions of dollars in fuel and paper through these practices:

- Measure the business impact of their initiatives and report results companywide.
- Pursue technologies that save energy and natural resources while reducing emissions and other waste products.
- Operate alternative fuel-fleet that includes hybrid electric, compressed natural gas, liquefied natural gas, propane, and electric vehicles to achieve fuel efficiency.
- Operate aircraft and manage operations to reduce environmental impact.
- One driver and one vehicle are used for air, ground, and international shipping as opposed to carriers that use three drivers and three trucks to handle the same volume.
- Most effective package routing reduces fuel use and emissions.
- Handheld devices record delivery information saving 7,308 trees annually.
- Vehicle washing policies save 365 million gallons of water.

They work to achieve better living for all, which is what sustainability is all about.

37

YOUR LEGACY COUNTS

"Live your life with class, dignity, and style so that an exclamation, rather than a question mark, signifies it!"

We all begin life at GO, and all roads lead to a final rendezvous. The difference is what we do en route as the paths chosen, actions taken, and a host of decisions made ultimately lead to a unique legacy. It's nonnegotiable: you will leave a legacy. The question then becomes: What legacy will you leave?

Your legacy comprises both ends and means. Is winning really winning when you are ashamed of how victory came? The means by which you move through your life provide the working platform that supports your goals. Style, courtesy, honesty, integrity, and respect—these are the qualities that make for an inspiring legacy. The way you live your life has an effect on how you are remembered. How can the ends of your efforts be respected if the means make you want to blush in embarrassment?

Your legacy is not age sensitive. Although we relate the two as one, the truth is far from that perception. Don't defer your legacy. It is never too early or late to consider how you want to be remembered. You should have an intimate obsession with your legacy, as it's the only one you've got.

Thinking of your legacy is like starting anything new—you are either gung ho or baffled. In order to break through the roadblocks, close your eyes and envision the outcome of a successful life—*your* successful life. What do you see? What do you hear? Who are you with? How do you feel? This picture may appear a bit fuzzy at first, but stick with it. Contemplation brings clarity, and when the picture is in focus, study what you see—your legacy.

As you age, the clock and calendar remind you that your time here is finite, which forces you to make a move. We have limited time to build something of substance, something that will transcend our own existence. Time does not permit dallying with options. Your goals must be clear, responsibilities fulfilled, intentions and actions honorable. You must decide: If not this way, there is no other way. Otherwise, kiss the legacy you envision goodbye.

Leaving a legacy is substantially more important than leaving an inheritance. The ultimate test of the impact of an individual or group of individuals is twofold: whether the world they left is qualitatively different from that which they inherited, and what contribution they made to that change. Be worthwhile and do something virtuous with the time you have.

You can dodge the questions for quite some time. Why am I here? What do I want to do with my life? How can I contribute? What will I leave behind? But eventually, we all reach our own philosophical puberty and realize that these questions call for—in fact, demand—answers. At some point, we all have to give our lives meaning. We must find or create reasons for living. To arrive at the point that you think seriously about your legacy, you must first reach a level of reality and commitment that represents an eternity to follow.

Few things in life are more interesting to us than the question of what will come at life's end. Death is a mystery that has defied the greatest minds in history. *If we dread death, it is for a few reasons:*

We have the fear that behind the curtain lays retribution for a lifetime of transgressions, and we have even greater fear that there is *nothing* there at all. Is death an irreversible and impersonal end to one's activities? Or is it a place we survive to be rewarded or punished for the lives we lead on earth? Or—and this is possibly the most threatening—will we live eternally the life and person we fashioned on earth?

What becomes of me after my death? Even if there are no answers, the result of such self-questioning gives some answers to another question: Before I die, what shall I do with my life? Consider your legacy to be something that is visceral and immediate rather than distant and speculative.

If we are going to leave an admirable legacy, we must pass on to succeeding generations both faith and love. Do you have a faith that is worth handing down? If you hand down your faith the way you are living it now, will your children be the better for having received and accepted your lifestyle?

Retire into yourself and think. Spend every day seeing the world as your classroom and paying very strict attention. The wonderful part of considering your legacy is the clarity it brings to daily decisions. Each decision moves you closer to or further from your legacy, and your legacy offers advice on how to live in the present in order to be remembered well when you are gone. It is a sort of symbolic immortality. Take the long view and consider how the work that you do will impact the next seven generations. We continue in some way to participate in the lives of others when we are gone. Just what will that participation be?

Rather than jewelry, property, or money, let your character and the example of a life well lived be your family heirloom to future generations. More importantly, foster an attitude in those future generations that will allow them to appreciate the gift of your legacy more than that of a shining jewel.

Make this life of yours into a work of art. Your legacy is a self-portrait, the signature of your life's meaning. It will be summed up in a few words—let those words be good and true. Remember, *they will talk about you when you are gone.*

We only live once, but once is enough if we do it right. Live your life with class, dignity, and style so that an exclamation point, rather than a question mark, signifies it!

So what legacy awaits you? When you take your final bow, who will you be? How will you enter eternity? Will you be just a footnote in history? Every day the plot thickens, the cement hardens, and the mystery deepens. Live to answer and honor these questions, because when it comes to your legacy, everything counts!

LEGACY COUNTS—CALL TO ACTION

To explore your own commitment to making your legacy count, ask yourself these questions:

- Do you believe it's important to think about how you want to be remembered? What do you want to be remembered for?
- Do you have a long-term perspective on your daily actions, and how each supports or detracts from your desired legacy?
- What step will you take to leave a lasting legacy? How committed are you to that legacy?

PORTRAIT OF A LASTING LEGACY

Pat Summitt

"You become the best by learning to do your best, you work at becoming better. You never quit learning."

These words by Pat Summitt, the head coach of the University of Tennessee's women's basketball team sum up the work ethic that has made her a legend to young women and basketball fans everywhere—nearly 1,000 wins, eight national championships, national coach of the year multiple times, and elected to the Basketball Hall of Fame.

She was a great player in college and played in two Olympics despite a knee injury that would have sidelined a less-determined player.

As a coach, she is known for her hard work and determination.

Her players say their success is due to her high expectations for them. She's tough and caring. She pushes them on the court and she demands that they perform well academically.

Every player who has stayed with the Tennessee program under Summitt has graduated.

Her work ethic and relentless commitment to results are qualities that have taken her to the pinnacle of the coaching profession—qualities that should be the standard in business and politics.

Summitt says that her greatest inspiration comes from helping young basketball players perform at their best.

Her legacy grows larger because many of her former players are becoming world-class coaches and they in turn are inspiring new generations of young women to greatness.

38

LOYALTY COUNTS

"Being loyal to something or someone apart from one-self means that self-interest is not all that governs such a person's behavior or lifestyle."

It is counterintuitive for some, yet crystal clear for others: regardless of your feelings or inclinations about it, loyalty counts. There are few words in the world that carry such weight and influence on character as *loyalty*. Wherever you may be, whatever language you speak, we are all called to understand and practice this noble virtue.

Semper Fidelis is Latin for "Always Faithful." It's a way of life that should be a shared responsibility for a civil society. It's a loyal and shared commitment to ourselves, the others upon whom we rely for our success, the companies for whom we work, and the communities and countries where we live.

We don't hear much about the virtue of loyalty these days. The word sounds old-fashioned and rather passé, but nothing could be further from the truth. Loyalty pertains to matters of truthfulness, faithfulness, and integrity. Perhaps the reason we don't hear very much about it is because we're not entirely certain we really aspire to it, or don't want to be held accountable for disloyalty.

Loyalty is an unswerving allegiance, faithfulness, and fidelity to a commitment, person, nation, or a cause. It provides the gold standard for relationship excellence. It's steadfast in good times and tested in bad. Loyalty is found in what you do, not what you say. It is willingly given, with a person's whole heart and soul. Loyalty and faithfulness also involve some degree of sacrifice. A loyal person is faithful to their bond, and demonstrates this in action, service, and sacrifice.

Where do your loyalties lie? How do you demonstrate your loyalty? Is that demonstration consistent in both good times and bad? We are immensely pleased with ourselves when we demonstrate loyalty, but loyalty is something you give regardless of what you get back. Giving it begets more, and out of loyalty flows other great qualities. Loyalty is best observed when it is beheld as a two-way commitment—if you are loyal to your compatriots, and they in turn are loyal to you, the summative effect is an order of magnitude above the sum of the individual parts. However, your own sense of loyalty cannot be dependant or conditional of that which you receive in return.

The absence of fidelity, loss of reputation, contaminated peace of mind, and diminished self-worth are the punishments of disloyalty. Ask yourself, "What would be missing if I chose to be disloyal?" The answer is your integrity and ability to be authentic. It's not only what you take away from the other party, but also what you rob from yourself when you choose not to be loyal.

Loyalty is a supreme moral virtue. Without it, we lack a moral center for our life. It is a universal good that binds people to the moral order and to one another. Hence, a conflict of loyalties is disastrous. It is like a civil war in the moral order.

We know instinctively that healthy relationships are built upon both a conscious and unconscious commitment to loyalty. It's an organic ingredient of healthy human chemistry. Think of your abiding friendships and love relationships—aren't faithfulness and loyalty essential?

If friends meet in times of comfort and prosperity, but leave when hardship and difficulty strike, it is clear that their friendship is not genuine. It is not fair, right, nor admirable to benefit from someone's company in good times but abandon them in bad times. Remaining true to our deepest commitments is lifelong work for all of us, as it is for every organization of which we're a part. Yet loyalty often takes a back seat to the less noble virtues of convenience, expediency, and self-interest. This fickle loyalty to our highest purposes is one of our greatest vulnerabilities.

Loyalty is a word that should remind all of us to honor our commitments to others and ourselves. It gives life a fundamental meaning and direction. Each of us must understand that without a robust loyalty to our loyalties, our lives and credibility are greatly diminished.

It's a pretty radical word, because it requires a radical level of commitment that takes a lifetime of discipline to follow. There is great glory imbedded within loyalty. Embracing it shows us our best selves and allows us to engender the best human qualities, like courage, integrity, compassion, and fidelity. It adds dignity, credibility, and transparency to our character. It's the glue that holds relationships together, making families functional and businesses profitable. Loyalty is the fabric of society. Yet, we are living in a generation that has incredible indifference to, and difficulty in establishing, loyalty. Relationships have become based on performance and need satisfaction, which results in anger, suspicion, and isolation from institutions.

As a virtue, loyalty can be complex and elusive. Its complexity is due to the fact that the value of loyalty depends both on the constancy of one's commitment to something or someone, and to some extent on the value of that to which one is faithful. This is where chicken meets egg. Is it that people are disloyal? Or is it that people don't engender loyalty? Unfortunately, the answer to both is yes. We need to give serious consideration to how we can demonstrate greater loyalty while earning the loyalty of others. This is a thought for every business and citizen to ponder.

Loyalty is also elusive in our rapidly changing culture, and in the unfolding of our lives as well. Our alliances and allegiances simply change over time, sometimes because of their nature or ours, but not always or only because we lack the virtue of loyalty. Being loyal to something or someone apart from oneself means that self-interest is not all that governs such a person's behavior or lifestyle. They will endure the inconvenience their commitments may impose; they will not just jump whenever something better comes along; they will hold fast to a promise or a vow even when it works against their own interests to do so. Thus, loyalty shows its best side when faced with temptation, or when conflicted by a choice.

We all become weakened by defections among customers, employees, friends, and family. If the primary objective of any relationship is value creation, than we must never betray nor neglect the virtue of loyalty, as value and loyalty feed one another. Each of us has to face the matter—either loyalty, or hypocrisy. Breathe the fresh air of loyalty, as there is no middle ground. Build your life on great strength, great fidelity, and great loyalty. Semper Fidelis!

LOYALTY COUNTS—CALL TO ACTION

To explore your own commitment to making loyalty count, ask yourself these questions:

- Do you demonstrate loyalty at all times, or only when convenient?
- Do you believe that loyalty is a desirable trait, or do you believe it's overrated? Why?
- What step will you take to demonstrate greater loyalty, and to whom?

PORTRAIT OF LOYALTY

Semper Fidelis

Since the 1400s, people have used the Latin phrase "Semper Fidelis" (Always Faithful) to signify loyalty.

The United States Marine Corps adopted this motto in 1883.

Marines take this pledge seriously—loyalty to corps and country—and they stake their lives on it.

Why do these words have so much meaning to people who embrace them?

Latin expressions seem to lend credibility and respectability.

Doctors use Latin terms to describe illnesses in words only doctors can understand. It sets apart those who can understand from those who cannot, thus both signifying the value that doctors provide as well as creating a group of people who identify one another by their similar values and education.

The Marine Corps motto achieves the same purpose. Semper Fidelis is a way of life for those who accept it. The Marines are a group that is separate and unique from any other.

Believers point out the phrase is "Always Faithful" not "Sometimes Faithful." Not "Usually Faithful," but always. Not negotiable. Not relative, but absolute.

Things do not need to be spelled out; they know what it means and what to do about it.

Marines are imbued with Semper Fidelis. They live it and cannot accept any less from others.

Semper Fidelis is much more than a military motto. It serves as a positive model and philosophy for all.

UNIVERSAL CONCEPTS

39

TRUTH COUNTS

"Confront truth and reality as it is, not as it was or as you wish it to be."

Death and taxes are not the only guarantees in life; the truth counts as well. Deny the truth, and you will soon discover that life is a game that can deliver a whole lot of undesirable consequences.

Facts are facts, perceptions are perceptions. Each is powerful, and each serves a purpose. But you MUST know the difference between them. True honesty, self-respect, trust, and character are built on truth, not on perceptions. The acceptance of truth is not an option, but a moral obligation. Lies destroy progress, compromise character, and ruin relationships with others and ourselves.

Truth is what it is—the truth. Your health, wealth, relationships, and peace of mind are what they are. Stick with the facts ... the truth. Every decision about your life must be based on it.

Unfortunately, truth often becomes a piñata for those unwilling to accept reality. This applies to those unwilling to admit to an addiction, a bad marriage, a competitive liability, a criminal act, or an ethical injustice. To resist the truth over a period of time results in an inevitable backlash. The truth is often viewed as a blunt instrument. It is the thing that many people resist at all costs, often waiting until all options are exhausted before accepting or acknowledging its irrevocability. While progress is desirable, the truth is often the first casualty thrown overboard without a life preserver.

Everyone must understand that the truth is out there, and it consists of facts, not perceptions. Most often, the truth is not the path of least resistance, but that which offers a challenge and could even make you uncomfortable (especially if you do not like it). While everyone has the right to believe and accept what he or she wants, the truth doesn't discriminate; it is not different for different people. Not once has truth excused anyone for good intentions, ignorance, or stubbornness. It shows no mercy, accepts no excuses, issues no pardons. Truth does not turn the other cheek. This does not mean that truth is cruel, merely that *truth is.*

Confront truth and reality as it is, not as it was or as you wish it to be. Without the ability to see the world in the purest, most transparent way possible, you cannot make decisions on a rational basis. You must embrace this profound virtue, as you simply cannot make legitimate progress by evading facts. Accept the true facts of reality as an absolute.

Truth nibbles, scratches, rubs some the wrong way, and yes, sometimes it even bites. However, you must accept it for what it is, because in the end, that's all that matters. Accept, confront, and embrace truth; it is the foundation of reality.

Once you come to terms with the truth, then you must act decisively. Most mistakes and self-engineered fiascos that people create, regardless of position, arise from not being willing to face the true reality of a situation but acting on it anyway. Though accepting truth might sound simple, it isn't. It requires that you remove the filters that screen out the things that you might not want to see, acknowledge shortcomings, and accept the need for change. And acting with truth often means saying and doing things that are not popular.

In order to lead and make well-informed decisions, true and accurate information is essential. Whether you *like* that information is irrelevant; the quality and integrity of information is what counts. You need integrity of data and the willingness to operate with it. It is essential to understand that reality isn't necessarily going to be the way you wish things to be or the way they seem to be; reality is the way things actually are. Life will occasionally be reduced to the lowest level in Maslow's hierarchy of needs—survival.

You have both strengths and weaknesses; there is no escaping who you are. Your personality, disposition, and reputation follow you around. You cannot reinvent yourself by changing location. You will deal with the same issues no matter where you wind up.

So, what are you pretending not to know? What truth are you hiding from? What part of your reality do you find undesirable? Denial drives us to such lengths, but an examination of the truth will bring us back to center. Refusing to see or acknowledge what is right in front of us—truth—is a way of coping, but in the end, you only survive. You do not thrive.

Get this and you've got it all: while truth moves you toward your goals, denial moves you away. Denial is self-imposed deception; a convenient cover, yet a poor alibi. Self-delusion can grip an entire organization and lead the people in it to ridiculous conclusions. Denying truth or reality, for any reason, leads only to stress and frustration and takes you away from your goals. Period!

Know yourself in the most intimidate and extreme way. Honesty is the best policy, as lies and deception corrupt the soul. Do you like to be lied too? How does it make you feel? Then why do we so often lie to ourselves? In fact, we lie the loudest when we lie to ourselves. How many years of self-denial will it take before you accept the truth as it is?

Success demands that you have an honest relationship with yourself and others. Refuse to make excuses, as they are nothing more than lame attempts to corrupt and submerge the truth; their aim is to prevent truth from exposing sin or revealing one's true behavior. Don't deny the truth in any way. Changing the label on a bottle of arsenic does not make it any less dangerous. In fact, it amplifies the risks, thus making it worse.

Truth can be inconvenient, especially for those that deny it. We tend to reject that which is not easy to digest, but truth can be a bitter pill. For the most part, people don't want to hear painful truths. It *seems* easier to ignore the facts, even if we succeed only in delaying the inevitable. But make your bed with blankets of denial and you are guaranteed a lousy night's sleep. By protecting a lie or false perception, you succeed only in dishonoring the truth and undermining your own credibility.

Anyone serious about achieving excellence and personal mastery must develop the habit of examining premises and beliefs; otherwise, one risks dining on delusions. When truth is harsh, the exit ramp of denial looks appealing. But don't go there. Take the high road of truth. Denial is addictive; perhaps that's why so many indulge in its fruits. Denial is propaganda, a blindfold, and a retreat from truth. If you are going to avoid anything, avoid the always present, ever-tempting world of denial.

Be willing to experience discomforts associated with the relentless pursuit of truth. Dealing with truth requires intellectual honesty, discipline, and commitment. Honoring truth pays dividends: The tighter the grasp on both truth and reality, the better the results and therefore your quality of life.

Truth has meaningful influence. To function optimally you must, in every instance, maintain an up close and personal view of the truth. Aim for a lifetime rendezvous. Your success is dependent upon it. When it comes to the truth, everything counts!

TRUTH COUNTS—CALL TO ACTION

To explore your own commitment to making the truth count, ask yourself these questions:

- Do you confront or avoid uncomfortable realities? Are you happy with the choices you make about dealing with the truth?
- Do you understand that real consequences are levied on your peace of mind, character, and the integrity of your relationships when you lie?
- What step will you take to bring more transparency to your life as it relates to the truth?

PORTRAIT OF TRUTH

Walter Cronkite—The Most Trusted Man in America

He was the man who told us that President Kennedy had been shot, that we had put a man on the moon, and that we couldn't win the war in Vietnam.

During the 20 years he anchored the evening news on CBS, Walter Cronkite became a daily presence in the American home. He brought CBS to the pinnacle of prestige, popularity, and trust in television news.

He was often cited in viewer opinion polls as "the most trusted man in America" because of his professional experience and kindly demeanor.

Consequently, CBS News acquired a reputation for accuracy and depth in its broadcast journalism.

From the age of 12, he knew he wanted to be a journalist. It was the only career goal he ever had, and he achieved it by becoming the first important news anchor on American television.

He earned recognition and praise through hard work, a passion for accuracy, and an insistence on impartiality (being neutral).

Cronkite was quite concerned with not becoming part of the story he was reporting. He stated, "I built my reputation on honest, straight-forward reporting. To do anything else would be phony. I'd be selling myself and not the news."

Cronkite raised television news broadcasting to a level of professionalism praised around the world.

40

JOY COUNTS

"Joy is a choice. It's not the absence of problems; joy is the attitude that you carry regardless of your problems."

Joy is an aphrodisiac; anyone who has experienced it will crave it again and again. Joy is a choice; it's an emotion that can be found in any circumstance. Joy is a natural state; it's best demonstrated by children. Joy is everywhere; it presents itself in abundance throughout each day. Joy is contagious; it's a gift we give to ourselves and spread to others. Joy is inside of us; it's a spirit we liberate and find spiritually liberating. Those who live in, share, and spread joy possess true wisdom.

An essential part of your journey is the pursuit of happiness. You are accountable for all that you do, as well as for the pleasures that you fail to enjoy during your lifetime. Count the days, weeks, and life experiences lost if you have not been moved to laughter.

Contrary to popular opinion, it's perfectly okay to have fun in everything you do. It's not selfish, insensitive, or self-centered. Wanting life to be joyful is natural, normal, and healthy. Every aspect of life blends better with joy. Joy and laughter can lubricate the most tedious chore and infuse even the most serious of situations with the lightness of love. And the mere thought of joy should bring you back to your core values. One of the earliest lessons we subconsciously learn is that the joy is in the journey. As children, we found joy in playing with our food, learning how to walk, and taking a bubble bath.

But what happened to this kind of joy? Where did we lose it? Many of us eschew the simple pleasures known to children, because we have tapes running in our heads that say: *Grow up. Quit acting like a child. Be serious.* When we regain the childlike joy of simple pleasures, the process of living more simply becomes much easier. We therefore see that there is little need for complexity in living, and much joy in simplicity.

Joy must once again become the core value that it was during our youth. Joy is the horse that pulls every aspect of your life or wagon. It needs to be incorporated into every decision you make, every relationship you enter, and every activity in which you engage. When asking the question, "Does this decision fill me with joy?" the answer should be transparent.

Joy, compassion, love, and respect are not insignificant issues; they are *the* issues. We are not to be businesspeople who are joyful and compassionate; we are to be joyful and compassionate people who happen to operate within the world of business. Putting business first will always distort our joy.

Joyful living is truly the good life. Our work—along with all the things we do with our personal time and bodies—should be done because they are joyful, not because they serve some serious purpose. If you are not doing something that is enjoyable on its own account, you should look for something that is.

Just as a scale is used to measure weight, it can also be used to measure joy. How would you measure the quality of your most significant relationships on a scale from emptiness to complete joy? No one should ever be involved in a relationship that is not completely joyful. And much like peace and quiet, joy and happiness will not come looking for you. It's a present, meant to be lovingly unwrapped, but one that you must seek. Sometimes you just have to open your eyes to opportunities, as daily life provides fertile ground for living joyfully:

- Morning coffee, fresh fruit, and a newspaper can make for a joyful start to the day.
- Waking your kids up and sending them off to school can be a glorious part of your day.
- Lying in bed and enjoying the sounds of rain droplets can bring joy.
- Teaching your daughter to ride a bicycle can bring a smile to your soul.

- Working through a challenging project can be a joyful process.
- The rising or setting sun is a sight worth enjoying.
- Watching a puppy with a new toy is pure natural enjoyment.

Joy is a virtue that bears the fruit of enlightenment. It hides in plain site, so open your eyes, be observant, and cultivate the pleasures of finding joy in places you least expect.

The ideal lifestyle begins with an ideal emotional state. Your outlook on life is not determined by your circumstances, but rather by your focus. A joyful focus is joyful living. Unfortunately, most people don't enjoy life; they simply *endure* it. They think that they can't be happy because of all their problems, and that life has to be perfect before they're happy. But a problem-free life does not exist, so if you're staking your joy on the absence of problems, you'll never be joyful. If you're ever going to learn to be joyful, you've got to do it amidst life's issues. Joy is a choice. It's not the absence of problems, it's the attitude that you carry *regardless* of your problems.

Is the day coming when your doctor will tell you to take two good belly laughs and call in the morning? Maybe not, but joy and laughter are natural healers for mental and physical health. Yet joy and humor aren't just useful for getting some laughs. They're essential components of longevity, job satisfaction, personal fulfillment, peace of mind, and life balance. Indeed, laughter *is* the best medicine.

Consider this: If stress, worry, and negative emotions can make us ill, then why can't joy, laughter, and positive emotions help us heal? *Stress* and *burn out* have become household words that are as familiar as the common cold. Taking yourself too seriously can have some nasty side effects. If you are going to take anything seriously, take your play seriously. Joy is no laughing matter.

Keep in mind that it's impossible for distressing emotions and humor to occupy the same psychological space. A joyful disposition—along with a sense of humor—helps you to find the lighter side of deadlines, conflicts, and hardships. They are tools that help us let go of the moment's frustrations and upsets. And the growing conviction that stress levels are running high makes a joyful spirit and sense of humor *mandatory* conditions.

Joy is the fabric of happy memories; a life filled with joyfulness is one well lived. Yet too many of us forget to take the time simply to slow down, enjoy the journey, and have a good laugh. Joy adds years to your life and life to your years, but we must make it count one day, one moment at a time.

JOY COUNTS—CALL TO ACTION

To explore your own commitment to making joy count, ask yourself these questions:

- Do you believe that people work most productively in a joyful or stressful environment? Why?
- Do you actively build a joyful environment and demonstrate childlike enthusiasm in your work and relationships?
- What step will you take to make joy a core value in every activity?

PORTRAIT OF A JOYFUL MAN

Richard Branson, founder Virgin Group

Sir Richard Branson is the poster child for putting the joy back into business.

He's ballooned across the Atlantic, floated down the Thames with the Sex Pistols, and been knighted by the Queen. His megabrand, Virgin, is home to more than 360 companies, from gyms, gambling houses, and bridal boutiques to fleets of planes, trains, and limousines.

Branson has built the Virgin Group into an international conglomerate combining for more than $8 billion a year in sales.

The man even owns his own island—Necker Island where he shares his passion and joy with leading entrepreneurs from all over the world.

His ever-present grin and full flowing hair give him the appearance of always plowing through the wind at the helm of a great sailing ship.

Now Richard Branson is moving onward and upward into space (tourism): Virgin Galactic's spacecraft are carrying people into space at $200,000 a ticket.

"The reason I went into business originally," he says, "was not because I thought that I could make a lot of money, but because the experiences I had personally with businesses were dire and I wanted to create an experience that I and my friends could enjoy."

Branson also has a philanthropic streak. He's pledged 10 years of profits from his transportation empire (an amount expected to reach $3 billion) to the development of renewable alternatives to carbon fuels.

It's clear that he always believes his best days are in front of him.

41

SIMPLICITY COUNTS

"Without conscious, sustained effort focused on simplicity, the opposite—increased complexity—is almost certain to manifest itself."

Simplicity is a beautiful word that can define a person, place, or thing. Yet the beauty of simplicity is, as the saying goes, in the eye of the beholder. What seems simple to one person might seem complex to another. The mere mention of simplicity has the potential to create a sense of relief and freedom in this increasingly complicated world; this is reason enough to believe that simplicity counts.

Simplicity and complexity are at the extreme opposite ends of life's spectrum. In fact, all other extremes are just manifestations of these two qualities. Complexity—whether in product design, decision-making, or any daily function—is to be avoided at all costs. Complexity is the curse of the digital age; it is the intellectual smog that smothers clear thought and directs negative benefits on worker productivity, customer delight, and corporate profitability.

On the other hand, simplicity is the property, condition, or quality of being simple or uncombined. It often denotes beauty, elegance, sophistication, purity, and clarity. Simplicity is a virtue worth striving for, but so often it seems all too hard, if indeed we have time to think about it at all. And that's where the problem starts, for simplicity doesn't just *happen*. In fact, without conscious, sustained effort focused on simplicity, the opposite—increased complexity—is almost certain to manifest itself.

Throughout history, the tools and technology we use have always shaped our bodies, our arts, our architecture, and ourselves. Now, the digital tools we use are changing us as well. Our modern world generates complexity at warp speed. Where we once communicated with the outside world by fixed phone or mail, we now have to deal with phone, mobile phone, fax, e-mail, voice mail, Internet discussion groups, web casts—the list goes on. Where we once had a filing cabinet, we now have a desktop, laptop, palm-held, and mobile to coordinate our complexity. Yet these examples relate only to technology—consider the complexity imposed on us by the endless number of choices available to us at every turn.

Life is complicated enough; technology should not add to the problem. Manufacturers should be committed to creating technology that makes sense, is easy to use, and is designed around how people live and work. In other words, technology that's pure and simple. The driving force of innovation and technology should be grounded in simplicity.

Simplicity is a good thing. It does not precede complexity; rather, it follows it. It removes waste from our value chains. It saves time and money. It improves decision making to give you a new competitive advantage—a leg up on less efficient and effective firms who fail to peel away the complexity of their organizations. It is the new competitive advantage.

As a matter of course, modern evolution contains the seed for complexity. It certainly doesn't encourage simplicity. Have you ever seen anybody advertising a television "now with less features"? How about an automobile manufacturer offering a product "downgrade"? Wall-to-wall complexity is here to stay, which leaves us with two choices:

1. We can be swept along on this wave of complexity, becoming increasingly rushed as we try to fit everything in and absorb everything thrown at us.
2. Or, we can make conscious decisions and hard trade-offs to start simplifying our businesses and our lives, to begin pruning away the unnecessary and getting back to basics.

Achieving *absolute* simplicity is something none of us will ever achieve. However, if we don't make some concerted effort—train ourselves to look for ways to make things easier—we can guarantee that our lives will become more complex, busier, less efficient, and more stressful. Although the pull toward simpler ways of living is strong, the attraction toward a more cluttered life seems equally compelling. Most people are not voluntarily choosing to live more simply from a feeling of sacrifice; rather, they are seeking deeper sources of satisfaction than are being offered by a high-stress, consumption-obsessed society.

Regardless of motive, the solution calls for radical acts of simplicity, new rituals, and good old-fashioned common sense. The opportunities for radical simplicity abound when we know where to look, which of course is right under our nose.

PERSONAL ACTS OF RADICAL SIMPLICITY

- Simplicity requires a reduction of options. Ask: "What must be removed in order to gain greater quality of life?"
- An uncluttered simplicity means cutting back on trivial distractions. Therefore, find ways to simplify the mechanics of ordinary, everyday life.
- Simplicity means organizing our collective lives in a way that enables us to live lighter and sustainable lives.
- A natural simplicity feels a deep reverence for the community of life on Earth and accepts that the nonhuman realms of plants and animals have dignity and rights.
- Frugality and careful financial management bring increased financial freedom and the opportunity to choose our path through life more consciously.
- Simplicity fosters "natural capitalism," or economic practices that value the importance of natural ecosystems and healthy people for a productive local and global economy.
- Simplicity means cutting back on meaningless consumption and spending that is not truly serving our lives.
- Simplicity means choosing your path through life consciously, deliberately, and of your own accord. Choose a path that emphasizes freedom, peace, joy, and total immersion.
- Simplicity hinges as much on cutting nonessential features as on adding helpful ones.

It is imperative to understand that the simple life itself is not simple. Temptation will always present itself in better features, greater speed, cool designs, new heights in luxury, and other fascinating gimmicks. But if we are to create a significant bounce or leap forward in the quality of our lives, it will surely include a shift toward simpler, more sustainable and satisfying ways of living.

Simplicity is not the process of dumbing down; nothing, in fact, could be further from the truth. When we embrace simplicity in our lives and bring it into our businesses, true genius is at work as the effort to make the complex simple is an example of superior thinking. So go ahead, practice simplicity, and make it count.

SIMPLICITY COUNTS—CALL TO ACTION

To explore your own commitment to making simplicity count, ask yourself these questions:

- Do you believe that simplicity is a worthy goal—one that significantly adds to the quality of your life?
- Do you look for ways to simplify your business, prune away the unnecessary, and get back to basics?
- What steps will you take to simplify your life, and when will you begin?

PORTRAIT OF SIMPLICITY

Philips Electronics—Sense and Simplicity Initiative

Royal Philips Electronics, a 123,000-person global electronics giant has refocused its business on improving people's lives based on simplicity.

Philips' research into customer preferences found that 30 percent of its networking products were returned because people couldn't get them to work. In addition, 48 percent of people interviewed had put off buying a digital camera because they saw them as complicated.

Gerard Kleisterlee, CEO of Philips said, "We discovered that people want the benefits of technology without the hassles . . . products that make lives easier, simpler, better."

Philips decided it was time to do something and they came up with a new strategy they named "Sense and Simplicity."

They decreed that every new product, every patent, and every business initiative, to see the light of day, must be designed around users, be easy to experience, and make use of advanced technology.

Annually, Philips hosts a "Simplicity Summit" where their thousands of their customers can see how their new products fulfill their commitment to simplicity. They are fully committed to developing products that improve people's lives through technology that makes sense; technology designed around the way people live and work.

When Philips launched its "Sense and Simplicity" campaign, their total brand value was $4.4 billion. Four years later, Interbrand, which rates brand value, said that Philips' brand value had risen to $8.3 billion, proving that simplicity pays.

42

INCONVENIENCE COUNTS

"Becoming uncomfortable is not a nuisance, but a necessity to growth, excellence, and success."

Success requires those who seek it to develop an enormous threshold for discomfort and inconvenience because of the many sacrifices involved. This truth applies to every definition of success; it applies to everyone and to every endeavor. In short, to be successful, you must get comfortable being uncomfortable.

Inconvenience and discomfort are part of the foundational building blocks of achievement. Every person who has ever been legitimately successful has nurtured the habit of doing things that others don't like to do. Unfortunately, our society has placed such a high premium on convenience and expediency that it has enabled weakness, while also creating an inability for many to perform at peak levels.

The acceptance of inconvenience and discomfort explains why people with every apparent qualification for success become disappointing failures, while others achieve outstanding success in spite of many obvious and discouraging handicaps. In other words, we've got to realize right from the start that success requires an unconventional approach, and a much different philosophical view.

True success is something that only a minority of people manages to attain. It is unnatural, and it's not realized by following our natural likes and dislikes. Nor is it guided by our natural preferences and prejudices. We have to accept that becoming uncomfortable is not a nuisance, but rather a necessity to growth, excellence, and success. While the list of things by which most people don't want to be inconvenienced is much too long to entertain, saying that they all emanate from a willingness to embrace easy and convenient solutions to just about any situation can dispose of them all.

I present the following as an exercise to spotlight inconvenience and expose behavioral convenience for the fraud it really is:

- It's inconvenient to work out when you're tired; it's convenient and easy to make an excuse.
- It's inconvenient to be forgiving when someone has hurt you or a family member; it's convenient and easy to hold a grudge.
- It's inconvenient to love when someone has acted inappropriately; it's convenient and easy to be angry.
- It's inconvenient to ask for help or assistance; it's convenient and easy to use guilt.
- It's inconvenient to teach your child how to tie their shoes; it's convenient and easy to do it for them or give them a pair of Velcro sneakers.
- It's inconvenient to prepare and cook a well-balanced meal; it's convenient and easy to go to a fast food restaurant.
- It's inconvenient to be tranquil in a traffic jam; it's convenient and easy to get stressed out.
- It's inconvenient to accept 100 percent responsibility for your behavior; it's convenient and easy to blame someone else.
- It's inconvenient to tell the truth to others and to ourselves; it's convenient and easy to lie or engage avoidance.
- It's inconvenient to go the extra mile for a client; it's convenient and easy to say that it can't be done.
- It's inconvenient to prepare and practice; it's convenient and easy to be unprepared while offering a cop out.
- It's inconvenient to confront problems head on; it's convenient and easy to pretend that they don't exist.

207

- It's inconvenient to sacrifice and enforce self-discipline; it's convenient and easy to be lazy and procrastinate.
- It's inconvenient to break free from a comfort zone; it's convenient and easy to stay where you are.
- It's inconvenient to speak up when injustice occurs; it's convenient and easy to look the other way.
- It's inconvenient to swallow your pride and admit a mistake; it's convenient and easy to be stubborn and insist that you're correct.
- It's inconvenient to be open-minded and understanding; it's easy and convenient to be judgmental and myopic.
- It's inconvenient to be empathetic and understanding; it's convenient and easy to be callous and cynical.
- It's inconvenient to do the right thing; it's convenient and easy to be selfish.
- It's inconvenient to practice the golden rule; it's convenient and easy to be self-centered.
- It's inconvenient to tell people what they *need* to hear; it's convenient and easy to tell them what they *want* to hear.
- It's inconvenient to put the needs of others first; it's convenient and easy to focus only on our personal needs and wants.
- It's inconvenient to deal with the issues involving global warming and environmental policy; it's convenient to make believe the problems aren't that serious.

Perhaps you have been discouraged by a feeling that you were born subject to certain dislikes peculiar to you, with which highly successful men and women in our society are not afflicted. Perhaps you have wondered why it is that some people seem to like to do the things that you don't like to do. Well, they don't. The truth is that *no one* likes being inconvenienced; high performers just understand that the road to success is constantly filled with acts of discomfort. They simply choose to do what needs to be done, regardless of how inopportune the actions happen to be.

But if they don't like be inconvenienced for whatever reason, then why do they embrace it? Because they know that by doing the right things at the right time, they can accomplish the things they want to accomplish while feeling great about how victory was achieved. Successful people are influenced by the desire for pleasing results, while the overwhelming majority of people are influenced by the desire for pleasing methods. They are inclined to be satisfied with such results as can be obtained by doing things that they like to do, or simply what they find to be convenient.

Every single qualification for success is acquired through the habit of inconvenience. People form habits and habits form futures. If you do not deliberately form good habits, you will unconsciously form bad ones. You are the kind of person that you are because you have formed the habit of being that kind of person; the only way you can change is through the habit of inconvenience. As long as you live, don't ever forget that while you may succeed beyond your fondest hopes and your greatest expectations, you will never succeed beyond the purpose to which you are willing to surrender.

Furthermore, your surrender will not be complete until you adopt the winner's philosophy that all progress, change, and successes are based upon a foundation of inconvenience. When it comes to your success, it's imperative that you increase your appetite for discomfort, as every act of inconvenience counts!

INCONVENIENCE COUNTS—CALL TO ACTION

To explore your own commitment to making inconvenience count, ask yourself these questions:

- Do you believe that temporary inconvenience creates better or worse results? Why?
- Do your actions demonstrate someone who is committed to quality and excellence and going the extra mile?
- What step will you take to enforce temporary inconvenience in order to enjoy long-term growth?

PORTRAIT OF INCONVENIENCE

John Peterson

As told in a brilliant documentary entitled *The Real Dirt on Farmer John*, the story of John Peterson is an allegory for the many sacrifices and inconveniences of family farmers, and the triumphant return to traditional artisan farming that is giving new life to small-scale agriculture.

Peterson grew up on an Illinois farm in the 1950s, and watched his Uncle Harold use teams of horses to plow his fields decades after tractors had revolutionized American farming.

In the 1980s, as the conventional farming economy collapsed, Peterson lost much of the land that his family had farmed for more than 100 years. But through his unique and reflective approach as an artist and writer, through his passionate devotion to the land, Peterson made an important discovery: that in order to preserve tradition, he must change.

However, the farming community in which Peterson attempted to make these alterations was not as open to new ways as he was. The locals treated him with suspicion, fear, and anger by spreading rumors of drug use, animal sacrifices, and other odd rituals such as witchcraft.

But in the face of this resistance, and despite a range of personal challenges and emotions, Peterson persevered. And today, the Peterson family farm has become Angelic Organics—one of the largest community-supported agriculture (CSA) farms in the United States and a beacon of hope for the survival of family farming in the face of the enormous power of agribusiness.

John Peterson's story is a testimony of endurance, resilience, and passion in fighting for a new form of community regardless of the sacrifice or inconvenience.

DIVERSITY COUNTS

"To fully understand diversity and equality, one must see humanity in terms of both its similarities and differences."

The world consists of billions of people who come from different cultural, religious, and ethnic backgrounds, each of whom carries his or her own value system. These differences find their way into coffee shops, conference rooms, and classrooms. You don't have to get a brain cramp to realize the significance of diversity, its impact on the world, and why we must find a way to make it count.

We are all staring down the barrel of the same reality. Diversity is a serious competitive issue that requires a serious and sustained solution. By giving diversity little more than lip service, many people and companies are in danger of losing touch with reality. The time to stop paying lip service to diversity is long overdue; we cannot complacently allow past preconceptions to continue. Every member of society must become diversity-enlightened.

As our industrial society and global economy grows and continues to diversify, many of us fail to understand how diversity affects what we do and how we do it. By failing to recognize its relevance, by failing to resemble the national population, and by failing to reward the proponents of diversity, many companies will soon find themselves uncompetitive in a highly diverse world.

The mere term *diversity* carries a plethora of meanings, depending on whom you ask. For many, equality has traditionally meant sameness—a concept that ignores fundamental differences between people. We are distinguished and united by differences and similarities according to gender, age, language, culture, race, sexual identity, religion, geography, and income level, just to name a few. Such diversity challenges our intellect and emotions as we learn to work and live together in harmony.

In order to fully understand diversity and equality, one must see humanity in terms of both its similarities and differences. Humans share innate traits that unify us at the most basic level. Language, the ability to learn, the capacity to relate to one another, the passion to love and nurture, the need for food and shelter are all traits that every person has. And although these similarities are often overlooked, it is because of human nature's common aspects that we must search for a greater understanding of the nuances that differences in people play. It begs the question, "If we are all very much alike at our core, then why do our differences cause pain and conflict?"

Diversity doesn't just mean increasing visible differences in the workforce. It is about the strategic advantages that come from incorporating a wide variety of approaches and perspectives. An organization that wants to be successful in today's world must use diversity to their advantage, as the business case for diversity has two significant elements. First, the labor market has become increasingly competitive. Any company that fails to take steps to recruit among the full spectrum of potential employees is missing a strategic opportunity. Second, the changing world demographics mean that the public served by the business world is also changing.

When companies recruit and retain an inclusive workforce and value individual differences, diversity becomes an organizational strength that contributes to achieving results. It offers a variety of views, approaches, and actions for a company to use in strategic planning, problem solving, and decision-making.

Managing diversity is about creating an environment in which everyone can achieve his or her full potential. Employees are happier and more productive if they are appreciated and included, not assimilated or tolerated. When you combine powerful minds from all types of backgrounds, you create not just great ideas, but also unlimited possibilities. Embracing diversity creates the foundation for a strong future because it:

- Fosters a culture that encourages innovation and breadth of vision
- Promotes businesses to better meet the needs of their customers
- Attracts and retains employees with a broad range of experiences and values-based perspectives
- Helps provide the competitive edge needed to succeed in a global marketplace

Accepting diversity requires a change in corporate culture. Organizations need to embrace the fact that shared business values and a strong work ethic make an employee valuable, not whether they look the same or share a common history. This approach results in a wealth of fresh ideas and creative problem solving that allows a company to focus on the customers and markets they serve, the business processes and practices they use, and the products and services they develop.

Innovation is made possible by looking at situations through different lenses. It's the people who bring a new and different perspective to a problem or opportunity, and it's the people who pursue their ideas with passion that make truly innovative products. Teams that are diverse and inclusive find more innovative, feasible, and effective ways to overcome challenges.

If successfully managed, diversity can serve as a strategic tool to build a stronger, more flexible organization, just as individual differences create opportunities to build great work places, resilient organizations, and a better world. The most powerful tool to empower diversity is to eliminate bias at its roots before stereotyping develops. This requires education and accountability.

As the workforce evolves to reflect the growing diversity of our communities and the global marketplace, it becomes increasingly important to make an effort to understand, value, and incorporate differences. Diversity will cease to be an issue once we have learned to respect and accept dissimilarities, wherever and whatever they are.

To succeed in developing and sustaining strong diversity initiatives, companies must hold their executives, managers, and supervisors accountable for achieving results. They must build accountability for hiring, retaining, and developing a diverse, high-quality workforce into the performance management systems for managers and supervisors. In addition to making higher-ups accountable for building and maintaining a diverse, high-quality workforce, companies should also remember to recognize successes. Identify and reward

213

champions, and publicize their accomplishments. Seriously consider nominating staff for special, honorary awards to recognize their accomplishments related to building and maintaining a diverse, high-quality workforce.

Understanding the relevance of diversity must be our top priority and a goal that we all pursue. Market drivers want it. Customers support it. The global marketplace demands it. Therefore, it's in our best interest that everyone gets it—the message that diversity counts!

DIVERSITY COUNTS—CALL TO ACTION

To explore your own commitment to making diversity count, ask yourself these questions:

- Do you view diversity as a competitive advantage or as a necessary evil? Why do you feel this way?
- Do you take energy management for granted, and just simply deal with the highs and lows produced through your body?
- What step will you take to systematically spend and renew energy?

PORTRAIT OF DIVERSITY

Procter & Gamble

In 1837, William Procter and James Gamble formed a new enterprise with the simple purpose to touch consumers' lives with products that make life a little better every day.

Staying focused has enabled them to become one of the world's leading consumer products companies and one of the most diverse with over 110,000 employees in 80 countries.

Bob McDonald, CEO of this $83 billion giant believes that "growing with integrity requires respect for the individual and the decision to do what's right for the long-term."

Clearly they are doing it right.

Annually they are ranked among the industry leaders for the Most Admired or Best to Work For, for Working Mothers, and for Multicultural Women by all the experts.

No accident, as they expect their leadership to hardwire diversity into their business strategies, establish clear expectations, and demonstrate personal accountability.

The Top 40 executives conduct in-depth diversity reviews, have diversity results tied to their stock options awards, and have action plans for each region of the world to reflect the greatest opportunity for advancement of local diversity strategies.

P&G leaders are expected to build an inclusive work environment that welcomes and embraces diversity—an environment where people feel comfortable being who they are, regardless of their individual differences, talents, or personal characteristics.

Commitment to diversity is clearly one of their most important strategies for success.

44

FAILURE COUNTS

"You are rewarded with success based on your ability to understand and learn from failure."

The dreaded "F" word—failure—is so important, yet so misunderstood. Failure serves an indispensable function in the production of your success. It provides information and motivation for you to learn from and apply. It is a sign that points toward progress; however, depending on your perception, it either moves you closer to or further from your goals.

Few people choose to study their own failures, except to lament the consequences that bring them about and to formulate what they believe to be corrective solutions. While most tend to concentrate on the negative side of failure and ignore its positive contributions, the bright side of failure must be acknowledged for what it is and why it exists. Only then can failures and proposed remedies be properly understood and appreciated.

People are generally naive about failure's benefits. Incorrectly formulated assumptions about failure replace potentially accurate assessments of what is necessary to achieve success. Failure—which spends much of its life in the gulag of public perception—is, by all measures, *essential* to success. In fact, success depends on a constant stream of small and occasionally large failures, and unfortunately, failure usually gets a bum rap. But failure is not merely the output of an unsuccessful activity, it is also the input for a successful one. However, unless failure is understood and respected as an integral part of success, it will remain widely perceived as unnecessary and objectionable— something to be avoided at all costs.

A proactive response to failure is impossible when one sees failure only in negative terms.

You must expect to get dinged here and there as you pursue your goal. But like wine that gets better with age, you get better when you have failed a time or two and learned from the experience. While there is nothing inherently sexy or enviable about failure, eventually people find you more attractive and interesting because of the knowledge, wisdom, and maturity you gained because of it.

Anything worthwhile is worth pursuing, even though the risk is huge, the investment formidable, and failure a possibility. Failure lobs an occasional grenade at success. It asks for your resignation letter, it attempts to extract a pound of flesh, it goads and prods you into quitting, but success hangs in the balance.

Success and failure are forever connected—just like peanut butter and jelly, salt and pepper, night and day, plus and minus, and black and white. The most dynamic and progressive people and corporations are those making productive use of failures by motivating appropriate responses. These leaders view specific failures as the unavoidable consequences of both action and change. They see failure as necessary to their success. They digest its instructive qualities and productive consequences, while enjoying its inevitable association with success.

Failure is a temporary condition that applies to a particular situation, time, or place. If you don't let it devastate you, failure can be an opportunity for learning, for recovery, for the creation and demonstration of character. You must acknowledge that failure has an ulterior motive, not to get you to quit, but to stop you long enough so that you may learn something. Restrategize and relaunch again, more prepared for success.

To achieve success and excellence in any endeavor, you must expose your goals and ambitions to the elements of failure, rejection, and attack just as a forest is exposed to rain, sleet, and snow. It is primarily through solving problems, overcoming obstacles, and managing adversity that we grow strong and get to enjoy success and fulfillment. The pain and misery of failure, missed opportunity, or simply a bonehead move on our own part should be a lesson learned, and never repeated. Even if you lose, don't lose the lesson. Those who cannot learn from failure are condemned to repeat it. The lessons of failure are a terrible thing to waste. Failure may seem intolerable, but it's also inevitable, so embrace the lessons it teaches.

The best way to diffuse the negative effects of failure is to grasp the insight and information that they offer. Failure counts, because it provides relevant information and the new insights necessary to achieve success. You are rewarded with success based on your ability to understand and learn from failure.

Failure in your efforts serves much the same purpose as pain in your body. Although you do not want to endure pain, you respond to it as a warning. Just as pain and its threat help you to act in your body's best interest, failure and its possibility prompt action to avoid harm and promote progress. But failure is more positive than pain, which is primarily a signal of physical problems rather than vitality, because failure steers you in positive directions and is a necessary and direct result of success.

Unfortunately, when we encounter failure, we tend to concentrate on the pain that this failure has caused instead of examining the reasons *why* it has occurred. Failure speaks volumes, but only when the student listens intently. In a strange way, failure is the teacher's pet of success.

The dark side of failure is the inevitable misfortune and accompanying turmoil caused when performance lags behind its competition. The costs of failure are difficult for people to ignore. Failure's high price is commonly imposed through the harshness of bankruptcy, unemployment, cost overruns, lost clients, and other forms of pain. The bright side is that failure inspires product improvements, new technologies, and additional opportunities as reflected in the ever-evolving and expanding marketplace.

Failure occurs for many reasons: poor management, gross inefficiency, complacency, arrogance, insufficient planning, and poor execution. Yet, failures are inevitable, even if everything is performed in an excellent manner. So, how can it occur, under even the most ideal circumstances? The dilemma is that failure is not simply a matter of neglecting to meet well-defined and fixed standards of performance. Rather, failure is a matter of performance; failure to do better than others, not doing things faster, not producing a better product, not having more efficient systems, and not finding better solutions. Performance only changes and improves to the degree that you change and improve. The bright side of failure is that it inspires improvement, creativity, change, and most important, a commitment to excellence.

We must also be aware of the perfection trap. There is a real problem with adopting perfection as your standard for performance: Perfection does not exist. Nonetheless, the perfection mentality, deeply ingrained within society, leaves no room for mistakes. "Failure is not an option" is the battle cry. Meanwhile, mistakes are made—and punished—all the time.

Failure is rarely sanctioned as an alternative to perfection. When mistakes do occur with this mind-set, it's not surprising that no one shows up with a claim ticket. Indeed, success has many parents, but failure is always born an orphan!

The most compelling case for success in any endeavor depends upon your recognition that failure is an inherent feature of it. The biggest threat to your progress is the belief that failure should be avoided at all costs. Your success is failure-dependent.

Realizing that failure is unavoidable may or may not help you to sleep any easier. However, not being squeezed by the impossible standard of perfection is a welcome relief. When it comes to failure and its contribution to your success, everything counts!

FAILURE COUNTS—CALL TO ACTION

To explore your own commitment to making failure count, ask yourself these questions:

- Do you believe that it's possible to succeed without failing?
- Do you look for the lessons in failure, or do you simply curse the situation?
- What step will you take to understand better the important role that failure plays in your success?

PORTRAIT OF A SUCCESSFUL FAILURE

James Dyson—Inventor

James Dyson is a man who likes to make things work better.

He is an engineer and an inventor. Products he has developed account for over $6 billion in sales worldwide.

Perhaps his most famous invention is the "bagless" vacuum cleaner.

One day, James Dyson noticed that vacuum cleaner bags clog with dust. Fifteen years and 5,127 prototypes later, he had built the world's first bagless vacuum cleaner.

Major manufacturers turned James down but he found a Japanese company that agreed to produce and sell his revolutionary design.

Dyson says this about his years of failure:

"There is a myth about inventors that all you need is one good idea and you'll make your fortune. It doesn't work like that. You start with a problem and you start building prototypes—hundreds or thousands of prototypes. The final solution never looks like your first idea. Failure is the starting point. You start looking for why it failed and you can start thinking about ideas to overcome that failure."

Because our society has an instant-gratification thing, we admire instant brilliance.

Mr. Dyson thinks quite the opposite. We should admire the person who perseveres and slogs through and gets there in the end.

So the moral of the tale is to keep on failing because in failure you will find success.

45

SPORTSMANSHIP COUNTS

"Sportsmanship offers the athlete an opportunity to develop life skills and qualities such as character, teamwork, honor, discipline, and excellence."

Whatever happened to good sportsmanship? How is that from the pee-wee to the professional leagues, trash talking, fist fights, profanity, cheating, gambling, drugs, threatening game officials, and blatant disrespect for coaches, teammates, and competitors has become tolerated, accepted, and even glamorized?

The choice made by athletes to engage in sportsmanlike behavior depends in large part on how the sport is structured by coaches, parents, and fans. Good sportsmanship begins with an understanding that the principle nature of athletics, sports, and physical education are an integral part of the educational process. These activities offer innumerable opportunities to learn skills that last a lifetime.

Teaching good sportsmanship offers the athlete an ideal opportunity to develop life skills and qualities such as character; teamwork; honor and fair play; excellence and hard work; discipline; the ability to overcome adversity and failure; resiliency and perseverance; joy and humility; respect; maturity; unselfishness; responsibility; goal setting; planning; citizenship; and a competitive spirit. These success and survival skills are all the direct benefits of learning and teaching good sportsmanship.

Sports are an extension of our societal mores. If an athlete chooses to engage in unsportsmanlike behavior, we must pause and wonder exactly where the athlete may have developed such a trait. Both poor and admirable sportsmanship are learned behaviors. We see moral behavior from engaging with and watching others' behaviors, or by being taught through example. Therefore, teaching and modeling appropriate behaviors can enhance sportsmanlike behaviors.

Merely being involved in sport, however, is not sufficient to ensure that athletes will learn sportsmanlike attitudes and behaviors. Rather, it is the social interactions that are fostered by the experience that will determine the benefit of sport to athletes. This benefit requires that designated leaders within the sport take action to teach ethical and moral behavior in sport.

Restoring sportsmanship and civility to athletics must become a shared concern. Good sportsmanship dictates:

Respect—Athletes should display proper respect and courtesy, maintaining civility toward opposing coaches and athletes, game officials, and spectators at all contests. Most important, athletes must respect the game and uphold its virtues.

Listening—A player with good sportsmanship listens to and follows the directions of the coach and realizes that each player's decisions affect the rest of the team.

Communication—In the case of a player's disagreement with the coach, the player discusses the disagreements privately in a civil manner, away from the public eye.

Responsibility—Designated leaders bear the responsibility of teaching the value of sporting conduct in both word and deed to their athletes. The use of foul or vulgar language is inconsistent with this responsibility.

Discipline—There is no place in athletics for taunting, embarrassing, or humiliating an opponent or game official. Each player must be made aware of the consequences when failing to abide by the acceptable code of conduct.

Humility—Sportsmanship dictates that failure is part of the game. The player with good sportsmanship does not use a loss as an occasion to make excuses or blame. They maintain composure, learn from their mistakes, and prepare for the next competition.

Self-Control—Sportsmanship requires that one exercises self-control with game officials during competition and refrains from approaching officials to address them in a disrespectful manner. Part of the human condition is making mistakes.

Joy—Maintaining a "Fun is Number 1" attitude is key. When everyone is having fun, learning all aspects of the game is more enjoyable and rewarding. A good sport has fun because they enjoy playing the game more than they enjoy winning.

Rules—Part of good sportsmanship is knowing the rules of the game and playing by them. It is the athlete's responsibility to learn not only how to play, but how to play according to the rules, and to allow competitive games to be played in an orderly fashion.

Accountability—Coaches and athletes must live up to their own highest personal standard of sportsmanship, even when their opponents may not. Personal accountability and respect for one's own standards must be your first priority.

Honor—The responsibility to demonstrate and develop character and sportsmanship should never be subordinated to the desire to win. The vital lessons and intrinsic value of sports are acquired through the competition and honorable pursuit of victory, rather than the outcome itself.

Excellence—Personal mastery, increased skill development, and performing to the best of your abilities are the hallmarks of good sportsmanship. Everyone can be a success, because success relates to the effort put into realizing one's personal potential.

Teamwork—Good sportsmanship implies that any given player on a team is a team player. In other words, the player understands that his or her behavior reflects on the team in general. Moreover, a team player does not condone unsportsmanlike conduct from teammates.

Encouragement—Sportsmanship means praising teammates when they do well, and comforting them when they make mistakes. Criticizing teammates in the heat of battle simply distracts from the focus of working together and gives the advantage to the opponent, who develops a sense of confidence upon realizing a lack of unity in the midst of the competition.

Gratitude—Coaches and athletes must understand that competing in athletics is a privilege and not a right. Be grateful for the opportunity to compete; be grateful for challenging opposition; be grateful for your skills and talents. Never take any part of the game for granted.

Role Modeling—Modeling sportsmanlike behaviors within a competitive environment increases an athlete's demonstration of sportsmanlike behaviors. The coach's behavior on the playing field or in the gym sends a message to their athletes about what is considered acceptable behavior.

Rewards—Any behavior that is rewarded is repeated. It is crucial that we recommit ourselves to guiding our athletes, reminding them what sportsmanship is all about, rewarding them for showing good sportsmanship, and showing, by our example, that sportsmanship is still alive and valued in sports today.

Sportsmanship is everyone's business—from the coaches and players, to the parents and fans, we can all learn or relearn the principles of sportsmanship. If our young athletes are not exposed to and guided in developing a sense of good sportsmanship, we can all but guarantee that they will fall prey to the uncivilized conduct that they see modeled and reinforced by so many poor examples.

Sportsmanship is something we must actively seek to teach and reinforce through our words and our behaviors at every opportunity, because sportsmanship counts.

SPORTSMANSHIP COUNTS—CALL TO ACTION

To explore your own commitment to making sportsmanship count, ask yourself these questions:

- Do you teach and model good sportsmanship? If so, what are the supporting benefits and how can you apply the same lessons to more areas of your life?
- Do you believe that teaching good sportsmanship leads to more civilized conduct among kids and teens?
- What steps will you take to bring greater sportsmanship to your athletic pursuits as well as those of your children and community?

PORTRAIT OF SPORTSMANSHIP

Sarah Tucholsky

This story is about a home run memorable not for the distance it traveled or the game it decided but for the meaning it carried.

Here's the scenario: It's the last game of the season, two teams fighting neck and neck for the conference championship. For senior Sarah Tucholsky it was her last chance to hit a home run. She'd never done it before—not in college, not in her life.

With two runners on, the second pitch changed everything. She swung. The ball just went and went over the fence.

She ran fast. In her excitement, she missed first base. She turned back but in turning, tore her ACL. She could only crawl back and hug the bag—a long way from home plate.

The coach worried, could she put someone in for Sarah? Yes, but it would be a two-run single and no home run! Could her teammates help her? No, she'd be called out!

That's when Mallory Holtman, a player with more home runs than anyone in conference history spoke up . . . a player on the opposing team.

"Could we carry her?" Yes, said the ump, but why?

Mallory said, "She hit it over the fence; she deserves it."

Mallory Holtman lost a game that day. Sarah accomplished her goal—she hit a home run.

But for the spirit of sportsmanship, a greater victory was made on a long trot around the bases—a trip that truly touched them all.

46

RESILIENCY COUNTS

"Those with good resiliency skills have a significant competitive advantage over those who feel helpless."

Resiliency refers to the ability to cope well with high levels of ongoing disruptive change; to sustain good health and energy when under constant pressure. It describes someone who is able to bounce back quickly from setbacks and adversities; to change to a new way of working and living when an old pattern is no longer possible; and to do all of this without acting in dysfunctional or harmful ways.

Highly functional resiliency skills are more important these days than ever before. The volatile and chaotic period we are experiencing will not be ending anytime soon; in fact, it is likely to intensify. And it's precisely for that reason why resiliency counts.

When resilient people have their lives disrupted or blindsided in any way, they handle their feelings in a healthy, mature manner. They allow themselves to feel grief, anger, loss, and confusion when hurt and distressed, but they don't let

226

it become a permanent state of emotional distress. An unexpected outcome of adversity is that resilient people not only heal; they often bounce back stronger than before. They are examples of Friedrich Wilhelm Nietzsche's famous statement, "That which does not kill me makes me stronger."

In order to sustain a good quality of life for yourself and your family, you must understand the benefits and purpose of resiliency. Those with good resiliency skills have a significant competitive advantage over those who feel helpless or react like stressed-out victims. Possessing a resilient mindset does not imply that one is free from stress, pressure, and conflict, but rather that one can successfully cope with problems as they arise.

The type and amount of unpleasant stress and strain that any one person can experience is their subjective reaction. Your perception of what is happening depends on your competence to consciously own your reaction. When struggling with extreme pressures and disruptive changes in the workplace, your attitudes and habits create either barriers or bridges to a better future.

In a world of life-disrupting, nonstop change, corporations with highly resilient employees have an advantage over their less resilient competitors. And, during economic hardship, resilient people give their families a much better chance of pulling through and bouncing back stronger than ever. Resiliency is an essential life skill in every job sector—in corporations, small businesses, public agencies, professional services, at home—that is especially necessary during times of turmoil. Business and social environments are often complex, dynamic, and turbulent, which means that today's success formula can become tomorrow's Achilles' heel. Thriving—or even surviving—in this context requires that everyone embrace resiliency as a career and life skill. Resiliency must inhabit every area of our lives in response to ever-changing dynamics.

Resilient people and organizations are able to sustain competitive advantage through their capability, and to consistently deliver excellence in performance and results. In addition, they must effectively innovate and adapt to rapid, turbulent changes in markets and technologies. It is imperative that you accept this reality as well: when you are hit with life-disrupting events, you will never be the same again. You either cope or crumble; you become better or bitter; you emerge stronger or weaker. Self-confidence, self-esteem, and self-concept are the three essential strengths that control your access to higher-level resiliency abilities. If they are healthy and strong, they will allow you to develop a wide range of talents, abilities, and skills that blossom. If they are weak or you do not work at developing them, they will undermine you and make you vulnerable. Weaknesses that were not obvious in safe, protected environments will become much more pronounced in unstable, stressful environments.

The world is becoming turbulent faster than most people and organizations are becoming resilient. The pace and chaos in today's world is beyond the ability of most people to handle well; in fact, many leaders manage their organizations in ways that hamper resiliency. Changes in the workplace occur so often now that very few employees have up-to-date job descriptions. And it isn't just frequent, disruptive change that must be handled; morale suffers when friendships with coworkers are disrupted by reorganization, downsizing, and layoffs. Pride in one's work can be hard to maintain when a system you developed for doing things is tossed out, and a new one that doesn't work as well is imposed upon you.

Putting the impressive mission statements aside for a moment, most workers will tell you that they feel intense pressure to do more work of better quality in less time, with fewer employees, in new ways, using new technology and new methods on a reduced budget—while worrying if their jobs are safe. Negative emotions such as fear, anger, anxiety, distress, helplessness, and hopelessness decrease your ability to solve the problems you face, and they weaken your resiliency. Constant fears and worries weaken both your physical and psychological immune system and increase your vulnerability to illnesses.

Resiliency is a sustainable inner power that will effectively help you to handle change, challenge, and adversity confidently and calmly. Learning to be resilient will also allow you to experience more peace and joy in your life, while creating the positive conditions that will support you in achieving your goals and dreams.

Each of us lives in a constantly changing, dynamic environment. We can make our lives difficult by denying or resisting the ongoing process of change, or we can adapt and flow with changes by being flexible and resilient. It's our choice.

By accepting that unceasing change permeates our lives, and that many kinds of energy constantly swirl through and around us, we can free ourselves from being buffeted around like leaves in a storm. In fact, we are most resilient when we approach new situations with childlike curiosity, not fully knowing in advance what we will or should do, but confident that we will act in ways that lead to desirable means and ends.

Our greatest glory is not in not falling, but rather in rising every time that we fall. Resiliency, along with our inborn ability to keep learning new ways of interacting with the world, can lead us to learn how to navigate through rough times of change so skillfully, that we actually enjoy the journey.

RESILIENCY COUNTS—CALL TO ACTION

To explore your own commitment to making resiliency count, ask yourself these questions:

- Do you understand the benefits and purpose of resiliency? Do you consider yourself a resilient person?
- Do you believe that everyone should embrace resiliency as a career and life skill? Why do you feel this way?
- What step will you take to sustain good health and energy when under constant pressure?

PORTRAIT OF RESILIENCY

Trisha Meili

Trisha Meili, the "Central Park Jogger," was given last rites after the 1989 attack and savage beating that left her near death; a crime that appalled people all over the world. Multiple gashes split Meili's scalp; an eye socket was fractured in 21 places. She could not breathe on her own, lost most of her blood, and had severe brain damage. Only the soles of her feet were unbruised. Doctors doubted that she would survive.

But Trisha Meili didn't die. She awoke from a 12-day coma to an apparently shattered life. A Phi Beta Kappa with two graduate degrees from Yale, Meili had been on the fast track to a vice presidency at Salomon Brothers. Now she couldn't even walk, talk, read, or button her blouse.

Sixteen years later, this same woman drew a standing ovation after a polished speech on recovering from trauma. Meili didn't just survive; she thrived and grew. Now she's a motivational speaker and volunteer who talks about her healing to medical and mental health groups, patients, and other people recovering from traumatic changes. She revealed her amazing story of survival and recovery 14 years later in her best-selling memoir *I Am the Central Park Jogger: A Story of Hope and Possibility.* She is a true testament to the power of resiliency.

47

FUNDAMENTALS COUNT

"No one is above the law, and no one is above the necessity of the fundamentals."

Success, in all its forms, consists of simple fundamentals. Professionals respect them, while amateurs loathe them. Professionals master them, while amateurs neglect them. Professionals practice them, while amateurs undermine them. The common denominator for success in any field is a focus on the most basic components.

Whether you refer to them as the ABCs, 123s, rudimentary skills, nuts and bolts, foundational principles, universal truths, elementary steps, or simply as square one, the fundamentals are the initial building blocks on which all success stands. Success is neither magical nor mysterious; it is the natural consequence of consistently applying fundamentals.

A foundation anchors your house to the earth, holding it up, and just as importantly, holding it down. A well-constructed, rock-solid foundation will last several lifetimes, while a poor one will forever remain unstable. The foundation must be strong enough to shoulder the entire weight of the house, as everything built into the house becomes either vulnerable or strengthened by the quality of the foundation.

When well constructed, foundations escape notice; they are quietly doing their job below grade. But when they begin to fail, their weakness is quickly exposed along with the fingerprints of mediocrity and incompetence. A poor foundation is a serious problem that leads to numerous quagmires and considerable expense.

Nothing is more fundamental to constructing a house than establishing a firm foundation, and the same applies in every aspect of life. Anything of quality and durability is constructed carefully, patiently, and lovingly to ensure a proper result. Fundamentals are basics; they are important because they are something upon which other vital components can be successfully built.

Success in any sport, career, or hobby is built on a foundation of timeless, universal, and pragmatic principles. From accounting to astrophysics, education to engineering, fly-fishing to firefighting, computer programming to construction, rock climbing to rocket science, and from raising kids to raising capital—all consist of fundamental principles and each fundamental counts.

FUNDAMENTAL RULES ON FUNDAMENTALS

Fundamentals Come First: You must learn these before anything else. Strong foundations are built on strong fundamentals; there is no shortcut to mastery. You must crawl before you walk, learn the notes and chords before you learn a song, and ski the bunny hill before attempting the double diamond trails. Everything that you learn in life starts small, and builds from there.

Fundamentals are Simple: Anything and everything is based on a foundation of simple truths. Even quantum physics is simple—once you learn the fundamentals. Our minds create fallacies of complexity, which betray us so often that we fail to see the simplicity that is hiding in plain sight.

Fundamentals Require Patience: Rome wasn't built in a day, and they were using local, well-trained help. While fundamentals are always simple, they conversely require time and patience to be understood. The process of trial and error correction is different for each person.

Fundamentals Must Be Mastered: The objective is and will always be to become brilliant at the basics. In order to perform at the top of your abilities, you must become a master at your trade. There is no other way to personal excellence; you must pay your dues in advance and in full.

Fundamentals Require Practice: Everybody loves a great performance, and behind every one is the consistent practice and reinforcement of the fundamentals. Repetition is everything, as the quality of your performance will never exceed the quality of your practice.

Fundamentals Are Universal: Fundamentals truly operate in a one-size-fits-all world. The wonderful part about them is that they establish a level playing field. For anything to be mastered, everyone must pass the same test. No one gets a passing grade simply for showing up.

Fundamentals Once Lost Are Found in Humility: The minute a performer gets away from the fundamentals—whether it is proper technique, work ethic, or mental preparation—her entire game begins to break down. This inevitably leads to embarrassment, missed opportunity, and finally to a helping of humble pie. Humility leads you back home—to the fundamentals of success.

Fundamentals Never Change: There is nothing new under the sun. The fundamentals of investing, raising kids, mathematics, science, or accounting—you name it—have been identified, are set in place, and will not be changing anytime soon.

There is nothing more fundamental to success than making everything you do count. Meticulous attention to details; a focus on superior quality, proper preparation, and planning; a well-crafted strategy; consistency of purpose; flawless execution; exemplary character; uncompromising standards; and the discipline to honor each commitment is how we make everything count. In fact, the companies and individuals that become more successful year after year, and who sustain excellence, are brilliant in the basics. They make everything they do count, because they know everything has bottom-line consequences. When leaders are done learning the fundamentals, they pick them up and take them wherever they go.

In times of high uncertainty, companies understandably tend to get carried away by a dizzying array of management fads. But to avoid distraction, management must stay focused on the key essentials that shape the business landscape. We must never choose fad over fundamentals.

Getting back to basics requires that one be obsessive over quality and details. Many of the big problems in business stem from ignoring the smallest of details. When small things don't get the attention they deserve, customers get insulted. As a result, they use less of your products and services, and your reputation is undermined. This combination ultimately leads to a negative impact on profits and brand loyalty. Constant attention to detail, on the other hand, not only demonstrates professional competence, it also shows that you care about quality.

232

Fundamentals are the most crucial part of success in any endeavor. While attitude, enthusiasm, and potential are important, they lack complete effectiveness without solid fundamentals. Sweating the small stuff is not easy. It requires endless attention to detail, rugged determination, and consistency over time. There is no shortcut to success. But precisely because it is so hard, the competitive benefits can be huge.

Everything you do, have, and will achieve in the future can be traced back to the way you approach the fundamentals, and how you use your abilities to apply them. The fundamentals are bedrock principles from which other truths can be derived. No one is above the law, and no one is above the necessity of the fundamentals. Many people need to go back, revisit, and relearn the fundamentals of their industry.

Fundamentals are the basic building blocks or principles that make everything work, and that's precisely why the fundamentals count.

FUNDAMENTALS COUNT—CALL TO ACTION

To explore your own commitment to making the fundamentals count, ask yourself these questions:

- Do you believe that it's important to become brilliant on the basics? Why do you feel this way?
- Do you exercise patience when learning a new fundamental skill? Or are you in such a rush to get to the next step that you overlook the importance of mastering the fundamentals?
- What step will you take to make the fundamentals count in your life and career?

PORTRAIT OF SOUND FUNDAMENTALS

John Wooden

As the UCLA men's basketball coach, his teams claimed 10 national championships and once won 88 consecutive games.

233

John Wooden, hall of famer as both a player (three-time All-American at Purdue) and a coach (Indiana State and UCLA).

Sports Illustrated named him Coach of the 20th Century.

His players remember his strict attention to the fundamentals of the game—the small details that enabled them to win championships.

His focus on fundamentals can best be demonstrated by the first thing he taught his players (the best in the country): How to put on their socks!!

If they didn't get that simple act right, then they might get a blister. If they got a blister, they'd miss practice time. If they missed practice time, they wouldn't win championships.

Wooden authored a book, *Pyramid of Success*, about the fundamental philosophical building blocks for winning at basketball and at life. Here are seven of them:

1. Be true to yourself.
2. Make each day your masterpiece.
3. Help others.
4. Drink deeply from good books, especially the Bible.
5. Make friendship a fine art.
6. Build a shelter against a rainy day.
7. Pray for guidance and give thanks for your blessings every day.

Sound advice from someone who knew the value of practicing the fundamentals.

48

Every Dollar Counts

"Money is a reward you receive for the service you render, and the more value you offer, the greater will be your reward."

Like it, loathe it, save it or blow it—the choice is yours. But you simply cannot ignore it. Money is important—and it has few equals. When it speaks, people listen, often without interrupting. Money functions much as a sixth sense, without which you cannot make complete use of your other five. It can help you realize—or derail—your dreams. It most definitely, no pun intended, *counts*.

Money is said to be both a blessing and the root of all evil. Too much or too little emphasis on making and saving money can warp your perspective. The fact is that money is not the first priority in happy people's lives. Health, relationships with family and friends, career satisfaction, and spiritual growth are all more important. Still, money touches every part of everyone's life. You work hard for it. It is tied up with your deepest emotional needs for love, power, security, independence, control, and self-worth. It affects your relationships, the way you go about your everyday activities … everything.

Money is always moving, always on its way somewhere. What you do with it while it is in your keeping and the direction you send it in say much about you. Your treatment of and respect for money, how you make it, and how you spend it all reflect your character. The old saying may claim that "It is much easier to give than to receive," but when it comes to money, the mantra is more like, "It is much easier to spend than to save." The road to poverty is paved with the good intentions of those who wanted to save but never got around to it. Human beings are guaranteed to procrastinate; that's why the IRS created deadlines *and* extensions.

It's true that money does not buy happiness, but then again, neither does poverty. Money brings you food, not appetite; medicine, not health; acquaintances, not friends; servants, not faithfulness; and moments of joy, but not peace of mind. Yet despite ample evidence to the contrary, people still seem to think that money is a panacea that will solve most problems. It isn't and it doesn't!

Nonetheless, there are obviously things that money *can* buy: a sense of security, a comfortable retirement, and an ability to provide for your family. Yet to truly appreciate the value of money, you must have the experience of actually earning it. Money provides greater choices and possibilities, but *only* if it is understood and managed. The biggest mistake you can make with money is neglect. If you choose to overlook the fact that every dollar counts, you may just as well leave your wallet on a park bench. Money requires numerous skill sets because the methods that help you acquire it are vastly different from the ones that help you keep and grow it.

Yet in a world where money counts, why are so many people financially illiterate? There's a perception that investing is only for the pros, a sort of "Don't try this at home" mentality, but nothing could be further from the truth. When it comes to money, the more we learn, the more we earn. And to make every dollar count, we must make our education count. The earlier in life you learn the fundamentals of financial literacy, the better off you'll be.

Simply put: taking steps to become informed and better educated about finance will lead to better choices. There's NO substitute for education. You may never become an expert, but expertise isn't necessary. A general understanding, however, is. Money management requires you to do more than just stick to a budget (although that is an important part of the equation). It means that you must find ways to increase your income, maintain a steady cash flow, and plan for the future. When it comes to money, the fundamentals remain constant. The basics are simple; the truth has not changed. Though our environment and how we function continually varies, the fundamentals do not. Spring always follows winter, water always runs downhill, and the sun will always rise in the east. These fundamental truths have existed throughout recorded history. So, too, have the fundamentals that govern money. Paying yourself first, saving for a rainy day, and never spending more than you earn is solid wisdom for any age.

Unfortunately, many people prefer to skip right on by the basics. They don't do their homework, and eventually acquire knowledge through the bitter pill of experience. This is like learning to drive by having a series of accidents. Keep this in mind: if you do not profit from your investment mistakes, someone else will.

Money is a faithful, loyal servant, and we are its master. It allows us to do more for others and ourselves. However, when we get into debt, the roles change, and we find ourselves in the position of slave. The person who owes money is a servant to the person or to the corporation who lends the money.

So what is it with money? Where's the mystery? The paper you fold and place in your pocket is not money; it's paper with pictures of people on it. It *symbolizes* money, but it's certainly not money. Money is all about idea and value creation. The earning of money has nothing to do with the paper in your pocket.

Money is a reward you receive for the service you render, so the more value you offer, the greater your reward will be. Thinking of ways we can be of greater service to our customers, employers, and employees will not only help us earn more money; it will also enable us to grow intellectually and spiritually. A focus on value creation is the hallmark of success.

The three main income-earning strategies include:

1. **Bartering:** Bartering time for money is by far the worst of the three income earning strategies; however, the majority employs it. Both white and blue-collar professions—from poorly educated day laborers to highly schooled doctors—embrace this model. This strategy is based on time, which in itself has a natural built-in limitation—saturation point. Therefore, your earning power ceases to exist at the moment you stop working.
2. **Investing:** Investing money to earn money is used by a small group of savvy people. The people who effectively employ this strategy either are well educated financially speaking, or follow the advice of a trusted, knowledgeable advisor.
3. **Leveraging:** Leveraging yourself and your assets to earn money allows you to accelerate and multiply your earnings through the efforts of others. Establishing multiple sources of income is, without question, the very best way to increase your income.

Retirement, college expenses, buying a home, establishing a better quality of life, or starting and growing a business—whatever your expense is, start by knowing your goals. They are, after all, the foundation of your investment strategy. What are your financial goals? Being rich is not a goal; it's a vague dream. Be specific, create a detailed action plan, and religiously follow it.

Financial ignorance is not bliss. It is not something to take pride in, or something to pass on to future generations. What you don't know *can* and will hurt you. You owe it to yourself, your family, and your future to learn and apply the fundamentals of saving and investing. Only one thing separates you from the financial bunny slopes and the more advanced hills: knowledge. Knowledge is the great neutralizer; it removes the sting from the killer bee of fear and replaces it with a strong sense of control and mastery.

When it comes to money, everything—and that means every dollar—counts!

EVERY DOLLAR COUNTS—CALL TO ACTION

To explore your own commitment to making every dollar count, ask yourself these questions:

- Do you believe that money is a blessing or the root of all evil? What is your perception of money, and how has it influenced your life?
- Do you actively work to develop you financial literacy in order to make more informed money decisions; or do you neglect this responsibility?
- What step will you take to make every dollar you make and contribute count?

PORTRAIT OF FINANCIAL LITERACY

Clark Howard, Radio Talk Show Host

Every day across America, Clark Howard's voice is heard on more than 150 radio stations advising millions of consumers how to save more, spend less, and avoid getting ripped off.

You can learn how to protect yourself against costly financial mistakes and potential scams by tuning in to his show on HLN (formerly CNN Headline News).

Known as the CNN Money Coach, his advice on how to make every dollar count is for real because it is based on his real-life experience.

Mr. Howard retired at age 31 with a fortune made from his travel agency and found his way into the public eye almost by accident.

He was asked to be a guest on a radio show about travel and the response was so positive that he was given his own program, The Clark Howard Show.

From there he was soon giving financial tips for struggling families.

Howard has dedicated his life to helping Americans of all means get ahead financially in life.

He offers books aimed at helping parents teach kids real-world financial skills like how to use credit cards wisely, buy a car, save for college, and stay out of debt.

Clark Howard's sound, uncomplicated advice is helping people everywhere discover that how they manage money counts!

49

EVERY VOTE COUNTS

"Voting is a sustained obligation that accompanies and protects the liberties we enjoy."

Voting is a universal language that's applied in a myriad of ways. It's a process that takes place for a Pope, Union Leader, Team Captain, CEO, and even for a Board of Directors. As a group of jurors, we vote for innocence or guilt; as judges, we vote for beauty queens; as family members, we vote for what or where we eat dinner; and as citizens, we vote for political leaders. While the range and significance of each vote is diverse, one constant remains: every vote counts.

The duties or responsibilities of a citizen in a Democratic society can be separated into two groups: mandatory responsibilities, such as paying taxes; and duties not demanded by law, such as voting. The right to vote is a duty and responsibility, as well as a privilege. Modern democracies, including the United States, extend this right (suffrage) to almost all responsible adult citizens. This inclusive voting right is known as universal suffrage. Indeed, "one person, one vote" is seen as a hallmark of representative democracy.

Abraham Lincoln best described democracy as "government of the people, by the people, and for the people." For that government to be "by the people," however, the people must decide who shall be their leaders. Without free and fair elections, there can be no democratic society. Without the constant accountability of government officials to the electorate, there can be no assurance of any other rights. The right to vote is not only an important individual liberty, it is also a pillar of free government.

The right to vote is one of our most important civil liberties, and those who expect to reap the blessings of freedom must support the vehicle of freedom. By fulfilling your obligation to express yourself with the ballot, you have preserved the democratic system. Moreover, voting is a sustained obligation that accompanies and protects the liberties we enjoy.

People tend to ask: Does my vote really count? Is it worth it? All of us have asked these questions at one time or another. You may feel like the lone sane voice in a shouting match. But the answer to both of those questions is an emphatic *Yes!* Voting in any type of election—from local elections to Presidential primaries—provides an important way to voice your opinions regarding elected leaders and overall policies. Voting also helps you decide your own future by electing a person who might reflect your personal views.

The ability to vote exists as one of the most cherished rights; one for which our forefathers fought, marched, and died over the centuries. Wars still rage so that citizens of other countries can earn this right; one that many of us now take for granted. The act of voting is an entitlement that should be practiced with the utmost consideration and care. Voting is more than simply acting upon our right to be heard; it is a moral obligation. Because we live in a republic and enjoy the right of voting, we are not just people who elect the government. We are a small and integral part *of* the government.

Of all of our freedoms, the right to vote is perhaps the most important one. However, not all citizens vote. Why? The reasons have historically included apathy, disillusionment with the political structure, and people's common belief that their single vote does not really count in the long run. For these and many other reasons, citizens simply haven't bothered to vote, preferring instead to let others decide for them how their futures will unfold. Yet there are other democracies throughout the world where people are protesting, fighting, and even dying to attain this privilege. For centuries, we have seen people rise up and demand this right. Why?

Their initial motivation was the quest for freedom and empowerment of personal liberties. People strongly believe that their solitary vote *really does count.* For so many reasons, they are compelled to vote, preferring to vote for the leaders they trust, who will help them to enjoy newfound freedoms.

Representational government, or the electorate, is our country's foundation. Founded in the eighteenth century, the United States of America fought a rebellion against taxation without representation. The King of England imposed taxes on the colonies, which had no voice in the British government by which they might hope to change laws that affected their prosperity. After the Revolutionary War, great care was taken to craft a Constitution—a document to grant us the freedoms designed to ensure that each individual had an active voice in government. However, as with all rights and freedoms, the right to vote carries with it vital responsibilities. When citizens fail to meet this obligation, our system of government does not function as it should.

People offer a variety of reasons for ducking this responsibility, yet all of them amount to mere excuses. And those who refuse their duty feel no restriction on their right to complain. They will not voice their opinions when it matters, yet feel entitled to express them at all other times.

Democracy requires and demands an informed electorate. These two factors are so intertwined that the failures or inadequacies of one can render the entire system ineffective. If voters do not know what is going on in politics, they cannot rationally participate in government policy. Without their participation, their needs and wants cannot possibly be understood or realized. This is particularly troubling in times of war or major conflict; in large issues such as healthcare, foreign policy, education; and in so many other areas of social and political importance.

Inadequate voter knowledge has two major negative implications for democracy. First, it prevents any meaningful reflection of the will of the people in democratic government. Second, it imperils the instrumental case for democracy as a nation that serves the interests of the majority, as ignorance potentially opens the door for both elite manipulation and gross policy errors caused by politicians' need to appeal to an ignorant electorate in order to win office.

In order to vote with informed intelligence and exert meaningful influence over a given issue, voters at a minimum must take the time to:

- Become *aware* of the issue's existence.
- Develop an *informed position* on the issue.
- Understand the *opposing candidate's* position on the issue.

One measure of the strength of a democracy can be seen in the participation of its younger citizens. However, much of our country's youth is unfamiliar with the political process and the importance of voting, unless they happened to grow up in a family that was politically engaged, or took civics or a related course in school. We must impress upon younger citizens the truth: that voting is a social duty that directly affects their life and future.

Time, energy, and a focus on democratic freedoms must be invested in younger citizens. The creation of an entire generation of nonvoters could have detrimental consequences for decades to come. If concerned parties do not step up, the so-called "snowball effect" threatens to decimate the importance of voting to future generations. How can anyone expect today's younger citizens to advocate voting to their own children when they don't care enough to vote themselves?

All rights carry with them responsibilities and obligations. Our rights deserve our utmost attention and vigilant protection. Achieving the right to vote was a hard-fought accomplishment for all races and genders throughout history. Now that each and every citizen in our country has the right to vote in any election, they must exercise it, because every vote counts.

EVERY VOTE COUNTS—CALL TO ACTION

To explore your own commitment to making your vote count, ask yourself these questions:

- Do you take the time to educate yourself on important political issues? If so, do you look at opposing views to test and deepen your understanding?
- Do you think you should have a sustained voting obligation that accompanies and protects the liberties you enjoy? Why do you feel this way?
- What step will you take to be a better informed on the key issues to ensure that you are voting with understanding?

PORTRAIT OF VOTING RIGHTS

The Suffrage Movement

Though the right to vote is considered vital to free society, it took over one hundred years of dissent before women in the United States were granted this fundamental right.

It wasn't until 1920 that the U.S. constitution was amended to grant American women full voting rights bringing victory to those who led the "Suffrage Movement" to secure the right of "suffrage" for women.

Beginning in the early 1800s, Susan B. Anthony, the face of the Suffrage Movement, devoted her life to this struggle. Her motto was "Men their rights and nothing more; women, their rights and nothing less."

Anthony is said to have had an independent spirit from an early age. A single exchange with one of her teachers stuck with her during her long struggle. It was reported that she asked her male schoolteacher why he only taught long division to just boys.

He answered, "A girl needs to know how to read her Bible and count her egg money, nothing more."

She was not satisfied with that answer:

Although Susan B. Anthony devoted 50 years to the woman's suffrage movement culminating with the passage of the 19th Amendment to the Constitution of the United States, she died before she could see her work succeed.

She would be proud to know that through her effort, now every woman's vote counts.

50

CONTRIBUTION COUNTS

"Focusing your energies on how you can contribute affects the quality, content, and impact of your work."

When someone does something so right, so honest, and yes, so commendable, attention must be paid. A focus on unique contribution allows one to make deposits into their sphere of influence in such a way that looking away is not an option.

We must individually and collectively replace the pursuit of success and material objects with the pursuit of contribution and generosity. For this to occur, the critical question must move from, "How can I become successful?" to "What can I contribute that will significantly impact the mission, performance, and overall results of the institution or community I serve?" By focusing on what we can contribute, we automatically become successful.

Focusing on contribution places a premium on responsibility. As the key driver of effectiveness, our contributions to others allow us to do well by doing good. This is only accomplished by looking outward from our workload and upward toward more noble goals and objectives. However, the great majority of people miss this important point. They tend to focus inward and become preoccupied with what they feel they are "owed," what others should do for them, or what they can get out of any given person or situation. This type of thinking is shallow and self-centered, and eventually, the afflicted party renders themselves ineffectual and unwanted. You must instead concentrate your energies on how what you contribute affects the quality, content, and impact of your work. Your standards, reputation, and credibility rise, as do the size and scope of new opportunities. Your relationship with others takes on new meaning and your presence is welcomed wherever you travel.

Questions direct thinking, stimulate innovation, and therefore affect our actions and results. What justifies your existence? Why are you on the payroll? What are you called to do with the gifts and time you are given? What can you and no one else do which, if done really well, would make a real difference? When you change the focus of your questions and intentions from getting to giving, there's a boomerang effect that takes place in such a way that whenever you give through contributions, your rewards come back multiplied.

Everything in life wishes to reward its contributor. In fact, every contribution turns you into a benefactor, allowing you to enjoy the fruits of your contributions. By giving to the garden, the flowers reward you by blooming with bright, vibrant, and beautiful colors. By donating to your children's education, they reward you by becoming responsible, disciplined, and productive members of society. Working for your client's best interests rewards you with loyalty and ongoing prosperity. Giving money to your retirement fund provides you with both peace of mind and an enjoyable final chapter of your life. And contributing to the health and well-being of your body through exercise and nutrition will reward you with responsiveness, flexibility, longevity, and optimal performance.

Those who contribute their time, talents, networks, and personal experience will be repaid in one way or another. It may seem strange intellectually, but the world begins to conspire for you as whom or whatever benefits from your contributions wishes to respond. The lawn wishes to grow; the muscle begins to strengthen; and as the student's mind expands, she will wish to repay you with her own success, accomplishments, and contributions to others.

The most basic human need that we all have is to matter, and to make a difference. At an intuitive, gut level, we know that each one of us has our very own unique contribution to make in life. Making a difference where we live, work, go to school, and play must be where we focus our greatest contributions. Your contributions will become a larger part of your life's body of work.

To ask, "What can I contribute?" is to look for the unused, untapped, unlimited potential in the task at hand. And what is considered to be excellent performance in many positions is often but a minute portion of the full potential of contribution. Conversely, those who do not ask themselves, "What can I contribute?" are likely to aim too low, too narrowly, or at the wrong things, such as material gain.

Every institution needs performance, especially in the building and developing of children, teens, and leaders of tomorrow. If deprived of performance, potential will decay and die. To ensure strong communities and prosperous businesses, a focus on unique contributions must be built into the very fabric of society and citizenship.

Likewise, your contributions will help lay the foundation for some of the greatest feats, innovations, and performances the world has ever seen. Your contributions will live on indefinitely while helping the recipient plan for the future with the confidence that comes from knowing that they are supported at every turn. We must all be like farmers and plant the seeds for a robust harvest, though we may never live to see it.

A parent, teacher, or coach's focus on contribution by itself is a powerful force in developing young people. Like a muscle, we all grow and adjust to the level of the demands made upon us. Anyone who sets their sights on contribution raises the sights and standards of everyone with whom they come in contact. The most successful leaders focus on maximum contributions, which impose relevance on all events and results. They ask questions that focus all parties such as "What contribution from me do you require to make your contribution to the organization? When do you need this, how do you need it, and in what form?"

The definition of a success *must* include a contribution to the lives of other people. The heroes and heroines worthy of emulation are those who enrich our lives each day and each moment. Their contribution—their imprint upon our lives—is enduring and indelible.

Your commitment to contributing must therefore be a vow to responsible living and proper citizenship. A meaningful life requires meaningful contributions and to focus on contributions is to focus on creating a meaningful life. A focus on contribution is, after all, good etiquette in action. By giving together, you empower progress and help to fulfill your gifts. You add significant value to your community, strengthen your reputation, and inspire people to make greater contributions. Attention must be paid, as every contribution counts.

247

CONTRIBUTION COUNTS—CALL TO ACTION

To explore your own commitment to making contribution count, ask yourself these questions:

- Do you constantly look for ways in which you can expand your contributions and overall impact on others?
- Do you focus on ways to make a difference where you live, work, go to school, and play? What has been your greatest contribution in the last month?
- What step will you take to make a greater contribution in your career, personal life, or in your community?

PORTRAIT OF CONTRIBUTION

Timberland

Many companies say they believe in the importance of service to their communities but far fewer put this value into action. Timberland is one such company.

Already a well-respected manufacturer of high-quality boots, with $1.2 billion in sales and ranked 78th on the 2007 CNN Money top 100 companies to work for list, Timberland wants to do more than sell waterproof boots.

At Timberland, doing well and doing good are not separate efforts. The premise of service to a truth larger than what they sell is a demand more pressing than this quarter's earnings.

President Jeff Swartz says, "We believe that our place in this world is bigger than the things we put in it. So we volunteer in our communities to make things better."

As a third generation leader, Swartz applies lessons passed down about what it takes to run a business and live a purposeful life—a commitment to humility, humanity, integrity, and service to others.

In 1992, they formally launched The Path of Service program that galvanized the spirit of volunteerism and citizenship in the company.

248

It provides 40 hours paid time annually for employees to work on critical community needs and supports over 170 projects with volunteers.

The Path of Service is the canvas on which Timberland's ideals and beliefs are expressed.

As Marian Wright Edelman wrote, "Service is the rent we pay for being. It is the very purpose of life, and not something you do in your spare time."

51

HISTORY COUNTS

"Those who came before us have shaped us and we will influence those who succeed us after we too descend into the deep of time."

History is the chronicle of the length and breadth of humankind's activities—the manuscript of the memory of life itself. Every citizen, regardless of race, religion, or gender, must know the history of the land to which they pledge allegiance. Unfortunately, the vast majority of people are historically illiterate, which results in a sorry ignorance of our great past.

History serves as the study and interpretation of the record of people, societies, and civilizations. The term *history* comes from the Greek *historia*, which means "an account of one's inquiries."

But, you might wonder—why study history? What's in it for me? Because history is all we have to make sense of the present. It's important to know that the world did not begin the moment we arrived. We have a past and a history that helps judge the present and prepare for the future. History exists in all of our lives, and we each make our own through our choices, actions, and relationships.

Knowledge of history extends our vision, enlarges our mind and imagination, and expands the range of our thinking. If we are to understand ourselves, our country and the world, we must know history and those who made it, for our past is theirs, and their future is ours. Where there is history, we can acquire the knowledge and wisdom of old age. Without an understanding and appreciation of history, we remain childlike and unable to make informed decisions based on historical perspective.

History is a wise teacher that provides many lessons, such as:

- **Humility:** This aspect of history allows us to see and appreciate the fact that any success or achievement we enjoy is built on that of others. Each generation advances and builds on the discoveries of the previous generation. We are better able than they were to see things, not because our sight is superior or because we are taller than they, but because they raise us up, and by their great stature, add to ours. When we study history, we become humbled by genius, effort, and creative insights as we learn about the many modern ideas that were discussed long ago.
- **Gratitude:** We develop a sense of gratitude as we study history and begin to realize that every freedom we enjoy came at someone else's expense. Past lessons allow us to truly appreciate the battles that our forebears fought, the ideals that they championed, the sacrifices they made, and the enduring effects of their accomplishments. History teaches us to be grateful for the failures, the mistakes, and the inequities of our past; as only when armed with this knowledge can we appreciate the hard-won freedoms that are our birthright.
- **Perspective:** We gain a sense of perspective from history—one that helps us to recognize the ways that the past has authority over us. Historical consciousness is an awareness of the past, of things we never experienced firsthand, and of one's own connection to it. It is cultivation of respect for what cannot be seen, for the invisible sources of meaning and authority in our lives, for the formative agents and foundational principles that, although no longer tangible, have made possible what is worthy in our own day.
- **Connectedness:** History lets us feel a connection that provides meaning for our daily living. Understanding history is a matter of taking stock of the way we live, of what our pastimes and pleasures, holidays and traditions, families and marriages, habits and aspirations, all say about our connection to the past, and, therefore, about ourselves. Historical consciousness draws us out of a narrow preoccupation with the present and with our selves, and

ushers us into another, larger world—a public world that cultures us, in all senses of that word. Historical consciousness is, then, part of the cement that holds civilization together.

- **Awareness:** History makes us keenly aware of good and bad, right and wrong, past successes and failures of leaders, and their collective impact on our present time. It brings our attention to the problems, the triumphs, the solutions, and the failures that mark our own personal history. It allows us to understand the many forms of government and recurring themes in the human story, and allows us to develop an appreciation of the premises, limitations, and possibilities of our notion of progress; of a culture and civilization which sees the value of the past, understands the implications of economic and technological growth, the nature of human reason, its potential and limitations, and the intrinsic importance of life on this earth. Studying history causes us to recognize the factors that result in the rise and fall of nation-states or civilizations, motivations for political actions, and the effects of social philosophies. That kind of awareness is critical to understanding who and what we are because of our past, and where we are headed.

- **Intellectual Growth:** History extends human knowledge beyond what we can ever experience on our own. It affords an absolutely necessary enlargement of human experience; a way of getting out of the boundaries of one's own life and culture and of seeing more of what human experience has been. It is the necessary, unique way of orienting the present moment, so that you know where you are and where we have come from. In fact, history is the only resource we have for doing so.

- **Role Models:** History is rich in accounts of men and women of character, nobility, courage, leadership, and other divine virtues. Their example inspires us to be and do more with our lives, as the only clue to what man can do is what man has already done. One of history's many values, then, is that it teaches us what man has accomplished, and thus, what man is and has the potential to be. Over the years, we discover how much our paths and perspectives are shaped by people who have gone before.

  History is a grand mirror in which we are reflected, and the virtues of the great men and women who came before us serve as a sort of looking glass into which we may see how to adjust and create our own life. Historical role models can have an enormous influence on those who study history, as they are very real individuals whose efforts and emotions once moved and still motivate people. They represent the passionate beating heart of history.

- **Continuity:** History creates a sense of continuity, which is critical in all human affairs. It lets us see that we are heirs of the past, in the same way that those who came before us have shaped us, we too will influence those who succeed us after we descend into the deep of time.

Knowledge of history enlarges our human experience and increases our self-awareness by creating a link with those who have preceded us. Without some understanding of our roots and our place in the flow of history, we cannot fully understand our own personal opinions, prejudices, and emotional reactions.

History is the foundation upon which every curriculum of learning stands. We must ensure that we teach history to our youth so that they in turn understand why they must continue, protect, and safeguard liberty and justice.

All of humanity is a partnership between the dead, the living, and the unborn. It is our collective responsibility to preserve history and to fulfill our duty to this partnership because history counts!

HISTORY COUNTS—CALL TO ACTION

To explore your own commitment to making history count, ask yourself these questions:

- Do you believe that history has any relevance to the freedoms and quality of life you enjoy today? Why do you feel this way?
- Do you take the time to look at historical facts and events in order to gain more clarity of modern situations?
- What steps will you take to become better informed on certain historical events and what impact do you think it will have on your decision-making?

PORTRAIT OF A HISTORIAN

Doris Kearns Goodwin

Doris Kearns Goodwin, Ph.D., is one of our country's foremost historians.

Her presidential biographies illuminate the lives of our greatest leaders that we might better understand their private struggles and fully appreciate the sacrifices they make to preserve our way of life.

Early on, she attracted the attention of Lyndon Johnson when as a White House fellow she co-authored an article critical of his foreign policy. He gave her a job feeling that hiring a White House fellow who was critical of the administration might deflect the growing antiwar sentiment.

Her first book, *Lyndon Johnson & the American Dream,* was a compelling portrait of a man deeply shaken by the Vietnam War and fearful to the point of obsession about his legacy. It became a best seller and propelled her literary career.

Other presidential biographies followed, including:

The *Fitzgeralds & The Kennedys* stayed on the New York Times bestseller list for five months and was made into a six-hour miniseries for ABC Television.

No Ordinary Time: Franklin and Eleanor Roosevelt: The American Homefront During World War II was awarded the Pulitzer Prize for history.

Her *Team of Rivals: The Political Genius of Abraham Lincoln* showed Lincoln's genius in placing his rivals in his Cabinet to stifle their opposition and put their talents to work for the benefit of the country.

Her talent expands our knowledge of history, extends our vision, enlarges our mind and imagination, and expands the range of our thinking.

52

PEACE COUNTS

*"Every single moment is an opportunity for peace, as is
each act, word, thought, and feeling."*

Peace is a universal human ideal. It is one of the few positive symbols
that have meaning for the whole of humanity. Every major system of faith
and belief, whether religious or secular in nature, has in some way or another
promised peace as an outcome of the implementation of its precepts. This
means that everyone has a vested interest in making peace count.

The challenge of peace as a virtue presents itself in the question, "Are human
beings by nature violent or nonviolent?" If the answer is violent, then the concept of peace becomes nonexistent. While the answer is of course nonviolent,
peace has become so elusive that people have begun to question its existence.

Achieving peace does not mean that we will automatically find ourselves in
a place that is absent of noise, trouble, or hard work. To be at peace means to
be in the midst of all those things and still be cool, calm, and collected in heart,
mind, and spirit. Thus, peace is more precious than diamonds, rubies, or pearls.

Peace and understanding can only come about as the result of personal responsibility and awareness. Violence begets violence, toughness begets toughness, love begets love, and peace begets peace. Peace begins with a simple choice.

Lasting world peace is not likely to be initiated politically; it will begin first in the hearts and minds of each of us. Lasting peace can come only to peaceful people. Until we have peace within our families, our communities, and most importantly, ourselves, no politician or nation will ever have the power to bring about peace. There will be no future worth living unless everyone takes personal responsibility for his or her own lives. If you want a kinder world, then behave with kindness; if you want a peaceful world, make peace within. We can never obtain peace in the world if we neglect the inner world and don't make peace with ourselves. World peace must develop out of inner peace.

Every single moment is an opportunity for peace, as is each act, word, thought, and feeling. Peace is not an external process, even though there are external manifestations. Peace is always appropriate; to be truly peaceful, we must invite peace into every action we take. Joy and peace are found in loving acts, and every act of love is a work of peace, no matter how small.

Peace is not passive. It can be gentle, even silent, but it's also action-oriented. Ordinary daily activities such as smiling can be experienced with a whole new perspective by associating them with a peaceful consciousness. So, too, can extraordinary acts be peaceful. It is the consciousness of peace that manifests the acts that we call peaceful.

Peace is the foundation—the major building block—upon which a healthy, functional society stands. The character of a society can be seen through the collective consciousness of its members. Consciousness creates culture—its norms, values, and systems—and consciousness can transform culture. Our future hinges on each individual's capacity to embrace a commitment to universal peace and love. We must begin to transcend the barriers that keep us from seeing ourselves as part of a global family. We have to start caring about what really happens to people across the street, as well as around the globe.

Establishing a lasting peace is the work of education. If we are to reach real peace in this world, we must focus on cultivating it within our children. Peace education works to build a harmonious, just, and sustainable world for our children. School helps to shape a person's character. Classrooms and schoolyards are places where every child can be heard, where conflict can be resolved positively, and where critical skills and cultural diversity can be learned among friends. Teachers can teach peace by integrating values, songs, poetry, movies, and even cartoons, along with facts and methods of peace and global education, into their curriculum. These skills and values are essential for survival in an increasingly interdependent world. Just as we teach reading, writing, and arithmetic, we must teach students to learn to think critically; respect diversity and the integrity of the Earth; understand global, cultural, and economic interdependence; analyze media; examine the nature of violence; and learn ways for us all to live more peacefully. Such learning cannot be achieved without the intentional, sustained, and systematic education for peace.

Terrorism, hatred, violence, bigotry, prejudice, and aggression do not happen by accident; they are a direct result of a culture—a dysfunctional culture that for some has been passed down and mutated through generations. The only way for those outcomes to change is through a change in culture. The intentional development of a culture of peace—one that promotes and indoctrinates love, understanding, cooperation, and humility—will help to build a new generation of young leaders and enlightened citizens. It's in our collective best interests, as well as a moral duty, to bring out, uplift, and celebrate compassion, tolerance, and active demonstrations of peace and forgiveness in our children.

Peace is not possible without forgiveness, and forgiveness is not possible without education. Forgiveness is not a situational or conditional act; it is a permanent attitude. The only way children can learn the habit of forgiveness is by seeing it modeled by adults, especially their parents. The freedom to be at peace in our own skins—that's what forgiveness allows. We relinquish this freedom when we hold onto anger and resentment. Enormous amounts of energy are wasted when we suppress our love, hold onto hate, and harbor acrimonious feelings. The only remedy is letting go, and being willing to forgive.

A culture of peace relies on love as a common bond to bring about unity and cohesion among its citizens to form in a united front. This is necessary in an enlightened culture that upholds individual rights, privacy, and promotes peace for all. Peace must be maintained and nourished constantly. Ongoing peace education is the way.

We must come to see that peace is not merely a distant goal, but that it is a means by which we arrive at that goal pursuing peaceful ends through peaceful means.

PEACE COUNTS—CALL TO ACTION

To explore your own commitment to making peace count, ask yourself these questions:

- Do you think that peace means to be in a place that is absent of noise, trouble, or hard work? How do you define peace?

- Do you have a peaceful spirit? Would others describe you as someone at peace with themselves and with the world?
- What step will you take to make the world, your office, and home more peaceful?

PORTRAIT OF PEACE

Alfred Nobel—The Nobel Peace Prize

Alfred Nobel, chemist, inventor, and philanthropist, never attended university. He was home tutored by the best minds of the day and worked for his father, developing mines, torpedoes, and other explosives.

A factory explosion in 1864 killed his younger brother and four other people and launched his search for a safe way to handle nitroglycerin.

Before age 30, Nobel achieved an important goal—he reduced the volatility of the nitroglycerin and produced what he called dynamite.

This was an era of large infrastructure projects like railways, ports, bridges, roads, mines, and tunnels, where blasting was necessary and dynamite was of vital importance in the construction of many projects. His products were in great demand making him a wealthy man.

His will decreed that his estate would fund the Nobel Peace Prize. Less famous are the prizes for physics, chemistry, medicine, and literature.

The Peace Prize is awarded each year "to the person who shall have done the most . . . for fraternity between nations . . . for the holding and promotion of peace congresses."

Most people think he chose the category of Peace to make up for the destructive use of his inventions in war, yet none of his explosives were used in war during his lifetime.

He simply believed that through his advocacy of peace, we could achieve peace throughout the world.

TOP TEN REASONS TO VISIT EVERYTHINGCOUNTS.COM

GARY RYAN BLAIR HAS THE TOOLS TO HELP YOU MAKE EVERYTHING COUNT!

1. **Access**

   When you visit Everything Counts, you'll have immediate access to a virtual library of world-class ideas, strategies, and resources that will help you on your journey towards excellence and mastery.

2. **Self Study Guides**

   Here you'll find a great way to fully immerse yourself into the Everything Counts philosophy. The purpose of these study guides is to give you a deeper understanding and format for implementing the lessons learned throughout the book.

3. **Teleseminar Series**

   Enjoy and participate in a series of content rich teleseminars. You'll have access to some of the best minds in the world all at the speed of sound and from the comfort of your home or office. See the entire series at www.EverythingCounts.com/teleseminar.

4. **Free Stuff**

   Visit our free download center and enjoy a massive feast of audios, screensavers, applications and other great material. It is our desire to provide you with some great ideas, all of which inspire, promote, and celebrate excellence.

5. **Community**

   Everything Counts is a community of people and organizations who are committed to living a life of excellence and displaying exceptionably high standards. You'll be able to network and collaborate with some very special people who embody excellence.

6. **Reader Only Resources—exclusive to readers only**

   This is a special password protected site that features bonus chapters, how-to articles, case studies, and other cool stuff. To gain access to this Readers Only Resources go to www.EverythingCounts.com/resources and enter the word "excellence" for the—password.

7. **Best Practices**

   If you want to know how other people and organizations are using the Everything Counts philosophy to transform their life and business than you simply must log in today to see how you can implement these best practices.

8. **Newsletter**

   The Everything Counts newsletter is all about inspiring excellence and driving results. The entire blog archive is available to you the moment you sign up and as a special bonus, you'll receive a free recording from one of Gary's presentations.

9. **Assessment**

   Let this online assessment and Excellence IQ Test help you plan and prioritize your Everything Counts plan for excellence. Log on now at www.EverythingCounts.com/assessment to access this powerful tool.

10. **Training and Speaking Resources**

    If you liked the book, you'll absolutely love the training program and keynote speech. Our programs take this special message to an entirely different level. You'll be challenged, enlightened, and compelled to raise the bar and commit to excellence.

CONTACT INFORMATION

For information on Gary Ryan Blair's speaking availability or his consulting services, please call 877-462-5748 or email Info@EverythingCounts.com.

ABOUT THE AUTHOR

Gary Ryan Blair has been called one of the world's most influential thinkers on excellence and productivity and has been a keynote speaker and facilitator for such organizations as IBM, Federal Express, Subway, and the U.S. Army, and he conducts workshops for individuals and organizations around the world.

He is the president of The GoalsGuy and has more than 20 years of experience helping business owners, corporate executives, and sales professionals manage their time, set their priorities, and stay focused so they can achieve their goals, grow their business, and build sustainable competitive advantage.

His work has been featured in the *New York Times*, the *Wall Street Journal*, *USA Today*, *Rolling Stone*, and many other publications. He is a dynamic and entertaining speaker who makes the heart sing, the mind expand, and the spirit soar. For more information, please visit www.EverythingCounts.com.

INDEX